Distilling the Influence of Alcohol

UNIVERSITY PRESS OF FLORIDA

Florida A&M University, Tallahassee
Florida Atlantic University, Boca Raton
Florida Gulf Coast University, Ft. Myers
Florida International University, Miami
Florida State University, Tallahassee
New College of Florida, Sarasota
University of Central Florida, Orlando
University of Florida, Gainesville
University of North Florida, Jacksonville
University of South Florida, Tampa
University of West Florida, Pensacola

Distilling the Influence of
Alcohol

❖❖❖❖❖❖❖❖❖❖❖❖❖

Aguardiente in Guatemalan History

Edited by David Carey Jr.

FOREWORD BY WILLIAM B. TAYLOR

University Press of Florida

Gainesville · Tallahassee · Tampa · Boca Raton
Pensacola · Orlando · Miami · Jacksonville · Ft. Myers · Sarasota

Printed in the United States of America. This book is printed on Glatfelter Natures Book,
a paper certified under the standards of the Forestry Stewardship Council (FSC). It is a
recycled stock that contains 30 percent post-consumer waste and is acid-free.

17 16 15 14 13 12   6 5 4 3 2 1

Library of Congress Cataloging-in-Publication Data
Distilling the influence of alcohol : aguardiente in Guatemalan history / edited by David
Carey ; foreword by William B. Taylor.
p. cm.
Includes bibliographical references and index.
ISBN 978-0-8130-4162-9 (alk. paper)
    1. Drinking of alcoholic beverages—Guatemala—History. 2. Alcoholic beverages—
Guatemala—History. 3. Guatemala—Social conditions. 4. Alcoholism—Guatemala—
History. 5. Guatemala—History. I. Carey, David. II. Taylor, William B.
HV5329.D57 2012
363.4'1097281—dc23   2012009808

The University Press of Florida is the scholarly publishing agency for the State
University System of Florida, comprising Florida A&M University, Florida Atlantic
University, Florida Gulf Coast University, Florida International University, Florida
State University, New College of Florida, University of Central Florida, University of
Florida, University of North Florida, University of South Florida, and University of
West Florida.

University Press of Florida
15 Northwest 15th Street
Gainesville, FL 32611-2079
http://www.upf.com

Contents

Illustrations

Foreword

Close to fifty years ago I had a first glimmer of how important alcoholic beverages have been in the history of Mesoamerica when *Juan the Chamula* by Ricardo Pozas was recommended to me as a little book worth reading. Told in the first person, it is the artful, deceptively simple story of Juan Pérez Jolote from San Juan Chamula in the highlands of Chiapas from about 1900 to the 1940s. Juan fled the community as a boy because his father beat him—but only when he was sober, reports Juan—and was swept into the Mexican Revolution (1910–20) before returning in the 1920s, eager to be Chamula again.

Juan's earnest efforts to gain acceptance become Pozas's window onto community life. At every significant step in Juan's remembered past, cane alcohol (*aguardiente de caña*) was in play, as a medium of exchange and obligation, as well as a convivial beverage. The *zinacanteco* couple that took him in when he ran away passed him on to a widow in their community in exchange for a bottle of aguardiente. When he went to work on a coffee plantation for the first time, he spent his advance on bread, peaches, brown sugar, and a bottle of aguardiente for his mother. In the community, a jug of aguardiente was always handy for sale, hospitality, and other ceremonial needs. When Juan returned to San Juan Chamula after the Mexican Revolution, he found that his father was about to move to town as an elected official and needed to take along three essentials: corn, firewood, and a jug of liquor. Juan, himself, would serve many times as a community official—becoming something of a super-Chamula. As he observed, "You can't govern the village or settle disputes or give the people justice without drinking *aguardiente*. The authorities gather in the town hall, and whenever the Mayor takes a drink, they drink, too. If you want to make a complaint or if you've been caught doing something wrong, you bring the authorities a litre or two of *aguardiente*, and the Mayor takes a drink and then the others drink. . . . Everything is settled by drinking, by getting drunk."[1]

Drink flowed freely during community feasts; exchanging bottles of aguardiente and binge drinking sealed a marriage contract; drinking was part of healing rituals, with some of the liquor spilled on the ground as an offering; and aguardiente was used to clean the staffs of office for the annual initiation of new officeholders. As Juan moved from one office to another, he found that drinking was an agreeable imperative. When he became a church officer, he recalled, "I bought a large jug, and every Sunday I went to the plaza to sell it. All my friends offered me a drink when they bought *aguardiente* from me, and I got drunk again and again. I couldn't help drinking. I was *alférez* of the Virgin of the Rosary, and since she's a woman, that made me a woman, too, and I was invited to drink with all those who take care of the saints that are men."[2]

At the end of the book, Juan acknowledges that he has paid a high price for embracing public service and all things Chamula. "My son Lorenzo and my wife Dominga keep telling me to stop drinking, but I can't. Sometimes I don't eat anything all day long. That's how my father died, from not eating. But I don't want to die. I want to live."

From his worm's eye view, Juan has little to say about the production and distribution of aguardiente, the wider politics of liquor, women, and much else, although he does mention that liquor consumed in the town hall had to be purchased from the secretary (an outsider appointed by the state government), and that a jug of his aguardiente was once confiscated because he bought it from the wrong supplier in the provincial capital of San Cristóbal.

Since *Juan the Chamula* first appeared (in Spanish in 1952 as *Juan Pérez Jolote: Biografía de un Tzotzil*; then in English in 1962), a few scholars have taken up the subject of alcohol in the history of Latin America in broad strokes or for polemical purposes, concerned mainly with social and cultural questions. But now, with *Distilling the Influence of Alcohol: Aguardiente in Guatemalan History*, we have a collection of deeply researched essays by anthropologically minded historians and historically minded anthropologists that engage the subject for Guatemala in more encompassing and revealing ways. The authors make a bold claim for aguardiente production and consumption as central to the history of nation building, as well as economic and social life, especially in Maya communities. The case is made in intriguing ways beyond the familiar story of alcohol serving as a means of recruiting Maya workers onto coffee plantations. Taxation on legal production and sale of aguardiente became a major source of revenue for the fledging nation in the nineteenth century and beyond, yet clandestine production and distribution were widespread and significant. In this way, Mayas resisted the impositions of the state through its shifting monopoly and licensing practices. The transportation of bootleg aguardiente from Chiapas became a hallowed "custom," and local moonshine was always present, much of it produced and sold by Maya women. But in this process of resisting state direction and resorting to more ritual drinking of aguardiente de caña during the late nineteenth century, Mayas were also becoming Guatemalans, increasingly affected by and responsive to politics and power outside their communities.

Beyond the solid contributions these essays make individually to a history of alcohol in Guatemala that is more than just another neglected subject, I find two features of the collection especially appealing. First, the chapters shine a bright light on the strategic importance of domestic economic activity during the nineteenth and twentieth centuries, when our gaze so often now is drawn to enclave economies and transatlantic or inter-American transactions. This is most welcome, but the second feature is the one that warms my scholar's heart: the authors have learned from each other and put their essays in conversation. The result is a more connected history, rich in episodes, people, and ironies that are understood together, synoptically. As E. P. Thompson liked to say, "History is made up of episodes, and if we cannot get inside these, we cannot get inside history at all. This has always been inconvenient to the schematists."[3]

William B. Taylor
Muriel McKevitt Sonne Professor Emeritus of History,
University of California–Berkeley

Notes

1. Pozas, *Juan the Chamula*, 52.
2. Ibid., 106.
3. Thompson, "Peculiarities of the English," 275.

Acknowledgments

Emerging out of a panel at the 2008 American Historical Association annual conference in New York City, this project was a collaborative effort from the start. Appropriately, the idea to publish an edited volume was first proposed over drinks after our panel. I count myself fortunate to have such wonderful colleagues with whom to pursue the past. In addition to each of the contributors, a number of other people made crucial contributions without which this volume might never have come to fruition.

Chris Lutz was among the first to encourage us to pursue publication of our collective works and explore the connections between them. Critical comments from the two outside reviewers, Frederick Smith and Todd Little-Siebold, strengthened the manuscript. Walter Little, Judie Maxwell, and Allen Wells also provided insights that sharpened aspects of earlier versions and portions of the manuscript.

At the University Press of Florida, Meredith Morris-Babb and Amy Gorelick both believed in the project from the start and helped to shepherd it through the editorial review process. Shannon McCarthy began to guide the manuscript through the production process even before it landed on her desk.

With her eye for detail, administrative assistant extraordinaire Rie Larson provided technical and formatting support that was essential for preparing the manuscript for submission. The Hemeroteca Nacional Guatemala in Guatemala City and the Latin American Library at Tulane University in New Orleans kindly allowed us to reproduce images from their collections for this book.

Finally and most important, I want to thank my wife, Sarah, and daughters, Ava and Kate, who always seemed to know just when to encourage me and just when to distract me as I was working on this volume.

Introduction

Writing a History of Alcohol in Guatemala

DAVID CAREY JR.

Despite its persistence and prevalence in the lives of most Central Americans, alcohol has received relatively little attention in Central American historiography. As a commodity that was produced and consumed locally (and often illicitly), *aguardiente* (distilled sugarcane liquor or rum) was frequently at the center of economic, political, and social conflicts within and between local communities and between communities and the state. The proceeds from alcohol manufacturing filled government coffers, fueled local economies, and fortified family livelihoods. Yet in a region where historians have emphasized the impact of such export and subsistence commodities as coffee, bananas, and corn, scholars have neglected the crucial role of alcohol.

With an eye toward shedding new light on ethnic, gender, class, and state-subaltern relations, *Distilling the Influence of Alcohol* deconstructs alcohol drinkways (production, commerce, and consumption habits) and the ways the state legislated and policed alcohol sales and consumption during Guatemala's colonial and national history. Comparisons with other Latin American locales inform the interpretations of alcohol drinkways in Guatemala and how alcohol was a marker of social position and cultural identity, a crucial component in community and state building, and a commodity around which different cultural traditions and policing policies developed and evolved.

In contrast to the rich corpus of literature on Europe, Africa, Asia, and the United States, Latin American historiography addressing alcohol is relatively sparse. In Central America and Mexico, for example, extant studies tend to be anthropological, not historical.[1] Like recent U.S. histo-riography that situates the production and consumption of alcohol within larger economic, political, and social contexts,[2] this volume uses the study of alcohol as an entrée into the seat of Spanish colonial power in Central America and a window into the tumultuous process of nation building in Guatemala thereafter. With its indigenous, European, African, and Asian influences and diverse mix of peoples—Mayas, Garifunas, creoles (Hispanic elites), and ladinos (nonindigenous Guatemalans)—Guatemala presents an excellent case study to examine how the alcohol economy pro-vided a site of critical social interaction among the contested categories of ethnicity, race, class, and gender.

Distilling the Influence of Alcohol fits squarely in the broader literature of Atlantic history that uses commodities, such as sugar and chocolate, as prisms through which to view social, political, and economic trends.[3] Of-ten these studies focus on commodity chains—the effect these commodi-ties had in Europe even when they were produced in the Americas and the linkages the commodity exchanges formed between the Old World and the New. In contrast, the authors in this volume are most concerned with understanding what alcohol—its production, sale, and consumption—meant to the servants, peasants, workers, professionals, and elites who lived in the locales where it was produced. How did it affect their lives and the formation of their communities, colony, and finally nation? Drawing from archival sources and oral histories, the contributors to this volume attempt to uncover subalterns' knowledges regarding the use of alcohol. African American immigrants living in the Caribbean coastal regions of Guatemala, for example, understood alcohol consumption differently than their indigenous counterparts in the western highlands. In contrast to creole and ladino portrayals of "*indios*'" inebriation as a manifestation and cause of their backwardness, Mayas often articulated the crucial cer-emonial and ritual roles that alcohol played in their communities.[4]

Studying alcohol in Guatemala offers an opportunity to examine closely the give and take between power brokers and subordinates. As Tom Gjelten suggests in *Bacardi and the Long Fight for Cuba,* alcohol played an integral role in forging nations.[5] Such was the case with aguardiente in Guatemala, as these chapters show. By exploring how accommodation, defiance, and resistance shaped Guatemala, this study builds on the bur-geoning historiography of nation-state formation. As historian Florencia Mallon argues in her seminal work *Peasant and Nation,* to understand the consolidation of nation-states, scholars must take peasants' alternative nationalisms seriously.[6] Applying Antonio Gramsci's notion of organic intellectuals to the ordinary men and women whose contact with the state often occurred under extraordinary circumstances, such as when the police persecuted them for the illicit production, sale, and consumption of alcohol, reveals their economic and political influence.[7] Although creole and ladino leaders in Guatemala defined citizenship in ways that excluded Mayas throughout much of the national period, the latter constantly contested this definition and continued to claim the nation as their own. In this sense, alcohol provides a window into the broader history of Guatemala, where a Hispanicized state confronted its predominantly indigenous subjects at every turn.

The historiography of postcolonial Guatemala has long been dominated by another liquid commodity: coffee. When conservatives began creating the conditions for the commodification of coffee in the 1850s, they established an export economy that connected Guatemala to Europe and the United States. Coffee revenues funded the expansion of Guatemala's physical, economic, and political infrastructure.[8] At the same time, in responding to Todd Little-Siebold's call for "decaffeinating" Guatemala's postcolonial history, one of the first avenues we might pursue is alcohol production and consumption.[9] This book does just that and more by tracing alcohol's historical significance back to the colonial period when indigo was the Kingdom of Guatemala's major export.[10] Because aguardiente consumption during the colonial and national eras was almost entirely domestic and generally inelastic, revenue from it was not subject to the whims of the international market.[11] Both colonial and national governments depended on it. Unlike coffee, which was largely an enclave economy that demanded large pools of labor only during the few months of its harvest (October to December), the alcohol economy was integral to local, regional, and national life year-round. By exploring alcohol's impact in Guatemala specifically and other Latin American nations more broadly, these essays demonstrate for Guatemala and suggest for other countries that subjects, citizens, and authorities had more frequent and complex interactions and relations with each other and the state than previously imagined.

Prior to the Spanish invasions, Mayas fermented their beverages from honey and maguey cactus (among other substances), but these drinks generally were reserved for elites. For their part, Spaniards had long followed the Mediterranean tradition of drinking wine as part of their daily life. With the introduction of sugarcane and the process of distilling (vaporizing then condensing fermented solutions to be collected as a purified liquid), alcohol became cheap, plentiful, and more potent. As historian David Christian notes, the new technology had a powerful impact: "This changed profoundly the economic and social role of alcoholic drinks, for distilled drinks were to fermented drinks what guns were to bows and arrows: instruments of a potency unimaginable in most traditional societies."[12] In many ways, Guatemala's experience with these changes mirrors that of the rest of the world. Although distilling was known to the Greeks and Romans and advanced by the Arabs, it did not enter Europe until the eleventh century. Even then the mass production of spirits did not begin until the late fifteenth century, when books on distilling appeared. By the eighteenth century, distilled liquor had become the addictive drug of choice (best pictured as "Gin Lane" in William Hogarth's 1751 print) and later the opium of the working-class masses. Widespread lower-class consumption of distilled alcohol sparked the nineteenth- and twentieth-century temperance movements in Europe and the Americas that (among other things) offered coffee as an alternative to booze.[13] Ironically, Guatemala turned its agricultural export focus to this caffeinated alternative in the nineteenth century even though it remained dependent on the vice itself for state revenue and the provision of labor.

The gendered aspects of the long history of alcohol in Guatemala also reflect trends in the Atlantic world and the Americas more broadly. As *clandestinistas* (moonshiners), vendors, tavern owners, and consumers, Guatemalan women were at the center of the alcohol economy. Like those in Peru, Bolivia, and Mexico, indigenous women in Guatemala were crucial to the alcohol economy even before the Spanish invasions.[14] Prehispanic Mesoamerican women contributed significantly to the domestic economy as petty commodity producers and market vendors. As a potentially lucrative variant of this general pattern, women increasingly turned to aguardiente production and sale over the course of the colonial era and became even more involved in such enterprises with the emergent modern economies of the nineteenth and early twentieth centuries that made access to cash and income all the more critical.[15] As early as 1608, the Crown recognized the gendered (and ethnic) components of alcohol sales when it ordered that "only one respectable old woman be licensed to sell *pulque* for every one hundred Indians."[16] Selling alcohol provided an avenue for survival and sometimes success for widows, single mothers, *solteras* (bachelorettes or spinsters), and otherwise poor or marginalized women. Recognizing their struggle, at times colonial regimes allowed such women to operate *pulperías* (store-taverns) without paying taxes.[17] Combining their traditional roles as petty merchants and producers with the profitability of aguardiente, Guatemalan women (like their counterparts elsewhere in Latin America) defied presumptions of their business incompetence, advanced their class position, influenced national identity, and pressed for their emancipation through the alcohol economy.[18]

Using alcohol as a lens through which to examine the past sheds new light on gender relations, roles, and constructions. As René Reeves demonstrates in chapter 2, nineteenth-century women involved in the alcohol trade were well informed of national politics and trade policies. Their expanded mobility outside the home often led to domestic struggles over power within it. Despite warnings by intellectuals that alcohol weakened and depraved women, many working-class women drank with fervor, which at times led to bouts of disorderly behavior that landed them in jail.[19] Of course, men too were involved in aguardiente smuggling, trade, and consumption; often these activities framed masculine identities, as Stacey Schwartzkopf demonstrates in chapter 1.

As a driver of the economy and axis of social relations and hierarchies, culture, like gender, warrants significant historical study, as the field of cultural history has established. With its contrasting and at times complementary indigenous, creole, African, and ladino influences, Guatemala provides a window into the ways alcohol helped rituals and ceremonies to create community both within and across ethnic groups. Throughout Latin America, alcohol has long been offered as a ceremonial gift.[20] For Mayas, drinking was an important part of many community and family rituals over several centuries, although its significance changed over time.[21] As Schwartzkopf shows in his chapter, during the colonial and national periods, Mayas used their rituals and traditions to negotiate with the state over the criminalization of alcohol production and trade. Although some Mayas considered excessive drinking a crime,[22] few judged the production and sale of aguardiente, clandestinely or otherwise, to be criminal. Indeed, many considered it vital to the preservation of local cultural and religious traditions. Perhaps more than any other area of the judicial record, bootleggers' trials point to how one's socioeconomic position affected their interpretations of the law and crime. By outlawing moonshine, the state altered definitions of crime. By maintaining this cottage industry, bootleggers challenged definitions of deviant behavior.

Latin American and European intellectuals associated crime with inebriation, and at times authorities conveniently used this rhetoric to cover up their own shortcomings.[23] Coming out of Europe, the most influential treatise attributing the rising crime rate to the excessive use of alcohol was Henry Fielding's *An Enquiry into the Causes of the Late Increase in Robbers* (1751). In turn, colonial Latin American elites such as the seventeenth-century intellectual Carlos de Sigüenza y Góngora and eighteenth-century Archbishop Pedro Cortés y Larraz decried the excessive consumption of pulque and other alcoholic drinks by indigenous people.[24]

After independence, Guatemalan intellectuals and elites cultivated images of indios as backward and drunk as part of a discourse of state formation, thereby introducing an ethnic dimension to the association of alcohol and crime. Just as intellectuals crafted a narrative around alcohol consumption that privileged elite consumers and criminalized poor drinkers, creoles and elite ladinos portrayed indios as alcoholics who were prone to crime.[25] For turn-of-the-century Mexico City, historian Pablo Piccato argues, "Criminality and alcoholism appeared within a particular set of cultural values and references that promoted their persistence."[26] In Guatemala, these cultural values and references were grounded in ladino norms. Although scholars of colonial and modern Latin America have shown there is little correlation between alcohol and crime,[27] indigenous defendants who attributed their transgressions to inebriation perpetuated this myth. Aware of the legal value of this defense, they made good use of it; until 1926, Guatemalan law recognized inebriation as a mitigating circumstance.[28]

The mountainous and fragmented topography and long history of authoritarian rule that characterized Guatemala during the colonial and national periods shaped the various economic systems through which alcohol flowed. Producers and vendors operated in both the formal and informal economies and oftentimes in both. Aware that some bootleggers kept a low profile by purchasing sugarcane locally from valley growers, at times authorities (particularly during the Ubico administration) destroyed small sugarcane crops.[29] Other moonshiners traded with small growers on the coast or went to Guatemala City to get supplies. When entrepreneurs went through the proper channels to legalize their establishments, their businesses could grow. In contrast, clandestine producers and vendors who could not afford to pay the state's licensing and other fees succeeded only by keeping their enterprises small and themselves mobile. Few aspects of the Guatemalan economy were untouched by alcohol.

Beginning in the colonial era, alcohol buoyed local, regional, and national economies in Guatemala. To both control and profit from its consumption, the Spanish Crown established a monopoly on the sale and production of alcoholic beverages. After independence, alcohol revenue played an increasingly important role in the nation's budget. During the Central American Federation (1823–39), such proceeds helped to fund militias and judges (*jueces de letras*) within the revamped judicial system.[30] Throughout the nineteenth century, the state looked to the alcohol monopoly system as a primary source of income and by the late 1840s began enforcing alcohol laws in earnest, as Reeves demonstrates in his chapter.[31] In the 1890s, revenue from the legal aguardiente economy provided between a fourth and a third of Guatemala's national budget.[32] At the turn of the century, the dictator Manuel Estrada Cabrera (1898–1920) used alcohol revenue to help create the first Guatemalan police state. Guatemala was not alone in capitalizing on alcohol revenue. Throughout the Americas, governments counted on alcohol revenues to operate.[33] As James Alex Garza argues for Porfirian Mexico City, "pulque was big business."[34]

Yet Guatemalan governments' dependence on aguardiente revenue—in the form of taxation and proceeds from the prosecution of bootlegging—often undermined their stability. For example, even after widespread opposition to the state's regulation of alcohol production and sale helped to bring down the Conservative regime in 1871,[35] the Liberals who subsequently assumed power established their own aguardiente licensing regulations, fees, and taxes. So desperate were they to access alcohol revenue that these new leaders risked engendering the same resentment that precipitated their predecessors' demise.

In addition to generating revenue, alcohol lubricated labor systems. Even as they regulated the consumption of aguardiente and fermented beverages known as *chicha*, colonial officials admitted that the consumption of such regional homebrewed liquors was "useful and necessary for the health and life of the workers."[36] Many officials and landowners believed alcohol was the key to a pliable (and available) labor force. As one ethnographer working in highland Guatemala in the late 1920s noted, "Work leads to rum, and rum leads to work."[37] Like their counterparts in the Yucatán, by the end of the nineteenth century, *enganchadores* (labor brokers) used alcohol to entrap Mayas for work on agro-export plantations.[38] If they were not paid directly with it, often alcohol helped lure workers into signing labor contracts. Beginning in the colonial era, alcohol barter between indigenous peoples and landowners survived into the twentieth century.[39]

Besides being a cash nexus for moving labor and land, alcohol was a currency of local economies. Maya midwives, for instance, often were paid with aguardiente. In some regions, even local judges were paid with it (by the litigants), and those guilty of infractions could pay their fines with alcohol.[40] In addition to its paramount position in local and national economies, alcohol played a central role in regional economies, as Reeves demonstrates in his study of highland bootleggers who used sugar produced by small growers on the coast. The alcohol trade was also international, as nineteenth-century Mayas who transported and consumed *comiteco* (a type of aguardiente) from Chiapas, Mexico, evince in Schwartzkopf's chapter.

Because alcohol revenue was so valuable to government coffers, officials from the colonial to the national era dedicated increasing resources to repressing the prohibited production of alcohol. Throughout Latin America, officials enjoyed only limited success.[41] For example, historian William Taylor suggests that about 250 *pulquerías* operated without a license in Mexico City in 1639, "each of them surrounded by an 'army of Indians from dawn to dusk.'"[42] By highlighting the state-sanctioned production of alcohol and petitions concerning aguardiente in his chapter, Reeves raises a question that continues to elude researchers: how much clandestine aguardiente was produced and consumed? Vexed by the very phenomenon we study, the contributors to this volume (and other scholars) have attempted to portray the significance of bootlegging in the absence of clear quantitative data. Ironically, even evidence aimed at portraying authorities' success hinted at their failure. The mug shots of twenty-six clandestinistas (six of whom were women) who were captured during the last few weeks of 1932 in Sololá alone (see figure I.1), for example, is more suggestive of the extent to which the moonshine industry had proliferated than officials' ability to curtail it.

Strategies for controlling the production, distribution, and sale of alcohol varied over time and region. The colonial penchant for establishing alcohol monopolies gave way to stamp taxes in nineteenth-century Mexico

Figure I.1. "Twenty-six clandestinistas of both sexes." *La Gaceta: Revista de Policía y Variedades,* January 3, 1933. Image is reproduced courtesy of the Latin American Library, Tulane University, New Orleans.

and tax farming in twentieth-century Venezuela, for example.[43] In much of Central America including Guatemala, however, alcohol monopolies were alive and well throughout the nineteenth century. Even though the state's attempts to curtail clandestine production provoked unrest and at times rebellion, Central American governments so desperately needed the revenues generated from the alcohol economy that they refused to divest from it.[44]

Even though a large proportion of Guatemala's alcohol industry operated illegally in the nineteenth and twentieth centuries, as I argue in chapter 5, the role of *aguardiente clandestino* (moonshine) in local and regional economies created some ambiguity in the pursuit of bootleggers. Certainly the state wanted to maximize alcohol revenues, and many individual functionaries (and more than a few hired henchmen) pursued convictions with great zeal; at times they received a percentage of the profits.

But some officials also understood that most Mayas and poor ladinos could not afford to purchase liquor licenses or, for that matter, legal alcohol. Removing aguardiente clandestino entirely would cause upheaval in the countryside and upset the economic system by which enganchadores recruited laborers. Moreover, the sale of aguardiente clandestino was an important source of revenue for local and regional economic systems, as the chapters in this volume reveal. In short, to cut off aguardiente clandestino completely would have caused a contagion of negative intended and unintended consequences. The local collaboration and complicity that ranged from corrupt authorities looking the other way to officials establishing their own illicit operations was as much driven by personal interest as this knowledge. Nonetheless, this collusion stemmed partly from the state's ambivalence about the efficacy of its alcohol policies, which in turn made enforcement spotty by design.

Alcohol also seeped into politics, as the collusion between elected officials, clandestinistas, and locals evinces. Some politicians used alcohol to enrich themselves and to buy votes.[45] As occurred elsewhere in Latin America, politics influenced policy (such as the transition from state monopolies to alcohol taxes), which in turn shaped the state's relationship with its charges.[46]

As a cultural marker that influenced identity and social coherence, alcohol's value was as much social and cultural as economic. Informed by historian Christopher Lutz's assertion that a Guatemalan's identity could be determined by the booze they drank,[47] *Distilling the Influence of Alcohol* explores how the behavior of drinkers was the "product of expectations and culturally shared values."[48] Despite the trouble emanating from excessive use and alcoholism, alcohol remained the basic social lubricant of fiestas and celebrations where local knowledges and traditions were reinforced and reshaped.

As the funnels through which much alcohol made it to the lips of consumers, taverns, cantinas, pulquerías, speakeasies, juke joints, honky-tonks, and other (often illicit) establishments played a significant role in economic, social, and political relations. Even though they generated significant income for local and national economies, such businesses had an uneasy relationship with the state. Like officials before and after them, Bourbon reformers, for example, attributed their colonies' moral decline to taverns and the loose women and lusty men they attracted. Often the state feared that watering holes were the hotbeds of social unrest.[49]

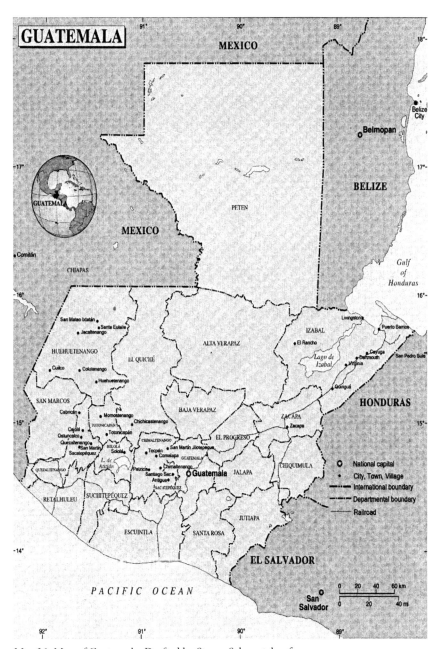

Map I.1. Map of Guatemala. Drafted by Stacey Schwartzkopf.

As venues where gossip was shared, taverns were often some of the most important places in communities and neighborhoods.[50] As microcosms of broader society, they provide a window into class, ethnic, generational, and gender relations. In chapter 3, Alvis Dunn puts to rest notions of colonial taverns as happy melting pots; rather, he shows how they reflected the social stratification of the larger society while providing an arena for dynamic interaction. With their regulations, local town councils both encouraged and upset these social hierarchies by, for example, prohibiting the consumption of imported alcohol by indigenous people but permitting Spaniards, mestizos (people of mixed European and indigenous ancestry), mulattos (people of mixed European and African ancestry), and even blacks to enjoy it. Saloons and their many counterparts were sites where one's accountability, vulnerability, power, and identity were contested, defended, and reconstituted.

*   *   *

Many of the chapters call attention to postcolonial Guatemala and the ways alcohol influenced state building. In chapter 1, with his command of the prehispanic, colonial, and early modern periods, Stacey Schwartzkopf establishes a framework for studying how Latin American indigenous peoples' alcohol consumption and production have changed over time. Careful not to generalize patterns and distinctions that occurred in different periods, places, and circumstances, Schwartzkopf compares indigenous peoples' drinkways in Guatemala, central Mexico, and the Andes to suggest the ways alcohol fueled economies and helped authorities to rule both before and after the Spanish invasions.

By examining the "highly divergent interpretations of alcohol use," Schwartzkopf identifies one of the central tensions between authorities and Mayas regarding alcohol production, trade, and consumption. Even if they seldom convinced authorities of their position, Mayas who emphasized alcohol's cultural and customary primacy in their negotiations with the state reveal much about competing worldviews in northwestern Guatemala. Although officials persecuted them whether they were engaged in the alcohol trade for profit or for use in their rituals, Maya involvement boosted local and regional economies, where the production of sugar and chicha were closely linked, and international trade when Mayas smuggled comiteco across the border from Chiapas. The continuation of these activities despite their criminalization can be read as Maya resistance to state monopolies and power.

In contemporary San Juan Ostuncalco and the surrounding towns in the predominantly indigenous department of Quezaltenango, many involved in the alcohol trade took a different approach. Although some simply sought to evade authorities, others addressed officials head-on in an effort to change government policies. As René Reeves points out in chapter 2, the goal was not simply to increase local profits but also to reduce the state's presence in their communities. Female vendors were often the leaders of these efforts. Excluded from formal political positions, they found other means to advance their agendas and in the process increased their exposure locally, regionally, and even nationally. Women involved in the alcohol economy enjoyed freedom, mobility, and influence. One need only consider the role that resistance to the state's hated alcohol monopolies played in bringing about the downfall of the Conservative regime to understand that women influenced the course of events. By framing his study from 1862 to 1886, Reeves adeptly explores the challenges and benefits of the alcohol economy for both the Conservative and Liberal governments in Guatemala and how that commodity influenced the fate of both regimes.

In a trend that changed over time, alcohol revenue was not always a significant contributor to state coffers. Unlike its successors after independence, the Crown's revenues from aguardiente in Guatemala rarely rose above 10 percent of its budget.[51] In his study of Santiago de los Caballeros (modern-day Antigua), Alvis E. Dunn demonstrates in chapter 3 that even this relatively minor income was sufficient to compel both the Crown and local town councils to condone alcohol consumption even as they lamented its detrimental effects on morality and health. By exploring how alcohol mediated relations between colonial authorities and subjects, Dunn provides a window into the way alcohol shaped colonial politics during the Bourbon era.

Focusing on the Caribbean coast and using alcohol as a lens through which to study a turn-of-the-century African American diaspora, Frederick Douglass Opie, in chapter 4, broadens both the geographical focus of and the historical approach to this collection. With an eye toward subaltern politics and power, he draws a stark contrast between African American migrant laborers on the Guatemalan coast who remained marginalized and sometimes trapped there and a small subset of that population that turned to the alcohol trade to establish more permanent and lucrative lives. For some, alcohol sales facilitated their upward mobility in ways that were not possible in the U.S. South or British West Indies; for most, alcohol consumption provided a temporary escape from their privations. Opie found that like Estrada Cabrera's dictatorship, private businesses such as the United Fruit Company too pursued the often-contradictory goals of turning a profit from alcohol sales and maintaining a sober work force. Perilous yet irresistible, the alcohol economy could just as easily disrupt as enrich both the state and the private sector.

Even though clandestine stills and inebriated denizens disrupted the efforts of Estrada Cabrera and President General Jorge Ubico Castañeda (1931–44) to portray Guatemala as a powerful and modern nation, these dictators lacked the political will to eradicate aguardiente clandestino, let alone legal alcohol. In a reflection of Opie's study, in chapter 5 I too find that profits were too lucrative and alcohol too central to social life for the government to outlaw its production or consumption despite pressure from intellectuals who decried its deleterious effects. As Reeves does for the nineteenth century, I demonstrate how women were often at the center of the struggle over alcohol's role in twentieth-century Guatemala's nation-state formation, despite being formally excluded from political power and citizenship. Even while calling the state's authority into question, moonshiners, consumers, and local citizens collaborated with officials and used the government's tools to further their own goals. Resistance and cooperation often went hand in hand.

Taken as a whole, the chapters in *Distilling the Influence of Alcohol* use alcohol as a lens through which to reconceptualize Guatemalan history. Because its sale, production, and consumption were steady throughout the year, alcohol, more than any other commodity—including coffee—was at the center of relations between Mayas, creoles, ladinos, Garifunas, black migrants, and the state in Guatemala. In many ways, this volume highlights the cultural diversity and historical complexity of Guatemala in the broader Atlantic world. Going beyond the Guatemalan case, *Distilling the Influence of Alcohol* demonstrates how approaching alcohol as a historical protagonist can open up fresh avenues to studying a nation's economic, political, cultural, and social development.

Notes

1. See, for example, Eber, *Women and Alcohol;* Siverts, *Drinking Patterns in Highland Chiapas;* Navarrete Pellicer, *El aguardiente;* Menéndez, *Antropología del alcoholismo;* Pine, *Working Hard, Drinking Hard;* Dennis, "Role of the Drunk"; Crump, "Alternative

Economy of Alcohol"; Adams, "Guatemala"; Brandes, "Drink, Abstinence." Historical studies include Taylor, *Drinking, Homicide, and Rebellion*; Mitchell, *Intoxicated Identities;* Hernández Palomo, *El aguardiente de caña*; and Bruman, *Alcohol in Ancient Mexico.* For Guatemala, McCreery, *Rural Guatemala, 1760–1940* and Woodward, *Rafael Carrera* both provide historical data about alcohol and descriptions of its use, but they refrain from examining its broader economic, social, or political importance. For historical studies of alcohol in other areas of Latin America, see, for example, Mora de Tovar, *El aguardiente y conflictos sociales* and Lomnitz, "Alcohol and Culture."

2. See, for example, Salinger, *Taverns and Drinking*; Burns, *Spirits of America*; Williams, *Rum*; Okrent, *Last Call.*

3. See, for example, Mintz, *Sweetness and Power;* Coe and Coe, *True History of Chocolate.*

4. The term *indio* or Indian was generally used by nonindigenous people to pejoratively characterize Mayas as dirty, drunk, lazy, and retrograde, though at times indigenous people complicated these meanings by self-identifying as indio.

5. Gjelten, *Bacardi.*

6. Mallon, *Peasant and Nation.*

7. Gramsci, *Selections from the Prison Notebooks*, 6, 15–16, 18.

8. Reeves, *Ladinos with Ladinos;* Gudmundson and Lindo-Fuentes, *Central America.*

9. Little-Siebold, "Decaffeinating Guatemalan History"; Little-Siebold, "Guatemala and the Dream," 254–72. In fact, scholars such as Gudmundson, Reeves, and Schwartzkopf have already begun doing this.

10. Woodward, *Central America,* 45–46.

11. Smith, *Caribbean Rum,* 220. In *La crisis de antiguo régimen*, Pompejano offers a fine analysis of alcohol's macroeconomic effects in nineteenth-century Guatemala.

12. Christian, "Alcohol and Primitive Accumulation," 33.

13. Schivelbusch, *Tastes of Paradise;* Courtwright, *Forces of Habit,* 11–13; Smith, *Caribbean Rum,* 78–79.

14. Eber, *Women and Alcohol*, 22; Hames, "Maize-Beer, Gossip, and Slander," 352, 358; Lacoste, "Wine and Women."

15. González Alzate, "State Reform, Popular Resistance," 131, 135; Taylor, *Drinking, Homicide, and Rebellion*, 37–38, 53–54; Ericastilla and Jiménez, "Las clandestinistas de aguardiente," 21; Dunn, "Aguardiente and Identity."

16. Taylor, *Drinking, Homicide, and Rebellion*, 37–38.

17. Rebolledo, "Pícaras y pulperas."

18. Reiche, "Estudio sobre el patrón"; Lacoste, "Wine and Women."

19. Carey, "Drunks and Dictators"; Fallaw, "Dry Law, Wet Politics."

20. Fallaw, "Dry Law, Wet Politics"; La Farge and Byers, *Year-Bearer's People*; La Farge, *Santa Eulalia*; Nash, *In the Eyes*, 186.

21. Reiche, "Estudio sobre el patrón"; Bunzel, "Role of Alcoholism," 384; Lewis, "La guerra del posh."

22. Bunzel, "Role of Alcoholism," 386.

23. Connell, "'Because I Was Drunk'"; Pilcher, *¡Que vivan los tamales!* 83–84.

24. Leonard, *Don Carlos de Sigüenza y Góngora*; Cortés y Larraz, *Descripción geográfico-moral*, 113.

25. Garrard-Burnett, "Indians Are Drunks"; Burkitt, "Explorations in the Highlands"; Connell, "'Because I Was Drunk'"; Lacoste, "Wine and Women"; Piccato, "'El paso de Venus'"; Carey, "Drunks and Dictators."

26. Piccato, "'El paso de Venus,'" 235.

27. Taylor, *Drinking, Homicide, and Rebellion*; Piccato, *City of Suspects*.

28. *Memoria de los trabajos realizados por la Policía Nacional durante al año de 1940*, 110.

29. Metz, *Ch'orti'-Maya Survival*, 60.

30. González Sandoval, "El estanco de bebidas embriagantes."

31. McCreery, *Rural Guatemala*, 87–88, 176–77; Reeves, *Ladinos with Ladinos*, 104, 116, 227n47; González Alzate, "History of Los Altos," 141–48; Bunzel, "Role of Alcoholism," 363, 386; Gudmundson, "Firewater, Desire," 254–55n30; Ingersoll, "War of the Mountain"; Schwartzkopf, "Maya Power and State Culture."

32. McCreery, *Rural Guatemala*, 177.

33. For example, from the 1790s to 1913 (when the sixteenth amendment, which allowed the federal government to levy an income tax without apportioning it among the states, was ratified), the United States government was dependent on excise taxes on alcohol. In some years, excise taxes accounted for as much as 50 percent of the government's domestic revenue. See Okrent, *Last Call*.

34. Garza, *Imagined Underworld*, 24.

35. Pompejano, *La crisis de antiguo régimen*; Reeves, *Ladinos with Ladinos*, 133, 135; Schwartzkopf, "Maya Power and State Culture."

36. Ericastilla and Jiménez, "Las clandestinistas de aguardiente," 14.

37. Burkitt, "Explorations in the Highlands," 59.

38. Fallaw, "Dry Law, Wet Politics."

39. Courtwright, *Forces of Habit*, 146–47.

40. Carey, *Engendering Mayan History*, 39; Lewis, "La guerra del posh."

41. Taylor, *Drinking, Homicide, and Rebellion*, 38, 53, 55, 56, 68; Scardaville, "Alcohol Abuse and Tavern Reform," 646–47, 651, 653, 654, 669; Lacoste, "Wine and Women," 377.

42. Taylor, *Drinking, Homicide, and Rebellion*, 38.

43. Márquez, "Stamp Tax on Alcoholic Beverages"; Yarrington, "Román Cárdenas."

44. Wolfe, *Everyday Nation State*, 45–79; Reeves, *Ladinos with Ladinos*, 115–35, 171–83. Even where national governments terminated alcohol monopolies, at times local officials were tempted to restore the monopoly, as was the case in Chiapas, Mexico, in the late 1940s. See Lewis, "La guerra del posh," 115.

45. Fallaw, "Dry Law, Wet Politics."

46. Yarrington, "Román Cárdenas"; Lewis, "La guerra del posh."

47. Lutz, *Santiago de Guatemala*.

48. Fallaw, "Dry Law, Wet Politics."

49. Brown, *Bourbons and Brandy*; González Alzate, "State Reform, Popular Resistance"; Connell, "Because I Was Drunk"; Lacoste, "Wine and Women."

50. Hames, "Maize-Beer, Gossip, and Slander," 357, 361.

51. Wortman, *Government and Society*, 153.

1

◇◇◇◇◇◇◇◇◇◇◇◇◇◇

Consumption, Custom, and Control

Aguardiente in Nineteenth-Century Maya Guatemala

STACEY SCHWARTZKOPF

In this chapter, I consider struggles over the meaning and practice of alcohol consumption by an indigenous group, specifically, the use of aguardiente among Q'anjob'alan Maya peoples in the Huehuetenango region of Guatemala during the nineteenth century. After a brief discussion of previous approaches to alcohol use among indigenous peoples in Latin America, I argue for an approach to Maya alcohol use in Guatemala that places the cultural construction of consumption at the center of the analysis of alcohol use among historic indigenous populations. This approach integrates often-divergent cultural and political economic perspectives on alcohol use within a single framework. I then draw on both anthropological and historical evidence to reconstruct key shifts in patterns of alcohol use among Q'anjob'alan communities in Guatemala over time, with a particular focus on the nineteenth century. Specifically, I argue that struggles over aguardiente consumption played a major role both in community ritual and in political relations between Maya communities and state projects promoted by colonial, conservative, and liberal governments in Huehuetenango during the nineteenth century. Furthermore, I argue that attention to such struggles reveals the larger historiographic significance of aguardiente in Guatemala over this time, namely, its fundamental role in state financing, private capital accumulation, and labor recruitment for coffee production. Finally, I suggest the relevance of this approach for the study of alcohol use among indigenous peoples elsewhere in Latin America.

Approaches to Indigenous Drinking in Latin America

Historical and anthropological studies of indigenous alcohol use in Latin America have largely tended to follow one of two major approaches. The first, which can be characterized as a sociocultural approach,[1] has been employed most often in ethnographic work among twentieth- and twenty-first-century indigenous communities.[2] This approach focuses on documenting the social and cultural context of alcohol use, as well as its biological, psychological, and social effects. A key emphasis of this research has been in culturally contextualizing alcohol use, including that regarded as pathological according to a biomedical standard of evaluation (that is, alcoholism), by relating drinking patterns to social and ritual practices found within particular indigenous communities. This emphasis has allowed anthropologists and others employing this approach to challenge lingering stereotypes of innate drunkenness among indigenous peoples, although it has left them open to charges of "deflating" alcohol problems among the groups they have studied.[3] A more serious flaw in this approach is its lack of systematic attention to the larger political and economic contexts that often shape patterns of alcohol use,[4] although the occasional study has explored this topic in greater depth.[5]

In contrast, the second approach, most often found in historical or documentary-based studies of indigenous alcohol use, can be characterized as a political economy approach precisely because of the attention it gives to the role of alcohol production and consumption in relation to issues such as state control over alcohol sales, prohibition, monopolization, taxation, crime (or criminalization), and rebellion.[6] Research using this approach has demonstrated the large and often overlooked part that (frequently illicit) alcohol production, sale, and consumption have played in rural and urban livelihoods, as well as the sometimes highly visible role of alcohol in political divisions ranging from debates over prohibition to outright rebellion. Although studies employing this approach are often sensitive to the social characteristics—in terms of class, race/ethnicity, and gender—of those engaged in political and economic struggles over alcohol, they rarely address the cultural meaning of alcohol consumption as it relates to specific groups.[7] As a consequence, research using this approach tends to take the question of the demand for alcohol as a given, rather than a subject for investigation in its own right.

A third approach, which avoids some of these limitations, is one that has been productively applied to the study of ingested commodities, including sugar, spices, tea, and alcohol, in historical settings in the United States, Europe, Africa, and the Caribbean,[8] but it has rarely been employed in Latin America. This approach, which can be characterized as a cultural commodities perspective,[9] effectively combines the concerns of the above approaches in emphasizing the construction of the demand for alcohol as a shifting social and cultural practice with profound political and economic implications. By placing demand within a cultural framework, this approach recognizes the multiple links that often exist between patterns of alcohol use and the reproduction of key social relationships within families and communities. This recognition is particularly relevant to Maya drinking patterns, which, as I discuss below, had deep roots in the prehispanic period in their associations with communal ritual events and social prestige, many of which were transformed in the succeeding colonial period and after. At the same time, this approach recognizes the multiple ways that drinking patterns connect individuals, families, and communities to other political and economic actors that seek to supply, limit, expand, or profit from this demand. Examining these connections involves tracing economic relationships of production and distribution, as well as political struggles over state prohibition, licensing, and taxation of alcoholic beverages. When both of these lines of investigation are followed within a single analytic frame, the full significance of alcohol use becomes clearer. Political, economic, and cultural dimensions are critical to understanding what anthropologist Christine Eber refers to as "rum's contradictions": its ability to serve social and ritual ends while simultaneously remaining a "devastatingly effective" tool of domination over indigenous groups.[10]

In order to trace each of these dimensions, this chapter reconstructs drinking patterns among Q'anjob'alan Maya groups in the northern Huehuetenango region of Guatemala from the prehispanic period to the twentieth century. For the remainder of this introduction I provide a brief outline of the most significant of these patterns before turning to the details of the evidence for each period in the following sections. First, a key shift in drinking practices during the early colonial period was the introduction of new crops, most importantly sugar, with which to make fermented brews, usually referred to by the generic term *chicha*. A second development during this time was the association of certain patterns of

Maya ritual activity, including the communal consumption of alcohol, with a broad area of negotiation between indigenous peoples and Spanish officials over custom or tradition (*costumbre*). As I have argued at greater length elsewhere,[11] within the colonial context custom came to serve for Maya peoples as a means to negotiate with royal officials and others over a wide variety of local practices, as well as their obligations as royal subjects, especially in the area of tribute and labor. Most important here is that Maya peoples used this understanding of custom to negotiate with royal officials and priests over local practices involving alcohol use, particularly during town fiestas and other ritual events. Although on several occasions the Crown and royal officials attempted to ban indigenous alcohol use outright, in practice a good deal of such customary drinking was permitted by royal officials and local clergy, especially if it involved fermented, rather than distilled, beverages.[12]

However, by the later colonial period the use of distilled alcoholic beverages (usually sugarcane liquor) known as aguardiente appears to have become much more widespread among many Maya peoples, and indeed among the population as a whole. This transition signaled a shift in consumption patterns, as distilled aguardiente began to supplement or replace fermented chicha for use in community rituals and other drinking occasions. Corresponding changes in production and distribution accompanied this shift, as individuals from a variety of ethnic and class backgrounds sought to supply this growing market. The later colonial period also witnessed more vigorous attempts at government regulation and taxation under the system of monopolies (*estancos*), which often met with stiff resistance by drinkers and the producers and sellers of alcohol.[13]

In the nineteenth century, issues of alcohol consumption, custom, and control were intimately connected to the political transitions of independence, Central American federation, and shifts in government between Liberals and Conservatives.[14] Throughout this period, available information indicates that colonial levels of alcohol consumption continued unabated, or perhaps even expanded, in the subsequent national period.[15] A major contributor to this greater freedom was the declining effectiveness of rural state power during the second quarter of the century, which limited government efforts to restrict, license, and tax alcohol.[16] At the same time, potential revenues from alcohol taxation were too tempting for governments of any political stripe to ignore for long. Revenues from alcohol licensing and taxation formed a growing proportion of state

Table 1.1. Guatemalan government income from aguardiente, 1827–1900

Year(s)	Income	% of total
1827	25,733 pesos	N/A
1831	38,383	N/A
1839	37,953	29%
FISCAL YEARS		
1843–44	30,474	5–16%
1844–45	20,518	5–16%
1845–46	22,190	5–16%
1846–47	21,928	5–16%
1847–48	39,339	5–16%
1848–49	39,568+	N/A
TWO-YEAR PERIODS		
1852–53	(128,156)[a]	N/A
1854–55	(83,370)[a]	N/A
1856–57	(91,104)[a]	N/A
1858–59	(99,973)[a]	N/A
1860	202,354	~26%[b]
1862	213,903	~26%[b]
1863	289,955	~26%[b]
1864	154,955	~26%[b]
1865	290,744	~26%[b]
1866	177,617	~26%[b]
1868	289,489	~26%[b]
1890	N/A	33%[c]
1892	N/A	34%[c]
1894	N/A	29%[c]
1896	N/A	23%[c]
1898	N/A	31%[c]
1899	N/A	35%[c]
1900	N/A	36%[c]

Sources: González Sandoval, "El estanco de bebidas embriagantes"; Woodward, *Rafael Carrera*, 406; McCreery, *Rural Guatemala*, 177.
a. Anticipated revenue.
b. Average percentage for years 1860–68.
c. Total alcohol tax.

income under both Conservative and Liberal regimes, particularly as state power began to be reasserted in rural areas after midcentury (table 1.1). Predictably, these greater efforts at control and taxation, which involved both public and quasi-public/quasi-private attempts to enforce alcohol monopolies, again resulted in widespread resistance and rebellion.[17]

By the late nineteenth century, three related trends had come to shape struggles over alcohol consumption. First was the ongoing consolidation of the legal alcohol industry under large producers, many of them politically connected members of Guatemala's wealthiest families.[18] Second, linked in some fashion to the first, was a great expansion in the enforcement of alcohol laws, which came to occupy nearly the full attention of the judicial system in rural areas during the final decades of the century and represented the increasing criminalization of small producers and distributers as moonshiners (*clandestinistas*) and smugglers (*contrabandistas*).[19] Finally, and most relevantly for many Maya peoples, were the ever closer links being established between indigenous consumption and labor recruitment for the expanding coffee industry.[20] Collectively, these trends shaped indigenous alcohol use against the background of continuing customary consumption, with profound implications for the exercise of state power, indigenous resistance, and the practice of community culture well into the twentieth century. For the remainder of this essay, I trace these patterns among Q'anjob'alan Maya peoples in Huehuetenango, before discussing their implications for the study of indigenous alcohol use elsewhere in Latin America.

Maya Alcohol Consumption in the Prehispanic and Colonial Periods

As noted earlier, one of the most significant questions relating to Maya alcohol use concerns the timing and nature of the transition from the production and use of primarily fermented alcoholic beverages based on maize, maguey, or honey to the dominance of distilled liquor made from sugar. Given the absence of available direct information on the issue within the Huehuetenango region prior to the seventeenth century, several inferences must collectively stand for more concrete data in reconstructing alcohol production and use in the prehispanic and early colonial periods. As all authorities agree that both sugar and distillation were unknown in the New World before the arrival of Europeans, alcoholic beverages made and used prior to that point were necessarily fermented from some other material.

Beyond this general statement, there was great variety within aboriginal Mesoamerica in preferred beverages, such that it is possible to delineate "drink areas" based on the predominance of certain plants used as the basis of fermentation. According to an exhaustive survey by Henry

J. Bruman, the Maya region was one of the most complex and internally diverse, containing drinks made from pineapple, *jocote*, *coyol* palm, and maize mixed with "bark from a certain tree . . . probably either a *Hibiscus* or *Heliocarpus*."[21] Unlike central Mexico, where pulque reigned supreme, in the Maya region relatively little use seems to have been made of maguey as a base, although it was sometimes used as an additive; rather, the dominant drink was made from honey mixed with the bark of a tree known as *balché* in Yukatek Maya, which gave the drink its name.

Early colonial sources describe the production of this mead among Maya of the Yucatán peninsula with honey collected from domesticated and wild bees.[22] These same sources, as well as prehispanic iconography, attest to the intimate role that this drink played in religious life, from rites connected to the practice of apiculture itself to the use of balché as an intoxicant in public rituals.[23] Production and consumption of balché, along with some of its associated rituals, continued well into the twentieth century among Maya-speakers in Yucatán, as well as among the linguistically related Lacândón in Chiapas.[24]

Based on this prevalence within the region, it seems likely that balché or a similar honey-based drink was made and consumed within the Huehuetenango region prior to the Spanish invasion, although this does not rule out consumption of other beverages as well. Some of the earliest sources concerning the area indicate that honey was produced in quantities sufficient to provide over a hundred large jugs annually as *encomienda* tribute during the first half of the sixteenth century.[25] Later colonial records also indicate that honey continued to be produced in several northern Huehuetenango towns in the parish of Jacaltenango into the early nineteenth century.[26] Far more prevalent by then, however, was the cultivation of sugar, which had been established in several towns in the southern Huehuetenango region by at least the late seventeenth century.[27]

All available information indicates that the latter sweetener quickly supplemented or replaced honey as the basis for making fermented drinks during the early colonial period throughout the Guatemalan highlands, including the Huehuetenango region. Thomas Gage, writing in the 1630s, provides an oft-cited recipe used by the Poqomam of Mixco, containing both sweeteners, as well as other plant or animal additives:

> Amongst themselves they use to make such drinks as are in operation far stronger than wine; and these they confection in such great

jars as come from Spain; wherein they put some little quantity of water, and fill up the jar with some molasses or juice of the sugar cane, or some honey for to sweeten it; then for the strengthening of it, they put roots and leaves of tobacco, with other kinds of roots which grow there, and they know to be strong in operation, nay in some places I have known where they have put in a live toad, and so closed up the jar for a fortnight, or month's space, till all that they have put in [it] be thoroughly steeped and the toad consumed, and the drink well-strengthened, then they open it, and call their friends to the drinking of it, (which commonly they do in the night time, lest their Priest in the Town should have notice of them in the day) which they never leave off, until they be mad and raging drunk. This drink they call *chicha*, which stinketh most filthily.[28]

Several points can be drawn from Gage's account. First, he clearly indicates the equivalence or admixture of honey and sugar in the creation of beverages in the central highlands by the early seventeenth century. Second, the term he used to describe this concoction, *chicha*, appears to have been used throughout highland Guatemala to designate such fermented sugar brews, not maize beer, as seems to have been the case in other areas of Mesoamerica and Andean South America. Third, he describes drinking as a social event occurring under the noses of local religious authorities, suggesting at best lax enforcement of royal prohibitions against alcohol use by indigenous peoples.

In the Huehuetenango region, the use of chicha is documented for the early eighteenth century in a March 1703 proceeding against a local indigenous official from the town of Jacaltenango.[29] This case also provides some of the earliest available information on the use of alcohol in connection with Maya community custom and ritual. The events leading to the whipping and removal from office of Sebastián Ros, Jacaltenango's town mayor (*alcalde primero*), involved accusations of drunkenness and physical abuse on the part of Ros during a Mardi Gras (*carnestolendas*) meal attended by the other town officials, local elders (*principales*), and three friars from the local convent. Specifically, Ros was accused of insulting and attacking one of the friars and several of the elders while drunk on chicha, or *agua de caña*, all the while proclaiming his dominance over the town. This drunkenness and self-aggrandizing behavior was apparently only the latest manifestation of a pattern Ros had maintained since being placed in office only a few months earlier. However, it was apparently the last straw not only for the three religious personnel, each of whom wrote letters condemning his behavior, but also for the other town officials and elders, who united in requesting his removal. Several of the latter, including his own brother Joachín, gave testimony against him, indicating that he had swindled his way into the office and that since then he had not only been continually drunk but had also incited others to drink, so that there was a continual carousal (*borrachera*) in progress within the town.

In his defense, Ros made the argument that, while he may in fact have been tipsy, "although not totally senseless," it was "the custom [*costumbre*] of the town that every year during carnival they have a fiesta as best they can, regaling the priests [with food] as is customary." Furthermore, he alleged, the elders were also drunk, as one of them "perhaps with malicious intentions" had handed him a gourd cup full of chicha just before he had entered for the feast. As for the alleged verbal and physical abuse, Ros claimed that it had all occurred in the opposite direction. When he had entered, the priests and elders were all seated, and upon being invited by one of the friars to take his seat, he had respectfully replied, "Father, my place is to serve the priests." However, as everyone was drunk, this deference went unnoticed, and suddenly the priest "went crazy and began to rush me, punching and slapping and much mistreating me, saying that he would deprive me of the *alcalde* [position] and break my staff [of office] into pieces." In light of such hostility, Ros offered to give up his staff on the spot and retire peacefully to his house. The colonial official who heard the case was apparently unconvinced by this account of events, as he sentenced Ros to twenty-five lashes before removing him from office and appointing another local official in his place.

Two points can be drawn from this case. The first relates to the (ineffective) claim made by Ros that the use of alcohol was customary, with the particular connotation that this term had in colonial Guatemala, as discussed above. This claim is an early example of a pattern that would remain common in legal disputes well into the nineteenth century, when a custom defense was (usually ineffectually) employed by indigenous individuals accused of smuggling, bootlegging, and other alcohol-related crimes. The second point relates to what the case indicates about the availability of sugar-based alcohol within the region.

As mentioned above, there is direct evidence that sugar had been cultivated on a small scale in the region since at least the late seventeenth century,[30] and based on more circumstantial information this date could perhaps be pushed back as much as a century or more. However, by itself the presence or absence of sugar cultivation does not necessarily indicate the production and consumption of sugar-based alcohol, as there is also the question of the materials and technical knowledge required for distillation, and of course alcohol could also be brought into the region from elsewhere. But most evidence from the late seventeenth century and after points to the co-occurrence of sugar crops and small mills (*trapiches*) for processing the sweetener into cakes (*panela*), chicha, and possibly aguardiente.[31] These small-scale operations were complemented outside of the region in the same period by a few larger sugar refineries (*ingenios*), usually owned by religious orders and utilizing large numbers of African slaves as well as (illegal) Indian labor.[32]

The most detailed information concerning eighteenth-century sugar production in the Huehuetenango region comes from a December 5, 1780, list of plantings (*siembras*) and mills, apparently undertaken for the purposes of taxing or tithing their production.[33] The report listed two dozen productive operations, nearly half of them owned or rented by local Spaniards and mulattos in the southern Huehuetenango region. The highest concentration of enterprises was in the area surrounding Cuilco, a large Mam-speaking town in southwestern Huehuetenango with a small nonindigenous population. With the exception of the large hacienda of Canibal, owned by the Spaniard Jossef Cossio and valued at four thousand pesos a year, most of these were relatively small individual or family operations on lands rented from the indigenous pueblo, each with an estimated production of fifty to two hundred pesos annually in brown sugar. Outside of this primary zone, a second and smaller area of sugar processing can be identified in the region surrounding the adjacent towns of Ixtahuacán and Colotenango,[34] in particular in Pétzal, a hamlet of the latter town, where again a few Spaniards and mulattos attempted to maintain various operations, largely on lands rented from the church or absentee owners. Unlike those in Cuilco, which seemed to have provided a more regular (and taxable) income for their resident proprietors, several of these operations were described as being in a state of deterioration or development and listed no income. Interestingly, in light of the dominance of religious orders in sugar production elsewhere in Guatemala, one of the apparently more successful operations in this area was run by a member of the clergy, the Mercedarian Fray Joseph Camposeco, in Ixtahuacán.

This pattern also held for the most profitable operation outside of these two zones, and the only one in northern Huehuetenango, the hacienda of Montenegro in Jacaltenango, similarly run by resident Mercedarians.[35]

However, for the purposes of the present chapter, the most useful information contained in the report concerns the documentation of indigenous planting of sugar specifically for the purposes of producing alcoholic beverages. In at least five instances, indigenous individuals or groups are indicated as growing sugar on small plots; in three of these cases, it is further specified that their purpose was to make drinks (*bebidas, brebajes*).[36] Although in most cases indigenous sugar plots were owned communally, in at least one instance two Maya individuals from nearby Santa Isabel were planting in the presumably more ecologically suitable Pétzal region. Frustratingly, the report does not specify whether the drinks being produced were chicha or aguardiente, nor does it indicate anything about their use. Circumstantially, given royal officials' apparent indifference to the production of these drinks, most of the alcohol was likely chicha, the use of which was usually tolerated among the indigenous population.[37] Nevertheless, given the explicit presence of hand mills (*trapiches de mano*) in the two indigenous operations in Pétzal, as well as the prevalence of sugar-processing technology in the region, it seems probable that some aguardiente was being produced by Maya peoples in late eighteenth-century Huehuetenango, although on a relatively small scale.

Custom, Comiteco, and Crime in the Nineteenth Century

Despite this evidence of sugar and alcohol processing within the Huehuetenango region, the area clearly also formed a substantial market for alcohol produced outside of the region. At least in relation to Q'anjob'alan Maya communities, the late colonial period witnessed a shift in consumption patterns toward alcohol produced in nearby Chiapas, which was produced in a distinctive fashion and became the preferred alcohol for the northern Huehuetenango region. Evidence for this assertion comes from various early nineteenth-century reports of widespread illegal alcohol trade or smuggling across the administrative border with Chiapas. In particular, several sources describe the contraband importation of comiteco, a type of aguardiente made with agave sap in the Chiapan town of Comitán. Such smuggling was particularly prevalent in northern Huehuetenango, where local Maya communities developed a preference for the comiteco brand. Thus, during an 1812 inspection, the provincial governor (*alcalde mayor*) specifically warned local officials in two northern Huehuetenango communities to guard against the introduction of "aguardiente de Comitán," and in one town he discovered and destroyed twenty-six jugs allegedly used to transport the alcohol.[38]

Contemporary accounts indicated that there were extensive economic ties between northern Huehuetenango and the Comitán region, including a livestock transport industry and a flourishing trade in wheat, maize, and salt extracted from wells in the town of San Mateo Ixtatán.[39] A substantial percentage of the profits from the latter seem to have been turned into comiteco. At least, this was the claim of the local priest Father Juan José Juárez, who in the context of an 1814 letter to the provincial governor concerning schools stated, "In this town [San Mateo] it is necessary that the teacher Y[our] L[ordship] appoints also be a dry, strong, and upright constable in order to contain those Indians in their continual drunkenness, larceny, and obstinacy. It is an incredible thing I am telling [you] that it surpasses 3000 pesos a year that are brought from the town of Comitán in aguardiente produced [i.e., through trade] from the salt [wells] that they have, by this disorder neglecting to comply with the most necessary obligations."[40] While there may be some reason to believe that these numbers are exaggerated,[41] there seems little doubt that some portion of the grains, livestock, and salt taken to Chiapas in the late colonial period returned to northern Huehuetenango in the form of comiteco. Although the existing data make assessing the economic impact of this trade difficult, the trade may have suppressed the development of local productive enterprises, as seems to have happened to a greater degree elsewhere in western Guatemala.[42]

These reports are early evidence of what would become an established practice in northern Huehuetenango by the mid-nineteenth century: the transportation of comiteco to the region in exchange for goods or labor. It is from this latter period that some of the most important accounts of aguardiente consumption are documented. To provide the context of these accounts, most of which come from criminal court cases located in the Court of First Jurisdiction (Juzgado de Primera Instancia) or the departmental administration (Jefatura Política) for Huehuetenango, I will first describe the status of the Guatemalan-Mexican border in the decades following independence. Despite the nominal establishment of this international border in 1823, following the decision of Chiapas to adhere to

Mexico rather than to remain within the Central American Federation, for most of the three decades following independence there was virtually no effective Guatemalan state presence in the border region. Indeed, sources from this period make it clear that regional officials were often uncertain as to the exact location of the border, and local residents regularly moved and traded across the frontier virtually unimpeded.[43] Only after 1850 did this situation begin to change, when a reviving Conservative government under José Rafael Carrera began to assert a state presence in the border region, establishing a minor official known as a *juez preventivo* to oversee a small contingent of soldiers assigned to guard the vast border region and to collect taxes on goods moving between the two nations.[44]

It is precisely in this context that we can turn to the accounts themselves, one of the earliest and the most detailed of which comes from a midcentury criminal case against one of these soldiers.[45] In 1853, Corporal Florencio Herrera was accused by his immediate superior of taking bribes, illegally confiscating goods, and stealing soldiers' pay while patrolling the border. These accusations touched off a long and involved criminal case that revealed widespread corruption, as well as considerable confusion over the legality of importing alcohol, its taxation, and, as mentioned above, even the physical location of the border. For our purposes, the most important data contained in the case are the detailed descriptions of customary practices related to the transportation and use of comiteco given by several indigenous witnesses over the course of the trial. In addition to these details, the case also reveals the highly divergent interpretations of alcohol use offered by indigenous peoples on the one hand and state agents on the other. The former steadfastly asserted that alcohol's customary status made the transportation of comiteco over the border legally exempt from regulation and taxation, while the latter viewed any such transportation as criminal smuggling.

The inclusion of so many indigenous statements concerning alcohol use in the case was the result of the fact that, in the days and weeks immediately prior to his arrest, Herrera and the soldiers under his command had encountered several small groups of Maya individuals transporting comiteco, which the soldiers had confiscated. Because the accusations against Herrera involved bribery and corruption, testimony was taken from several of these individuals, mostly young married men, in which almost all asserted the customary nature of this transportation and even described its intended ritual use. Additionally, over the duration of the trial, they and several indigenous officials petitioned the court for the return of their alcohol, again confidently asserting its customary status.

Collectively, these statements and petitions present a relatively coherent picture of alcohol trade and use within the context of rituals and practices related to the maintenance of family and community relationships. More specifically, three of the smugglers from San Mateo Ixtatán submitted a petition claiming that they had been sent by the governor of their community "to bring a keg of aguardiente from Comitán for the traditional customs in said pueblo; not to sell but for the use of the elders." They requested that their confiscated alcohol be immediately returned. A few days later, San Mateo's governor reiterated the request, stating that the alcohol was necessary for "their customs," this time offering to pay the taxes required. Around the same time, officials from Santa Eulalia made a similar appeal on behalf of one Felipe Diego, whom they had sent to bring a demijohn of comiteco for the festivities of Corpus Christi.

Finally, in perhaps the most unusual request, yet another petition was signed by the members of three different communities from the parish of San Pedro Soloma: Antonio, Dionisio, and Agustín Gonzáles and Esteban Martín of Soloma; Baltazar Gómes of San Mateo; and Pedro Juan of Santa Eulalia. This multicommunity appeal stated their account of the circumstances surrounding the "unjust embargo" of their liquor even more explicitly:

[O]n the 20th of last month [June 1853] we were returning from Comitán where we went to bring back a little aguardiente because of the approach of the titular fiesta of our pueblo [San Pedro] and because it is necessary to make use of this liquor to fulfill our customs; and in the place called Yulchen we were surprised by the soldier Valentín Vásquez who confiscated from us the aguardiente we brought and reduced it to two barrels, three demijohns, and three jugs of which only that which corresponded to us the natives (*indígenas*) of Santa Eulalia and San Mateo came without a manifest because we didn't know that it was necessary.[46]

They offered again to pay the taxes in return for the alcohol, arguing that its importation was not prohibited, as they had no intentions to "speculate" with it but only to use it for their customs, and that they had been inexplicably apprehended while traveling openly on the main road. They therefore requested the immediate return of the liquor, as they had already spent time in traveling to retrieve it, "causing us grave losses and damages."

Although all of these requests were ultimately unsuccessful in obtaining the return of the confiscated alcohol, their most intriguing aspect is the confidence with which Maya litigants asserted customary claims as a legal argument. Over the succeeding decades, such a custom defense was to remain a common feature of alcohol cases involving indigenous residents of the region, although the particular practices claimed under this heading varied from case to case. In the Herrera case, the ability of young, mostly married, men to retrieve alcohol for Catholic holidays under the direction of indigenous officials was being asserted as a vital, necessary, and (most importantly) legal element of their traditional rights.[47]

Indigenous defendants in later smuggling cases from the 1850s and 1860s made similar claims, although in some of these instances other ritual practices besides Catholic holidays were included as well. For example, in 1861 Mateo Lucas, a young married man from San Mateo Ixtatán, argued that the mule load of aguardiente that officials had confiscated from him was required for the annual change of town officials in his community. Because his father had been elected as an alderman (*regidor*), he was obligated to honor the other officials with alcohol and had sent his son to retrieve it.[48] In addition, town officials were not the only ones who might be so honored, as it was also customary to regale one's compadres with alcohol during each fiesta, as claimed by Baltazar García of Chaculá when a local customs official discovered comiteco in his home in July 1861.[49] A similar tradition prevailed in San Miguel Acatán, as reported by Pedro Sebastián, apprehended transporting comiteco along with three other indigenous locals in November 1862.[50] The latter, Tomás Francisco, Juan Sebastián, and Martín Tomás, all young married men from San Sebastián Coatán, each argued that their aguardiente was destined for a "*remate de casamiento*" for a brother or other male relative. Presumably this was a customary gift or ceremony within the marriage negotiations known ethnographically as a *pedida*.[51] Finally, ritual gifts of alcohol might be given in exchange for labor, as claimed by Juan Rámos, a farmer living in the town of Chaculá. He had sent his fellow townsman Juan Tadeo to Comitán to buy aguardiente "to give to the workers (*mozos*) that harvested his *milpa*, because it is customary; also to cure his son who is suffering from fevers."[52]

The latter justification highlights the fact that not all explanations for alcohol use in the northern Huehuetenango region involved claims of custom and tradition. In several instances local residents asserted other motivations for alcohol trafficking, including the treatment of illness and financial hardship.[53] These two defenses were frequently used by indigenous and nonindigenous individuals elsewhere in Huehuetenango, especially women, who often formed the bulk of alcohol sellers in the department capital and nearby communities and as a result often found themselves before the courts, as David Carey Jr. and René Reeves discuss in their chapters.[54] Nevertheless, the consistent use of the custom defense by men in the area is striking. This is all the more so given the fact that in virtually all of the cases mentioned above the accused were perfunctorily given the full penalty prescribed by law. Given its relative ineffectiveness as a legal strategy, the persistent invocation of costumbre indicates its key position in a larger struggle over the meaning of alcohol use within local social practices and, by extension, the social practices themselves. More specifically, in the face of increasing government and private efforts to criminalize the distribution and consumption of aguardiente, indigenous residents of the area contested state officials' interpretations of their actions at the level of both meaning and practice.

First, by continuing to purchase their alcohol across the border in Mexican territory, rather than in the state-sanctioned estancos, indigenous residents were simultaneously undermining the ability of government officials to control their economic activity and the national territory itself. Second, by defining their actions as a form of costumbre, local Maya peoples implicitly challenged the government's interpretation of their actions as criminal behavior.

Finally, local indigenous peoples, along with other residents, also took more direct action against those enforcing monopolies in the region. On nearly a half-dozen occasions during the 1850s and 1860s there were incidents or tumults that resulted in the destruction of monopoly stores (estancos) and distilleries as well as the verbal or physical abuse of their owners and operators.[55] Among the most serious was a three-day riot in the departmental capital of Huehuetenango in 1862, which required troops from the nearby department of Quezaltenango to restore order.[56] Very often the spark that set off these riots was some other issue (such as cholera or political divisions), but the hated monopolies were always a target of popular rage. Indeed, the Italian historian Danielle Pompejano has argued that resentment against the enforcement of monopolies played a role in bringing down the Conservative regime in 1871.[57]

Pompejano is also one of the clearest in pointing out the economic sources of this rising tension in the increasing consolidation of the alcohol industry in the hands of fewer and fewer large producers. This process culminated in the creation of the Compañía Anónima de Aguardiente in 1866.[58] Pompejano describes the partners and shareholders who made up this company as "representatives of the richest families of the country."[59] In the same year the company was granted the aguardiente concession for all of Guatemala, in exchange for a strict guarantee of large monthly payments into the Treasury. This centralization and rationalization of the relationship between wealthy private interests and the government benefited both: the former saw what must have been a phenomenal return on their investments while the latter saw a dramatic increase in annual revenue from alcohol concessions, which after average receipts in 1867 and 1868 climbed to a staggering 1.2 million pesos the following year.[60]

As noted above, although the incoming Liberal regime installed in 1871 initially promised to eliminate the hated monopolies, a decade later the restrictive licensing system they instituted in its place was being enforced even more vigorously, with correspondingly apparent benefits to state income. In addition to growing revenues (see table 1.1), evidence for this assertion again comes from Huehuetenango, where the number of prosecutions for alcohol-related crimes spiked dramatically in the last two decades of the nineteenth century.[61] From an annual average of less than a dozen prosecutions during the years 1850–71,[62] the last twenty years of the century witnessed regional courts processing hundreds of alcohol-related cases, and in many years these represented fully half of the prosecutions.[63] The widespread involvement of the judicial system in prosecuting such crimes, which included the apprehension of smuggled goods (*contrabando*) and moonshine (aguardiente clandestino) and the catchall "defrauding the branch of liquors" (*defraudación en el ramo de licores*), represented a significant escalation in state enforcement of alcohol laws. Seen from the perspective of Maya peoples, especially in light of the earlier cases discussed above, it also represented the systematic criminalization of customary practices that many communities regarded as essential to their ritual and social life.

While the benefits to state coffers and those members of the elite who held monopolies is perhaps sufficient to explain the government's motivation in vigorously prosecuting alcohol-related crimes, a third factor also likely played a role, albeit more indirectly. As is well known, the latter half of the nineteenth century witnessed the transformation of the Guatemalan economy around the production of coffee, which became the single largest export by 1870.[64] The need for seasonal labor on these plantations, mostly located outside of the highland zone, fueled a highland labor market in which alcohol played a significant role. As described in great detail by early twentieth-century ethnographers working throughout the Guatemalan highlands,[65] aguardiente was essential to the mechanisms by which coffee plantation recruiters, the so-called hookers (or *enganchadores*), acquired their laborers from highland Maya communities. In a typical pattern, prior to harvest season the recruiting agent would advance money for aguardiente (or the drink itself) in exchange for a labor contract, to be fulfilled shortly thereafter. The whole process was so smoothly integrated that one plantation owner described it to anthropologist Ruth Bunzel as follows: "Take *aguardiente* away from the Indian and what will become of coffee? Coffee plantations run on *aguardiente* as an automobile runs on gasoline."[66] This striking metaphor offered by Bunzel's informant highlights the increasingly close links between the production and consumption of two ingested commodities with very different effects: coffee and alcohol. Most critical for highland Maya peoples is that this trend exemplified the increasingly contradictory nature of their relationship with alcohol consumption as they entered the twentieth century. As described for other Latin American indigenous groups,[67] during the past one hundred years Maya peoples have increasingly come into conflict with one another over the significance of alcohol and the often-problematic nature of its use and abuse by both individuals and communities. In many communities, particularly during the latter half of the century, conflicts over alcohol use and prohibition were expressed through religious divisions that pitted wet traditionalists (*costumbristas*) against dry Protestants and reforming Catholics.[68] In addition to reflecting a generational divide, these divisions also sometimes indexed the economic interests of different groups, both internal and external to the community, in relation to their ability to profit from alcohol manufacture and sale. Yet it can also be understood as the manifestation of persistent practices and meanings attached to alcohol consumption that link it to both exploitation and resistance, as well as to the past and the present.

Conclusions, Comparisons, and Suggestions for Future Research

In this chapter, I reconstruct some of the most significant transitions in alcohol use among Maya peoples in highland Guatemala over the past five centuries by focusing on the shifting status of specific types of alcohol as cultural commodities. By building upon the prehispanic production of fermented beverages from honey and maize to be consumed in social and ritual contexts, Maya peoples during the colonial period developed new materials (sugar) and technologies for production, eventually including distillation. Over the same time, they also began to rely more heavily on alcohol produced by others and, along with the other consuming sectors of colonial society, increasingly formed a market for new alcohol producers. From at least the eighteenth century, competition over this expanding market pitted various social and political actors, including colonial and national states, against one another in the quest for profits, taxation, and control. This competition continued into the nineteenth century, when established customs of alcohol use continued to play a significant role in struggles between Maya peoples and state and private agents. These struggles involved both the meaning and the practice of alcohol use and pitted Maya claims of customary rights against the increasing criminalization of alcohol trafficking and use by police and the courts. At century's end, many of "rum's contradictions" were firmly in place. This included the irony of government and elite moralizing over "drunken Indians" while profits from alcohol sales poured into state coffers and private purses.[69] It also included increasing evidence of the fact that customary social and ritual uses of alcohol were not incompatible with its use as a tool of political and economic domination.

Two general points can be made about the approach adopted here and its applicability to understanding the history of alcohol use among indigenous peoples in Latin America. First, greater attention needs to be paid to specific details of alcohol production and consumption in the historical record. Put simply, until we have a better sense of when, where, how, and under what circumstances indigenous people (and others) began to drink specific kinds of alcoholic beverages, it will be difficult to appreciate the cultural meaning of alcohol use in any period. Although these types of investigation have been conducted on a limited scale for places such as colonial Mexico, where attention to the meaning of specific examples of alcohol use has greatly refined our understanding of the role it played in rebellion, crime, and punishment,[70] such studies remain the exception rather than the norm. Similarly, without a better sense of how alcohol use was shaped by struggles over profits and revenues generated by these acts of drinking, it will be difficult to fully understand alcohol's historical significance to economic transformation, state formation, and ethnic relations from colonial times to the present.

Second, while the outline given here for Maya peoples in Guatemala could be refined greatly, several of the transitions it identifies may be relevant to assessing the experiences of indigenous peoples elsewhere in Latin America. At the same time, each region had its own cultural history of alcohol that reflected the interaction among distinct prehispanic patterns of alcohol use, subsequent colonial developments relating to the introduction of distillation, and how these patterns of drinking were linked to labor practices, state formation, and ethnic relations in the period after independence. Comparisons with two of the best-documented regions, central Mexico and the Andes, reveal significant commonalities and contrasts with the experiences of Maya peoples in Guatemala in each of these periods.

In the late prehispanic period, one point of comparison among the three regions involves the ways in which alcohol production and consumption were integrated into elite strategies of rule. Because both central Mexico and the Andes were sites of empire building in the period immediately preceding the Spanish invasions of the early sixteenth century, it is perhaps unsurprising that one of the major findings of research from these areas involves recognition of the extent to which both the Aztecs and the Incas attempted to regulate alcohol production and consumption within their respective areas of imperial control. In both cases there is evidence that these attempts at regulation overlay older patterns of production and consumption. In central Mexico, for example, William Taylor contrasts two patterns of pulque drinking: a sumptuary pattern of noble drinking with severe punishments for commoners characteristic of the regions under direct Aztec control and, outside of these areas, evidence of mass community drinking that he argues represented an older pattern that Aztec leaders were seeking to suppress.[71] These attempts at imperial regulation also seem to have involved taxation of production, with several provinces to the north of the Valley of Mexico delivering substantial quantities of maguey syrup as tribute to the Aztec capital of Tenochtitlán.

Similar findings come from the Andes region, where the link between Inca expansion and chicha (in this case referring primarily to fermented maize) was perhaps even more direct. Recent research suggests that Incan control over chicha production and consumption was a significant component of their imperial strategy, specifically through their use of the *aclla*, women who produced maize chicha and other products as part of their dedication to the Incan cult of the sun. In addition to being a direct source of wealth, chicha produced in this fashion was incorporated into the ceremonial practices legitimating the Incan state, where again research has drawn a contrast between a restricted elite use of chicha and a more communal pattern found among commoner work parties.[72] In contrast to both of these patterns, alcohol production does not appear to have been as centralized during the late prehispanic period in the Maya area, where no single imperial power ever exercised hegemony over the region. This may help explain why in contrast to other Mesoamerican drink areas, such as the central Mexican pulque region, the Maya region shows some of the greatest internal diversity with regard to varieties of alcohol.[73]

Such contrasts in the degree of centralization may have been a factor, though clearly only one of many, in transitions to new forms and uses of alcohol, including distillation, during the succeeding colonial period. As discussed above, in highland Guatemala the incorporation of sugar into honey-based fermented drinks was occurring as early as the mid-seventeenth century, with the crucial transition to distilled aguardiente in some areas beginning by at least the early eighteenth century. In contrast, in the central Mexican region the dominance of fermented pulque over distilled mescal and sugar-based distilled alcohol among the indigenous population appears to have lasted through the late colonial period,[74] although the latter drink was certainly consumed widely and was increasingly commercialized and regulated during the late eighteenth century.[75] Nevertheless, most of the transitions of the colonial period among the indigenous population in central Mexico appear to have involved new ways of making, distributing, and consuming pulque.[76] Similarly, in the Andes, chicha (sometimes fermented using new grains such as wheat)[77] remained the preferred drink in many heavily indigenous areas into the colonial period and beyond, with distilled alcohol (here often known as *trago*) only making significant inroads into some communities in the twentieth century.[78] Recognition of these patterns is not meant to suggest that there was any greater continuity in other aspects of alcohol production and consumption in these regions than in Guatemala over time, only that the transition to distillation occurred at different times and under different circumstances in each case. This makes it critical to assess the historiography of this transition in each area with great care, while at the same time recognizing that the factors that accompanied or delayed the introduction of distilled beverages among colonial indigenous groups in Latin America may serve as a useful basis for comparison.[79]

Such caution is also warranted in comparing the most significant issues of the postcolonial period, about which we often know even less than the two earlier eras. Even given the current state of research, at least two related issues emerging from the Guatemalan case during the nineteenth and twentieth centuries appear to have parallels in Mexico and Andean nations. First is the persistence or expansion of prehispanic and colonial patterns of alcohol use within a context of shifting patterns of labor recruitment, namely, debt peonage, linked to economic changes of the postcolonial period. Although there is little readily available data from the nineteenth century, twentieth-century ethnographers have long noted the association between specific forms of alcohol use and patterns of debt in Mexico, Peru, and Ecuador that developed or intensified during the postcolonial period.[80] Second, at the same time that alcohol was being used to secure a labor force for new national industries, these same practices were increasingly being reviled within nationalist projects that played off stereotypes of "drunken Indians," in a pattern that had parallels in Central, South, and even North America.[81]

Apart from these evident parallels, several other potentially critical issues remain obscure and are more difficult to compare. Based on the Guatemalan case, the critical role of alcohol in state financing in Latin America would appear to be a key area for future research, as would more historical and archaeological studies of the distribution and transmission of alcohol technology over time and space. Again, however, such political economic questions need to be balanced by continued attention to the social and cultural meaning of drinking acts.

Notes

1. Heath, "Anthropology and Alcohol Studies."
2. Bunzel, "Role of Alcoholism"; Doughty, "Social Uses of Alcohol"; Navarrete Pellicer, *El aguardiente*; Menéndez, *Antropología del alcoholismo*; Aguirre, *País de alcohol;*

Eber, *Women and Alcohol*; Huarcaya, *No os embriaguéis*; Butler, *Holy Intoxication to Drunken Dissipation*; Jennings and Bowser, *Drink, Power, and Society*.

3. Room, "Alcohol and Ethnography." For discussions of this issue, see Heath, "Anthropology and Alcohol Studies"; Eber, *Women and Alcohol*; and Dietler, "Alcohol."

4. Singer, "Toward a Political-Economy of Alcoholism."

5. Crump, "Alternative Economy of Alcohol."

6. Hernández Palomo, *El aguardiente de caña*; Lomnitz, "Alcohol and Culture"; Taylor, *Drinking, Homicide, and Rebellion*; Scardaville, "Alcohol Abuse and Tavern Reform"; Mora de Tovar, *El aguardiente y conflictos sociales*; Fallaw, "Dry Law, Wet Politics"; Lewis, "La guerra del posh"; González Alzate, "State Reform, Popular Resistance."

7. Taylor (*Drinking, Homicide, and Rebellion*, 157) is a notable exception in his detailed attention to the "social meaning of alcohol."

8. Mintz, *Sweetness and Power*; Schivelbusch, *Tastes of Paradise*; Appadurai, *Social Life of Things*; Miller, "Consumption and Commodities," 141–61; Akyeampong, *Drink, Power, and Cultural Change*; Willis, *Potent Brews*; Griffiths, *Tea*.

9. Appadurai, *Social Life of Things*; Miller, "Consumption and Commodities"; Douglas and Isherwood, *World of Goods*; Van Binsbergen and Geschiere, *Commodification*.

10. Eber, *Women and Alcohol*, 244, 246.

11. Schwartzkopf, "Maya Power and State Culture."

12. González Sandoval, "El estanco de bebidas embriagantes."

13. Ibid.; Dunn, "Aguardiente and Identity"; González Alzate, "State Reform, Popular Resistance." For more on this period, see Dunn's chapter in this volume.

14. Pompejano, *La crisis de antiguo régimen*; Woodward, *Rafael Carrera*; McCreery, *Rural Guatemala*; Gudmundson and Lindo-Fuentes, *Central America*.

15. González Sandoval, "El estanco de bebidas embriagantes"; Pompejano, *La crisis de antiguo régimen*.

16. Schwartzkopf, "Maya Power and State Culture," 228–55.

17. González Sandoval, "El estanco de bebidas embriagantes"; Pompejano, *La crisis de antiguo régimen*.

18. Pompejano, *La crisis de antiguo régimen*, 37.

19. Archivo General de Centro América (hereafter AGCA), Juzgado de Primera Instancia de Huehuetenango (hereafter JPIH); Ericastilla and Jiménez, "Las clandestinistas de aguardiente."

20. Bunzel, "Role of Alcoholism"; Burkitt, "Explorations in the Highlands."

21. Bruman, *Alcohol in Ancient Mexico*, 91–92.

22. Tozzer, *Landa's Relación*.

23. Sharer and Traxler, *Ancient Maya*, 749–50.

24. Bruman, *Alcohol in Ancient Mexico*, 91–93.

25. Kramer, Lovell, and Lutz, "Fire in the Mountains."

26. AGCA, A1, Leg. 6115, Exp. 56343.

27. Fuentes y Guzmán, *Obras históricas*, vol. 3.

28. Gage, *New Survey*, 93.

29. AGCA, A1, Leg. 2891, Exp. 26647. Unless otherwise noted, all of the information concerning this case is drawn from this source.

30. Fuentes y Guzmán, *Obras históricas.*

31. Ibid.; "Relaciones Geográficas"; Cortés y Larraz, *Descripción geográfico-moral.*

32. McCreery, *Rural Guatemala*, 45.

33. AGCA, A1, Leg. 6097, Exp. 55503.

34. Here it is relevant to note that in the report produced a decade earlier by Archbishop Pedro Cortés y Larraz (*Descripción geográfico-moral de la diócesis de Goathelama*, 113) these two communities were among those singled out by their parish priests as having a "scandalous" level of drunkenness (*embriaguez*). This prompted the prelate's ironic rhetorical question: Given widespread accounts of this vice among the Indians, how much drunkenness must "there be in these towns [that] they designate it with the adjective of scandalous?"

35. For more about Montenegro, see AGCA, Sección de Tierras, Leg. 4, Exps. 7, 11; Schwartzkopf, "Maya Power and State Culture," 464–99.

36. AGCA, A1, Leg. 6097, Exp. 55503.

37. González Sandoval, "El estanco de bebidas embriagantes."

38. AGCA, A1, Leg. 6115, Exp. 56343, fols. 19–24.

39. AGCA, A1, Leg. 6115, Exp. 56343.

40. AGCA, A1, Leg. 6117, Exp. 56571.

41. Specifically, it should be noted that among San Mateo's "obligations" at this time was the payment of a substantial contribution to the royal administration's current war effort, backed up by the same receipts from the product of the salt industry. This may have exaggerated Juárez's concern, as well as his estimates of the amounts involved, as he was instrumental in brokering this arrangement. See Schwartzkopf, "Maya Power and State Culture," 231–46.

42. Reeves, *Ladinos with Ladinos*, 115–35.

43. Stephens, *Incidents of Travel*, 2:240–54.

44. Schwartzkopf, "Maya Power and State Culture," 312–16.

45. AGCA, JPIH Criminal, Leg. 4, Exp. 3. Unless otherwise noted, all information concerning this case comes from this document.

46. Ibid., fols. 44–45.

47. This pattern is strikingly similar to early twentieth-century ethnographic accounts from the Huehuetenango region that describe the retrieval of ritual items, such as dance costumes from the distant town of Totonicapán, as a necessary part of the preparations for town fiestas. See La Farge, *Santa Eulalia*, 85–86; and Oakes, *Two Crosses of Todos Santos*, 217–18. Such tasks were also a vital part of the movement of young men through the civil-religious hierarchy, or cargo system, described ethnographically for many Mesoamerican indigenous communities; as such, they played a key role in establishing community identity for adult males.

48. AGCA, Jefatura Política de Huehuetenango (hereafter JPH) 1861, Reg. 14.

49. AGCA, JPH 1861, Reg. 3.

50. AGCA, JPH 1862, Reg. 1.

51. La Farge and Byers, *Year-Bearer's People*, 87–88; La Farge, *Santa Eulalia*, 42–43.

52. AGCA, JPH 1862, Reg. 34.

53. AGCA, JPH 1862, Regs. 4, 34, 47.

54. For examples of female defendants, most of them nonindigenous, in and around the departmental capital, see AGCA, JPIH Criminal, Leg. 6, Exp. 3, 4, 14, 20. For examples of this gendered pattern among Mam-speaking communities in Quezaltenango, see Reeves, *Ladinos with Ladinos*, 115–35.

55. AGCA, JPIH Criminal, Leg. 6, Exp. 33; Leg. 12, Exp. 14; Leg. 13, Exp. 6; Ministerio de Gobernación, Leg. 28575, Exp. 36; Leg. 28595, Exp. 65.

56. AGCA, Ministerio de Gobernación, Leg. 28595, Exp. 65.

57. Pompejano, *La crisis de antiguo régimen*.

58. González Sandoval, "El estanco de bebidas embriagantes," 145–48.

59. Pompejano, *La crisis de antiguo régimen*, 37 (my translation).

60. Ibid., 16.

61. AGCA, JPIH, Criminal 1880–99.

62. Schwartzkopf, "Maya Power and State Culture," 401.

63. AGCA, JPIH, Criminal 1880–99.

64. Cambranes, *Coffee and Peasants;* Reeves, *Ladinos with Ladinos*; McCreery, *Rural Guatemala*.

65. Bunzel, "Role of Alcoholism"; Burkitt, "Explorations in the Highlands"; Wagley, *Economics of a Guatemalan Village*, 74–77.

66. Bunzel, "Role of Alcoholism," 363.

67. Doughty, "Social Uses of Alcohol"; Allen, "'Let's Drink Together, My Dear!'"; Butler, *Holy Intoxication to Drunken Dissipation*.

68. Smith, *Fiesta System and Economic Change*; Warren, *Symbolism of Subordination*; Brintnall, *Revolt against the Dead*; Annis, *God and Production*; Adams, "Guatemala."

69. Garrard-Burnett, "Indians Are Drunks."

70. Taylor, *Drinking, Homicide, and Rebellion*.

71. Ibid., 33–34.

72. Goodman-Elgar, "Places to Partake."

73. Bruman, *Alcohol in Ancient Mexico*, 87.

74. Taylor, *Drinking, Homicide, and Rebellion*, 55.

75. Hernández Palomo, *El aguardiente de caña*.

76. Taylor, *Drinking, Homicide, and Rebellion*, 34–57.

77. Mangan, *Trading Roles*, 76–105.

78. Jennings and Bowser, *Drink, Power, and Society*, 13–14; Butler, *Holy Intoxication to Drunken Dissipation*.

79. In contrast, because they lacked even fermented alcohol, most indigenous groups in the present-day United States and Canada first encountered alcohol in the form of distilled beverages. See Mancall, *Deadly Medicine*; and Ishii, *Bad Fruits*.

80. Eber, *Women and Alcohol*; Allen, "'Let's Drink Together, My Dear!'"; Butler, *Holy Intoxication to Drunken Dissipation*.

81. Garrard-Burnett, "Indians Are Drunks"; Weismantel, "Have a Drink," 257–77; Thatcher, *Fighting Firewater Fictions*.

2

◇◇◇◇◇◇◇◇◇◇◇◇◇◇

From Household to Nation

The Economic and Political Impact of Women and Alcohol in Nineteenth-Century Guatemala

RENÉ REEVES

On June 27, 1829, Catalina Escobar sent a complaint against Aniseto López, the local alcohol monopoly holder, to the *jefe político* (governor) of the department of Quezaltenango. She did not approach the municipal authorities of her town, San Juan Ostuncalco, probably because López was an important figure there, having served on the municipal council for several years, and because her complaint also involved Ostuncalco's current *alcalde primero*, a man named Bernabé Monterroso. In her petition, Escobar described how she had obtained an authorization from López to sell alcohol in exchange for paying him four reales, or half a peso, per month. She did this for several months, but in June she fell behind. López immediately went to the alcalde primero, who forced Escobar to pay up. To make matters worse, López's wife began to insult her. Outraged, Escobar asserted that López "was a thief [because] he obtained the monopoly for ten pesos but the townspeople pay him more than twenty." Furthermore, she added, "he was not empowered to give out authorizations [for others to sell aguardiente] since his monopoly license does not give him permission to do that. . . . All I ask," Escobar concluded, "is that you tell me honestly if this man will be allowed to violate the [aguardiente] regulations because he is rich and his money gives him power over the entire town."[1]

Catalina Escobar's complaint is revealing on many levels. It demonstrates that Aniseto López brazenly flouted the alcohol monopoly regulations by illegally subleasing, for lack of a better term, his monopoly license to an additional thirty-one people. It reflects the power he held in San Juan Ostuncalco, which allowed him to behave as he did, with the open connivance of the highest municipal officials. It gives important insight into how the alcohol monopoly functioned in actual practice, as opposed to how the legal statutes articulated its operation, in that despite the state's efforts to restrict or concentrate the alcohol industry in as few hands as possible, in Ostuncalco the monopoly was manipulated to include the participation of dozens of individuals. It also reflects a surprising incipient class consciousness on the part of its progenitor: Will Lópes "be allowed to violate the regulations because he is rich and his money gives him power over the entire town"? Finally, and perhaps most importantly, Escobar's complaint gives a snapshot of who was engaged in selling aguardiente in Ostuncalco in 1829: of the thirty-one individuals who had purchased permission from Aniseto Lópes to sell aguardiente, twenty-five—or slightly more than 80 percent—were women.

The purpose of this chapter is twofold. First, it shows that alcohol was a crucial part of Guatemala's domestic economy and that conflicts over its production and sale were intimately connected to the political developments of the nineteenth century.[2] Second, it demonstrates that women were the main distillers and vendors of alcohol and that this close relationship often gave them cause to weigh in publicly on political matters. Catalina Escobar's complaint provides a rare glimpse of the ways that alcohol and women meshed with the complex political and economic web that formed the contours of Guatemala's nineteenth century, a perspective that is missing from the historical literature of the era. Traditional narratives of nineteenth-century politics tend to focus on Liberals and Conservatives, which typically meant elite males, in contrast to the plebeian rabble, and even the revisionist literature, which allows a positive political role for men of mixed or indigenous backgrounds, pays little attention to the possibility that women were important protagonists in the political and economic trends of the period. Often, when women are mentioned as political actors, their presence is taken as a sign that society had reached the point of breaking down.[3] John Lloyd Stephens, a visitor to Guatemala in late 1839 and 1840, reflects this view in his description of the forces that made up the Carrera Revolt. He relates how a "gentleman" of the capital "told [him] that he never felt such consternation and horror as when he saw the entry of this immense mass of barbarians [into Guatemala City];

choking up the streets . . . and swelling the multitude were two or three thousand women, with sacks and *alforgas* [*sic*, saddlebags] for carrying away the plunder."[4]

To be fair, anyone who has ever attempted to uncover the activities and importance of women in centuries past knows that the methodological challenges are substantial, particularly when oral history is no longer a possibility. Oral history certainly has its own challenges, as David Carey Jr. makes clear in *Engendering Mayan History: Kaqchikel Women as Agents and Conduits of the Past, 1875–1970*, but written records are much more likely to be generated by men and to focus on them, their actions, or their thoughts.[5] If the women in question were plebeian rather than elite, the challenges are even greater, and if they were rural rather than urban, or indigenous rather than ladino, greater still. With very little direct evidence to go on, most researchers are reduced to "reading between the lines," or interpreting the empty spaces, something Eugenia Rodríguez Sáenz describes as listening for women "*entre silencios y voces*" (between silences and voices).[6]

Alcohol and Women: Lynchpins of the Rural Domestic Economy

In my research on the nineteenth-century political district of San Juan Ostuncalco I found very few sources generated by or about women that contained the kind of rich detail Catalina Escobar's complaint provides. Indeed, the most ubiquitous documents by far, beginning with the 1850s, are short one- or two-sentence notices or simple lists describing people who had been fined or imprisoned "*por clandestinistas*"—that is, for producing or selling alcohol illegally. Conservative officials first generated these lists when they took advantage of the political stability and growth the state had achieved by the late 1840s to implement new, more rigorous policies against illegal alcohol. Over the next several decades thousands of people were arrested and fined or imprisoned in the district of Ostuncalco alone for making or selling aguardiente clandestino—clandestine rum. Surprisingly, most of them were women. Despite the paucity of information found in these lists of clandestinistas, they do tell a story—a big, collective story, even if it lacks the thick description historians are wont to find—about a large number of women who were running afoul of the law as they tried to support themselves and their families by making or selling alcohol from their homes. The political implications could not have been positive for the Conservative authorities who implemented the increasingly repressive alcohol regimen, or for their ostensibly populist leader, José Rafael Carrera. Although the lists do not indicate explicitly what these women thought of the repression they were suffering, at least they give a rough approximation of *how many* were suffering. This information proved useful in reconstructing women's importance to the economy and politics of the era.

I focused my quantification efforts on the period from 1862 to 1886. These are the years with the most documented alcohol offenses and for which the sources appear most complete, with four or more monthly lists of clandestinistas for most years. In addition, this period spans the last decade of Conservative rule and the first fifteen years of the Liberal Reforma, allowing for a comparison between the two. Altogether, 813 people were documented clandestinistas during this twenty-five-year period, with a high of 109 in 1865 and a low of 9 in 1873. I could find no data for six of the twenty-five years included in this span, and even in the years for which documentation does exist, most are missing lists for anywhere from three to eight months.[7] As a result, the figure 813 is certainly under-representative. Still, what these numbers do show is the relative importance of women, who composed fully 77 percent of clandestinistas.

It is not necessary to embrace a rigid public-private spheres argument for gendered social divisions to accept that producing and selling aguardiente appealed to women.[8] In his recent article on viticulture and *pulperías* in Mendoza, Argentina, from 1561 to 1852, Pablo Lacoste notes that making wine and selling petty commodities "offered women the possibility of working from home."[9] The aguardiente industry, like many other forms of petty commerce and production, allowed women to blur the line between public and private while ostensibly satisfying the rigid demands of patriarchy and the material constraints of childcare. This was certainly true for nineteenth-century Guatemala, and Carey's chapter in this volume suggests that it held for the early twentieth century as well. Thus, in Justin Wolfe's words, writing about nineteenth-century Nicaragua, "The pervasiveness of home [that is, illegal] *aguardiente* production was exacerbated by the fact that women were the most common producers."[10] A similar association between alcohol and women appears to have prevailed in Andean South America, where women predominated in the *chicha* industry. Gina Hames describes their "small corn beer taverns" as "not much more than extensions of their homes."[11] William Taylor makes a similar observation about the sale of alcoholic beverages in colonial central Mexico: "Most villages had few formal *cantinas*; *pulque* and other local drinks were dispensed from the doorways of homes by a woman of the household."[12] Michael Scardaville, focusing on early nineteenth-century Mexico City more specifically, notes that "[w]omen, most of whom were Spanish and married, comprised the majority of the proprietors of illegal taverns. Commonly called *cuberas*, they sold intoxicants directly from their homes or apartments which contained the essential barroom paraphernalia."[13]

An even more accurate view of the extent of women's involvement with clandestine aguardiente in San Juan Ostuncalco can be gleaned by focusing on the years 1865 to 1868. Only two months lacked documentation during this four-year period. Of the 366 people listed as clandestinistas, 279 were women, producing an annual average of approximately 70 women punished for illegal alcohol. There were no documented clandestinistas in the towns of San Cristóbal Cabricán, Huitán, or San Martín Sacatepéquez, even though other evidence suggests that clandestine aguardiente was rampant throughout the entire district of Ostuncalco.[14] Moreover, as Scardaville reminds us in his article on alcohol in colonial Mexico City, arrests typically amount to only a small fraction of those involved in illegal activity.[15] Thus, it is not a stretch to argue that the annual average of 70 "known" female clandestinistas that prevailed in the late 1860s was indicative of a much larger number. Quite likely, several hundred of the district's 8,500 adult women engaged in the illegal production and sale of aguardiente at any one time, and similar ratios probably existed in the decades both before and after.

In conclusion, illegal aguardiente was clearly important to the domestic economy of many, many households in the Mam towns of western Quezaltenango. To put this importance in broader economic perspective, the entire department of Quezaltenango counted forty legal aguardiente monopolists in 1863, who produced approximately 23,300 pesos in direct revenues for the state.[16] That same year, the combined income of the aguardiente and chicha monopolies in all of Guatemala's fourteen departments and additional territories amounted to roughly 600,000 pesos, or well over half of the national budget.[17] Even as late as the 1890s, despite the fact that coffee production and coffee revenues far surpassed what they had been in the 1860s, income from alcohol continued to generate anywhere from 23 to 36 percent of the national budget, according to David

McCreery.[18] Frederick Douglass Opie, in his chapter in this volume, asserts that alcohol monies continued to be singularly important to the national treasury in the early twentieth century as well. In comparative terms, these numbers are similar to what Wolfe found for nearby Nicaragua, where aguardiente revenues made up anywhere from approximately 20 to 38 percent of treasury receipts in the years 1858 to 1900.[19]

My point in reviewing what we know about legal alcohol revenues is this. If legal alcohol typically generated anywhere from 20 to 50 percent of the Guatemalan national budget from the mid-nineteenth century through the early 1900s, imagine what the much more numerous clandestinistas were producing across the width and breadth of the country during this same period. The department of Quezaltenango alone likely counted several hundred illegal producers and sellers of aguardiente, in contrast to the forty who were legally authorized. The comments of Mariano Gálvez, Guatemala's chief of state during most of the 1830s, suggest that the same was true for other areas of the country as well: "[T]he entire department of Verapaz is a factory of aguardiente and between San Geronimo and Salamá there exist perhaps one thousand [illegal] factories."[20]

Taken together, the quantitative evidence and the anecdotal documentation such as Catalina Escobar's petition, with its list including twenty-five women, indicate that aguardiente was central to the economic calculus of many women throughout the towns of the district of San Juan Ostuncalco. Evidence from the provincial capital, Quezaltenango, as we shall see, suggests that women's predominance in the alcohol industry was not unique to Ostuncalco. Stacey Schwartzkopf, in the preceding chapter, reinforces such a conclusion, noting that women also were the primary aguardiente vendors in Huehuetenango and its environs, directly to the north of Quezaltenango. It seems fair to claim that innumerable women throughout the western highlands, and quite likely across the entire nation, were similarly involved in the alcohol industry during the nineteenth century. A growing historiography on women and alcohol elsewhere in Latin America would seem to corroborate such a conclusion. Wolfe notes that "women were the most common [aguardiente] producers" in nineteenth-century Nicaragua, and Hames does the same for the chicha industry of Andean South America between 1870 and 1930, writing that "[w]ith rare exceptions only women brewed and sold the beverage." Christine Eber makes a similar case for southern Mexico, while Taylor and Scardaville, writing about pulque and other alcoholic beverages more generally, provide ample documentation for central Mexico in the colonial era. Although Lacoste does not find a predominance of women in Argentine viticulture or as owners of Mendoza's pulperías, nevertheless, he does note their growing importance by the mid-nineteenth century.[21]

Ostuncalco's female aguardiente entrepreneurs, regardless of legal status, depended on access to sugar for their income. Sugar is the main ingredient in aguardiente, and thus the industry was symbiotically tied to those who cultivated and processed sugarcane. The latter likewise required the demand of the aguardiente producers to market their product.[22] Indeed, at least some families vertically integrated these complementary activities, echoing colonial Mexico's pulque industry as well as the colonial-era *chicherías* (corn beer establishments) of Lima, Peru.[23] Although the state taxed sugar and attempted to regulate its flow within the district by establishing a *garita,* or government checkpoint, in San Martín Sacatepéquez in the early 1850s, on the main path between the coast and the highlands, nevertheless, this did not seem to impede its movement between the two locales.[24] District men grew cane and refined it into sugar on the coast, then brought the sugar to the highland towns where their wives and other family members converted it into aguardiente. Family members then retailed the alcohol directly from the home or sold it in quantity to others who engaged in the retail end of the business.[25] In my view, this synergistic relationship between the aguardiente and sugar industries was the motor force of the local economy in many rural areas of Guatemala during the nineteenth century. As Carey concludes in his chapter about the early twentieth century, whether men liked it or not, women were in the driver's seat.[26]

State Alcohol Policy and Subaltern Politics

On July 11, 1834, San Juan Ostuncalco's municipal council met in extraordinary session with the parish priest and more than a dozen of the town's prominent citizens. By the end of the meeting, the participants had generated a stirring petition to Quezaltenango's departmental governor, begging him to reinstate an 1833 law that had "prohibited the free commerce in aguardiente."[27] By "free," the petitioners meant "legal," because it was understood by all that "free commerce in aguardiente" would simply mean a return to the monopoly licensing system that had been in effect in the town for much of the 1820s and early 1830s. This system, Ostuncalco's municipal officials asserted, had resulted in "pervasive drunkenness" and produced "grave injuries . . . not only to particular families, and to the people in general, but also to the public treasury, since that which the [aguardiente] licenses contribute [to the treasury] does not make up for the deficit they cause by delaying the industry and operations of agriculture for many days, representing the personal labor of perhaps one thousand men."[28] Although they did not refer to the political unrest that Alvis Dunn found colonial-era authorities linked to alcohol consumption, local authorities concluded that the aguardiente monopoly had "convert[ed] society into a labyrinth of beasts, which is what people become without common sense or reason, and [this is] what impels us to beg the Departmental Governor . . . to take whatever steps are necessary to exempt Ostuncalco from the effects" of legalized alcohol.[29] Parish priest José María Orellana reiterated the councilors' sentiments at the bottom of the petition, calling on the departmental governor to "take whatever measures he can so that this town shall remain exempt from the monopoly system."[30]

Clearly the aguardiente monopoly was not very popular in San Juan Ostuncalco in the early 1830s. Under this system the state auctioned off a small number of monopoly licenses for a specific population center to the highest bidder. The goal was to restrict aguardiente production and sale so that it could be more easily taxed and so that widespread public drunkenness and all of its attendant ills could be more easily prevented. Larger towns or cities like the departmental capital, Quezaltenango, were assigned two or four monopoly licenses, whereas smaller towns like San Juan Ostuncalco generally had one. The alternative for smaller towns like Ostuncalco was a complete alcohol ban, which is what Ostuncalco's town notables were requesting in 1834. Under the ban, any aguardiente was by definition illegal. State authorities did not consider the ban in the largest provincial towns, such as Quezaltenango, but at times they did allow the monopoly system to be replaced by less restrictive permits, which enabled many more people to engage in producing and selling aguardiente. Occasionally towns like Ostuncalco were also allowed to utilize permits in place of the monopoly.

In very general terms, one of these three alcohol regimes existed in all the towns of Guatemala during the 1820s, 1830s, and 1840s. The smallest, most remote, and most heavily Maya towns were typically considered for the ban, but depending on the time and place they might also be subject to the monopoly. Larger, more important towns like Ostuncalco were usually saddled with the monopoly, but as in the smaller towns their municipal council and priest could petition the state to replace the monopoly with a complete ban. At times the state required towns that desired the ban to pay the national treasury the amount that the monopoly would have fetched at public auction. Another alternative that existed prior to midcentury, as Catalina Escobar's complaint makes clear, was that Ostuncalco's municipal authorities would allow the resident monopolist to sublease his or her license to others. Although this was illegal, strictly speaking, the practice helped blur the lines between the monopoly system and the permits that typically prevailed in the largest provincial towns like Quezaltenango. By midcentury, however, monopolies had been firmly established throughout the department of Quezaltenango, and most likely all of Guatemala. Moreover, given the growth of the state over the preceding decade, monopolists were now provided with treasury personnel who were authorized to investigate and arrest suspected clandestinistas. This is precisely what led to the proliferation of documents listing people—largely women—arrested "*por clandestinistas*" from the 1850s onward. There was no alternative to the highly repressive and unpopular alcohol monopoly until the Liberal Reforma of 1871. Even then, however, after the erstwhile Liberal rebels abolished the aguardiente monopoly in the name of "free trade," they quickly replaced it with an increasingly restrictive permit system once they understood the importance of alcohol revenues for the national treasury.[31] Both Carey and Schwartzkopf reinforce this point in their chapters, and Schwartzkopf notes that by the early 1880s the Liberals had initiated a new level of state repression against alcohol-related criminality in the frontier zones of Huehuetanango, directly north of the district of Ostuncalco. Opie asserts that the licensing system remained ubiquitous into the early twentieth century.[32]

Returning to the 1834 petition submitted by San Juan Ostuncalco's notables, contrary to the petitioners' wishes alcohol remained legal and subject to either monopoly or permit regulations for the rest of the 1830s. Not until the last days of 1839, following Rafael Carrera's conquest of Guatemala City, was the alcohol ban restored.[33] In early 1841, however, barely a year later, it was lifted once again. Just as in 1834, Ostuncalco's leaders opposed lifting the ban. This time, however, it was the indigenous municipal government, recently separated from its ladino counterpart, along with the most important indigenous citizens—the *principales*—who "verbally expressed that they [would] not allow the monopoly system in [the] town."[34] What is more, they appeared to have the sympathy of the ladino alcalde primero, or at least that was how Miguel de Ara, the departmental treasury administrator, perceived it. He chastised Ostuncalco's alcalde primero: "[I]f the monopoly that has been auctioned and is going to be established is as noxious to that populace as you indicate, this should be presented in a legal manner to the authority of the Superior Intendant General of the public treasury, rather than insolently stating, as if a matter of fact, that said monopoly will not be admitted [in the town]. If the reasons that you and the opposition put forward are reasonable and fair, said superior authority will take the appropriate measures because you have come before him personally."[35] However this standoff resolved, the available evidence suggests that despite the treasury administrator's assurances the monopoly system continued to function in the town in subsequent years. It was not seriously impeded by the opposition of Ostuncalco's notable citizens, be they indigenous or ladino.

These two episodes—one in 1834 and the other in 1841—raise at least a couple of intriguing questions. First, why did the state twice overturn the legal ban on alcohol in Ostuncalco barely a year after it originally had been imposed, particularly when it appeared to have significant local support? Certainly the town's ladino and indigenous officials and leading citizens favored the ban. The 1834 petition from the municipal council to the departmental governor suggests the reason that likely prevailed at that moment. Anticipating criticism from higher-level state authorities for their opposition to ending the ban, local officials and notables admitted that "in months past [when the ban was in effect] there has been some aguardiente in this town."[36] Recall that under the ban, all aguardiente was considered illegal. The petitioners continued that if the governor would only give them another chance, "in the future [the municipal council] pledges to exhaust its resources and watch with the greatest care so that aguardiente is eradicated, sparing no effort to achieve this end."[37] Padre Orellana added his moral authority to the pledge, asserting that "the present Alcalde . . . will exhaust municipal revenues to ensure the total elimination of [all] aguardiente in this town."[38] By implication, however, he reinforced the preceding admission that the previous town government had been rather lax in rooting out the banned beverage. This, I would suggest, was the reason the alcohol ban was so rapidly reversed in 1834: far from ending the local production, sale, and consumption of aguardiente, it had simply terminated the legal portion of the industry, thus depriving the state of the corresponding revenues. Clandestine traffic, meanwhile, had persisted and perhaps even grown, and local officials had not been vigilant in preventing this outcome.[39]

The 1841 dispute provides even more direct evidence for this explanation of why the state would move so quickly to reverse the alcohol ban. After hearing from Ostuncalco's ladino first alcalde that the entire indigenous municipal government and its principales vowed to block the reestablishment of the legal aguardiente trade, the departmental treasury administrator retorted that "the interests of the public treasury have been robbed of their legal income because from the past year of 1840 until today the production and sale of illegal [aguardiente] has been tolerated in that same town, as is well-known and proven. . . . [T]he administration under my charge," he reminded the first alcalde, "clearly has preference in this area over the particular interests of the residents who engage in the [illegal] production and sale [of aguardiente] without contributing anything, and I don't have to point them out to you one by one, because you and the local populace know them better than I."[40] Indeed, at least some of the many clandestinistas were likely linked to town officials themselves, not unlike the situation that Wolfe documents for nineteenth-century Nicaragua and Carey for Guatemala in the early twentieth century.[41] In sum, the state was willing to consider a ban on aguardiente in Ostuncalco and other similar towns as long as local officials appeared to be serious in their efforts to eradicate the illegal traffic. If, however, the ban simply served as a cover under which clandestine aguardiente flourished, then the state demanded its share of the revenues, and that required legalization and renewed efforts to shut down the clandestinistas.[42]

The second question raised by the episodes of 1834 and 1841 is why Ostuncalco's municipal officials and leading citizens consistently, and with apparent unanimity, opposed decriminalizing alcohol if so many local residents relied on it for income. It was not just the many women subleasing monopoly licenses identified by Catalina Escobar who benefited from the industry. At least some of the town's powerful male political figures also profited. The Aniseto Lópes whom Escobar refers to was the town's primary monopolist for several years, and during that time he held numerous positions in the municipal government, including the position of alcalde primero. Other notables were linked to the alcohol industry through kinship, while still others owned coastal *trapiches* and relied on highland aguardiente producers to boost demand for their sugar.[43] Given these ties, why was there such significant and persistent local opposition to legalizing alcohol?

One possible answer is to take the claims of local officials and leading citizens at face value. Although they *could* have profited from legalization, in fact they preferred to try to prevent the pernicious effects of alcohol from "converting [Ostuncalco] into a labyrinth of beasts," as they had written in 1834. By completely outlawing aguardiente, the state gave them a potent weapon with which to eradicate the noxious beverage from their town. Yet if higher-level state authorities are to be believed, this is not at all what happened in Ostuncalco when the ban was in effect. Instead, municipal officers exhibited little zeal in persecuting clandestinistas, and the underground commerce flourished in a way that would have been impossible if alcohol had been decriminalized and local monopolists had been present to raise a ruckus about illegal competitors. As we saw in the 1834 document, town leaders and notables admitted as much even as they tried to downplay the extent of the illegal trafficking that occurred. "[I]n past months," they wrote, "there has been some aguardiente in this town."[44] Thus, although a complete ban on aguardiente may have pushed alcohol into the shadows and reduced the level of pervasive, open consumption that legal monopoly posts made possible, it most definitely was not effective in eradicating the beverage altogether.

A more compelling, if less straightforward, explanation for the extent of local opposition to "free commerce in aguardiente" is that what local petitioners really objected to when they used the term "free commerce" was the reimposition of the monopoly system. Although the monopoly system lifted the complete alcohol ban, removing the town in question from its dry status, it only legalized alcohol produced and sold by authorized vendors—that is, monopoly license holders. The monopoly system did not open the alcohol industry for all to participate in as they desired: quite the opposite. Only when aguardiente was completely illegal could local producers and vendors—the clandestinistas—operate with relative freedom. When a complete ban on alcohol was in place in Ostuncalco or any other community, all alcohol was illegal, and thus no monopoly license was issued for the town. As a result, there was nobody at the local level with a direct financial motivation to eradicate illegal competitors. Particularly prior to midcentury, when persistent penury meant that the state apparatus remained weak and remote in locales like Ostuncalco, the absence of a local monopolist also meant that the state lacked an additional window into the local community, reducing its surveillance and information-gathering capabilities. And as long as the state did not receive information indicating that clandestine alcohol was rampant, it was loath to send in treasury investigators given the small number of personnel at its disposal and the expenses involved. Although a complete alcohol ban certainly reduced state revenues, state officials apparently were willing to forgo this income for the moral good that resulted when a population became dry and thus protected from the corrupting influence of alcohol.

In sum, a ban on aguardiente meant one less reason for the state to intrude locally and one less channel by which it could do so. From the perspective of Ostuncalco's officials and notable citizens, this was good. It is not that they were being disingenuous when they proclaimed the evils of alcohol and opposed "free commerce." Rather, they had a more complex and holistic view of the monopoly system's negative consequences. Local monopolists not only promoted overt alcohol consumption and pervasive drunkenness, as Carey notes in his essay on the early twentieth century, but also raised political tensions by demanding that municipal officers persecute clandestinistas, noisily complaining to higher-level state authorities when they believed local officials were not doing enough and calling in aggressive treasury investigators for backup. This was upsetting to all concerned.

From the perspective of Ostuncalco's clandestinistas as well, a complete ban on aguardiente was clearly more advantageous than the monopoly system. A ban did not change the fact that their activities were illegal, because they had been illegal under the monopoly as well. A ban did mean, however, that the town would be free of monopolists who sought to destroy their clandestine activities, and it correspondingly diminished the likelihood that treasury personnel would be called in to investigate them. An alcohol ban also gave greater leeway to municipal leaders to adopt a more relaxed attitude toward the illegal production and sale of aguardiente because prior to midcentury, higher-level state offices remained remote and state coffers were too impoverished to field significant numbers of treasury personnel. Town officials who were directly or indirectly involved in clandestine activities enjoyed this reprieve from state oversight, but even those who did not approve of the illicit alcohol industry were loath to call for higher-level state interference provided the clandestinistas did not brazenly shatter the façade of an ostensibly dry, law-abiding town.

A happy coincidence of interests in Ostuncalco produced the consensus, or something close, among municipal authorities, notable citizens, and clandestinistas alike that "free commerce in aguardiente"—that is, the monopoly system—should be opposed and that the offending beverage should be legally banned from the community.

The exception to this happy coincidence occurred in provincial capitals like Quezaltenango. Here the central state did not contemplate replacing the legal alcohol industry with an outright ban. Even if it had, such a change would not have helped clandestinistas all that much, because the provincial capital counted a more developed state apparatus and the permanent presence of higher-level authorities who, notwithstanding the glaring failures Carey documents in the early twentieth century, would have enforced a ban more vigorously than Ostuncalco's municipal government. In Quezaltenango, then, a ban on alcohol was not an option anybody desired, and thus when the state moved to replace the existing permitting system with a monopoly in 1841, resident aguardiente traffickers wrote to Rafael Carrera asking him to block the change: "We beseech you, Señor General, to use all your beneficence and authority to reestablish the permit system of this city, simultaneously ordering the suspension of the monopoly auctions that have been scheduled for the 12th of the current month."[45] The monopoly, they insisted, "by depriving us of the only source of income we have to sustain ourselves, the income from this industry, has placed us in grave jeopardy and suffering."[46] Moreover, it would diminish aguardiente sales, thereby reducing sales tax revenues collected by the state and causing the "ruin of the farms and fortunes of more than 100 property owners."[47]

In contrast to the expensive and restrictive monopoly, the petitioners preferred the preexisting permit system because it was cheaper and there were many more permits than monopoly licenses. Whereas the monopoly was limited to a very small number of proprietors, typically one to four, and required an up-front commitment to pay several hundred pesos a year in monthly installments, in the case of Quezaltenango the permits cost twenty-eight pesos every six months and, more to the point from the perspective of the city's aguardiente producers and vendors, there were forty-six available. Despite state regulation, then, the permit system allowed a significant number to participate in the licit aguardiente industry. For those who claimed that the less restrictive permits would result in a "population that merits being called drunkards, in this case Señor

[Carrera]," the petitioners asserted, "the same could be said about the English people, the French, and many others from foreign lands where year after year the grain consumed in making alcohol rises to two million pesos."[48]

Implications for Women and Politics

Regardless of the policy alternatives preferred by specific subaltern sectors—permits in Quezaltenango or a complete ban in Ostuncalco—the evidence suggests that when the flourishing, female-dominated alcohol industry suffered under what were viewed by its participants to be onerous restrictions, women took political action. The 1841 document from Quezaltenango, for example, which pressed for the return of the permit system to that city, was authored by "*las mujeres del común del Quezaltenango*," that is, by the women of the provincial capital. In line with Schwartzkopf and Carey's findings, expressed in their respective chapters in this volume, the female petitioners placed economic necessity at the center of their appeal.[49] Yet they also went well beyond state alcohol policy in their critique of national political issues. For instance, they openly decried the oppressive gendered social norms that inhibited women's participation in the public sphere. "In years past," the women averred, "to deprive us of the profits of [the alcohol] industry, our involvement in it was reproached as a thing of infamy because our sex is said to be fit only for domestic activities such as sewing, embroidery, [making] cigars, etc."[50] They likewise criticized the "blind veneration of the era of Spanish rule," asserting that it "gave rise to the system of revenue monopolies that consistently undermined the growth of individual fortunes. . . . The government understood this simple truth better than us," the women continued, which is why "more than twelve years [ago] it implemented the dispositions issued by the legislature for the system of licenses that we know of popularly as 'permits.'"[51]

Antagonism toward Spanish colonialism and monopolies, and support for a more open system of permits, did not mean that las mujeres del común del Quezaltenango necessarily championed free trade. Betraying their ladino prejudices, they accepted the need to ban aguardiente from the overwhelmingly Maya towns that surrounded the provincial capital, "because [the Indians] are simpletons, and it would be a wrong deserving the most severe punishment to allow them to become intoxicated."[52]

Foreshadowing Carey's finding for the early twentieth century, the stereo-type of Maya excess with regard to alcohol consumption was apparently alive and well in the early nineteenth century as well.[53] The women continued by arguing for broad state regulation of foreign imports: "Last year, with reason and justice, Señor General Carrera had the legislature turn its attention to the petition that the artisan guilds elevated, requesting that their industries and crafts be protected, and that products coming from abroad that have damaged and ruined our country be restricted."[54] Domestic aguardiente producers were suffering the same kind of "damage" at the hands of foreign alcohol producers, who "export from the many ports they are known to have and introduce [their alcohol] on our soil, where because of the leniency of our customs laws for imported goods they pay a very small tariff in comparison to the quotas we have to pay, and after they make only this small payment all alcohol that they introduce circulates freely."[55]

The 1841 document amply demonstrates that Quezaltenango's women had a strong interest in, and had developed a cogent analysis of, the broader political debates and trends of nineteenth-century Guatemala. It also shows that their involvement in the alcohol industry gave them a compelling reason to take public political action. In Ostuncalco the documentary record is less overt, but there is no doubt that local women opposed the monopoly system, and when the Conservative state clamped down on the official monopolist's illegal competitors women were the ones who bore the brunt. Treasury investigators began to aid Ostuncalco's monopolist in repressing clandestinistas on a regular basis in 1849.[56] Paralleling Schwartzkopf's finding for Huehuetenango's frontier zone, a *juez preventivo* (district judge) was established in the town in 1853, along with a permanent detachment of the *"resguardo de aguardiente,"* or alcohol police, and together these new officials pursued clandestine aguardiente much more vigorously than municipal-level authorities had ever done in the past.[57] Women were fined and imprisoned in growing numbers, reaching as many as one hundred per year by the early 1860s. They also suffered inordinately from the repressive tactics of the alcohol police, who burst into houses unannounced and then proceeded to destroy all manner of dishware that might have been used to produce aguardiente.

On Christmas Day, 1856, Ostuncalco's juez preventivo, José Miguel Urrutia, wrote to Quezaltenango's *corregidor* (governor), complaining that "the tranquility of this population was almost shattered because of a mistake committed by the [alcohol police]." "[A]t around 1:00 p.m.," Urrutia continued, "approximately fifty Indians confronted me, complaining that the [alcohol police] had entered the house of the cofradía of the Sweet Name of Jesus [earlier in the morning], and had broken the kettles in which they were cooking tamales for the impending celebration."[58] Manuel Escobar, Ostuncalco's indigenous governor, described a similar incident to Quezaltenango's corregidor in October 1858. According to Escobar, the alcohol police moved into the *cantón* of Sechicul in early October, "entering the houses of the [residents] with swords and pistols in hand, terrorizing them, and climbing up into their storage lofts, breaking jugs, kettles . . . bowls, cups, griddles, and all manner of utensils used by women." In one house they even took time out from their frenzied "investigation" to help themselves to a pot of meat they found on the fire, further infuriating their unwilling hostess.[59]

The growing surveillance of state officials and the concomitant increase in harassment, fines, and imprisonment impelled Ostuncalco's women to act, both as individuals and collectively. Exactly one year after his appointment in July 1853, the new juez preventivo, Manuel Larrave, faced open rebellion. The leaders were Matilde Ralda and her husband Cayetano, close relatives of Yrinea Ralda, a notorious clandestinista whom the juez preventivo had been seeking for some time.[60] According to Larrave, Yrinea also happened to be the concubine of Ostuncalco's first *regidor* (town councilor), Leandro Galindo. When authorities attempted to arrest Yrinea on the night of July 30, 1854, Larrave claimed that Galindo "drew his sword against the soldiers and alcohol police, preventing them from taking [Yrinea] Ralda to jail as a clandestinista." This gave Matilde and Cayetano enough time to instigate an uprising that stymied further pursuit.[61] Over the next year, community opposition to the juez preventivo grew, forcing Manuel Larrave to resign his office in October 1855,[62] but not before Guatemala City took the unusual step of ordering that the town's ladino municipality be permanently disbanded at the end of the year. With regidores like Leandro Galindo, state authorities evidently believed that they could not trust Ostuncalco's municipal officials to behave responsibly.[63]

The replacement for Manuel Larrave, José Miguel Urrutia, was in his post barely one month before he was confronted with "a multitude of women" who pressed him for permission to collectively purchase Ostuncalco's aguardiente monopoly. Urrutia wrote to Quezaltenango's corregidor:

> This afternoon they came to my house with the purpose of convincing me to have you give them the right to purchase the town's monopoly. I told them that I had neither the obligation nor the desire to take part in this business, but if they wanted to make an inquiry they should direct it to Señor Afre, who they were sure had purchased the monopolies of the department. I warned them that if they did obtain their goal, they would be limited to two points of sale, and they would not have authorization to produce [aguardiente] here [in Ostuncalco].[64]

From what I can tell, nothing came of the women's efforts, despite the fact that the town's *síndico* (town agent) was sent to Totonicapán to meet with Señor Afre about purchasing the monopoly.

Although things did not turn out as Ostuncalco's residents had hoped— local women did not obtain the monopoly, and the ladino municipal council was dissolved in perpetuity—this record of events from the 1850s shows that the town's women were quite willing to enter the public political sphere to further their interests in the alcohol industry. They had invited the public into the privacy of their own homes to sell aguardiente, and when state policy threatened their economic survival, they left their homes to pursue public political goals. Despite their efforts, however, the repressive aguardiente monopoly remained in place throughout the district of Ostuncalco and the department of Quezaltenango for the remainder of the Conservative era. Innumerable women suffered its effects, including the many hundreds from the political district of Ostuncalco who were arrested and fined or imprisoned. Women from both Ostuncalco and Quezaltenango, often joined or backed by local men, challenged the onerous monopoly system, hoping for its replacement by either the less restrictive permits or a complete ban that would allow clandestine participation in the industry to continue relatively unmolested. I believe that the Liberal rebels who battled the Conservative state in the late 1860s were responding to the groundswell of subaltern opposition to the Conservatives' alcohol policies when they promised to replace the hated monopoly with free trade.[65] I also believe that the Liberal rebels' call gave Guatemalan women even greater cause to enter the public political sphere. While

I doubt they did so as combatants, they almost certainly voiced their partisan support for the Liberal's proposal to do away with the aguardiente monopoly, thus helping to erode popular backing for the Conservatives, the party of Rafael Carrera.[66]

When Liberal rebels vanquished Conservative forces outside Guatemala City in June 1871, retaking control of the state after a more than thirty-year absence, popular antipathy toward the Conservatives' repressive alcohol policies was but one factor among many that aided the Liberal cause. This antipathy was indicative, however, of how the Conservatives' luster had begun to tarnish over the preceding years, particularly after the death of their very popular leader, Rafael Carrera, in 1865. Hidden behind Carrera's popular image was the fact that under his watch Maya communities located in or near the Pacific *boca costa*, the Verapaces, and other piedmont regions had lost control of huge portions of their community territories to ladino peasants and cattle ranchers, sugar growers, and coffee planters. Similarly hidden was the fact that Carrera had initiated a sweeping return to the colonial-era *repartimientos*—referred to in midcentury Guatemala as *mandamientos* (forced labor drafts)—drawing on large numbers of Maya men to cultivate and harvest coffee and to build the mule paths and cart roads that would transport the *oro*, or golden beans, to market or port. To add insult to injury, many of the Maya men who found themselves ensnared in the mandamientos had only recently been dispossessed of their *milpas* (corn fields) by Conservative land policies. Thus, when Carrera died in 1865, depriving the Conservatives of his popular mantle, he left behind a rather dismal legacy: dozens of Maya communities collectively deprived of hundreds of thousands of acres of community land; tens of thousands of Maya men forced to labor on behalf of the coffee barons; and thousands of women, both Maya and ladino, arrested and fined or imprisoned for trying to support their families by producing or selling alcohol without proper authority.[67]

Popular anger at the Conservatives' land, labor, and alcohol policies was not enough to spark a mass uprising against Conservative rule of the kind that had vanquished the Liberals in the late 1830s and brought Rafael Carrera to power. But it was enough that when Liberal rebels threatened Conservative control of the state, announcing their determination to rid the country of the hated alcohol monopoly, popular sectors were ambivalent about where to throw their support or whether to get involved at all. They certainly did not flock to defend the Conservatives as shock troops, rearguard, and fifth column as they had in the military conflicts of the late 1830s and early 1840s. And although the Liberal rebels were rarely greeted by the kind of popular throngs that besieged Rafael Carrera whenever he visited the countryside, they did receive at least tepid support in many communities.[68]

In sum, Liberal rebels did not inspire a popular uprising on behalf of their insurrection in the months leading up to victory in June 1871, nor did they provoke one bent on defending the Conservative regime and preventing it from being overthrown. Instead, most popular sectors remained only tenuously involved in the conflict, watching it unfold more as spectators than participants. The fact that the Liberals imposed a fairly restrictive permit system shortly after abolishing the Conservatives' hated alcohol monopoly, and made it progressively more restrictive over the next several years, as Carey and Schwartzkopf attest—in effect betraying their promise of "free trade" in alcohol—does not diminish the importance that widespread unhappiness with the alcohol monopoly had in undermining the Conservatives' popular base.[69] This hatred had never been enough to spark a mass uprising against the Conservatives, and the Liberals' betrayal of their rebel platform demanding "free trade" in alcohol, and the resumption of arresting women in significant numbers, did not inspire widespread insurrection against Liberal rule in the months and years after 1871.

Conclusions and Comparisons

In this chapter I argue that women were the main producers and sellers of alcohol in nineteenth-century Guatemala. I also argue that as such they made a major contribution to the Guatemalan economy during this period, at the level of the household, the region, and the nation. Finally, I link women's participation in this vital enterprise to the broader political debates and conflicts that swept the country during the nineteenth century. As alcohol producers, and more often than not clandestinistas, women had a major stake in arguments over not only domestic alcohol regulations and laws but also international trade policy and national-level political rivalries that pitted Liberals against Conservatives.

Alcohol is a particularly useful lens by which to see behind the veil that hides the past activities of Guatemalan women from the present-day observer. There are a number of reasons for this, but among the most important is the fact that a large proportion of Guatemala's nineteenth-century alcohol industry operated illegally. Because this operation was of necessity clandestine, hence the label "clandestinistas" given to those involved, state officials at all levels concerned themselves with an activity in which women happened to be the main protagonists. Official concern, in turn, generated a written legacy that subsequent investigators would be able to consult. Few of women's licit activities attracted such administrative or legal scrutiny or produced even a fraction of the paperwork, even though these activities invariably made up a larger proportion of women's daily lives than producing or selling alcohol. Still, this should not diminish the importance of the industry to the lives of everyday Guatemalan women. They may have spent more time making tortillas than alcohol, but the evidence shows that women participated in the alcohol industry in large numbers, that it was widespread, and that its economic impact was massive, in terms of both households and the nation as a whole.

The other reason for alcohol's importance in tracing the outline of women's lives in nineteenth-century Guatemala was that it lent itself so easily to the requirements of their gendered world. It could be produced and sold in the home, the center of child rearing and other domestic activities, and it meshed well with women's traditional roles as food preparers and petty commodity producers and vendors. It also complemented male cane cultivation and sugar production. In an era when few other activities open to women could command such lucrative returns, the benefits derived from making or selling alcohol illegally far outweighed the risks.

This combination of alcohol's illicit nature and its complementarity to women's lives explains why the beverage was so useful in uncovering the role of women as economic and political subjects in nineteenth-century Guatemala. Emmanuel Akyeampong makes excellent use of these connections in his study of the development of anticolonial popular culture in Ghana, in which the producers and sellers of illegal gin, or *akpeteshie*, many of whom were women, played such a crucial role.[70] For these same reasons, I am convinced that alcohol will prove to be an equally fruitful entrée into the past economic and political activities of women in many other areas of Latin America. A growing body of scholarly literature has begun to demonstrate this claim. Taylor hinted at this in his classic *Drinking, Homicide, and Rebellion in Colonial Mexican Villages* more than three decades ago, and in 1995 Christine Eber placed it front and center in *Women and Alcohol in a Highland Maya Town.*[71] In more recent years, Gina Hames, Pablo Lacoste, and several contributors to Justin Jennings and Brenda Bowser's *Drink, Power, and Society in the Andes* also have focused on the linkages between the alcohol industry and women.[72] Several authors anchor these linkages in the pre-Columbian era even as they note that significant changes have occurred in response to historical trends and specific events such as the Spanish conquest.[73] Frances Hayashida, for example, emphasizes that Spanish colonialism repressed state-sponsored alcohol production for ritual consumption but facilitated the expansion of alcohol commerce in predominantly urban zones.[74] Clearly, further research is needed to fully understand Latin American women's evolving participation in the alcohol industry across time and space. Yet this does not diminish the broad continuities that exist between the pre-Columbian era and more recent times. Wolfe's comment on "[t]he pervasiveness of home *aguardiente* production" in which "women were the most common producers," written about sugar-based alcohol in nineteenth-century Nicaragua, aptly describes the context in which many intoxicating beverages were produced in various regions of Latin America at different moments in history. Likewise, his claim that "the criminalization of *aguardiente* production created a whole new class of criminals in Nicaraguan society, [and] threw a large number of women into that group" was true of many American locales in the colonial and postcolonial eras.[75]

In sum, women were important, if not the most important, producers and distributors of alcohol in many areas of Latin America from pre-Columbian times to the twentieth century. During the colonial and national periods, extant legal restrictions and prohibitions generated documentation that reveals women's alcohol-related activities, whether they were official purveyors authorized by the state or law-breaking clandestinistas who failed to avoid detection. Legal or not, however, alcohol production and sale as a petty commodity was eminently suitable to the home and thus easily integrated into women's lives. These overlapping factors connected the state to domestic economic activities, making the alcohol industry one of the most productive avenues for present-day scholars to mine women's historical importance as household providers, commercial players, and political subjects in Latin America's past.

Notes

1. Archivo Municipal de San Juan Ostuncalco (hereafter AMSJO), Correspondencia, Bulto 1826–29, "Co. Jues Politico Antonio Corso," June 27, 1829. Monterroso is identified as the first alcalde in AMSJO, Correspondencia, Bulto 1826–29, "San Juan Ostuncalco Mayo ultimo de 1829," May 31, 1829.

2. Most of the existing historiography, focused as it is on coffee, does not suggest the importance of alcohol to the myriad conflicts that rent Guatemalan society or the financial calculi of state officials and innumerable households that sought to sustain themselves from its revenues. Pompejano's *La crisis de antiguo régimen en Guatemala (1839–1871)* is the major exception, at least in macroeconomic terms. Although both Mc-Creery, in *Rural Guatemala,* and Woodward, in *Rafael Carrera and the Emergence of the Republic of Guatemala,* provide useful information about alcohol (discussed elsewhere in this chapter), neither one undertakes a more thorough analysis of the commodity or its broader economic and political importance. Against the tendency of the literature on nineteenth-century Guatemala to focus on coffee, Little-Siebold suggests that we will not reach a more accurate understanding of the era until we succeed in "decaffeinating" it. See his "Guatemala and the Dream," esp. 254–72.

3. For a fuller discussion of the evolution of the historiography of nineteenth-century Guatemala, including the innovations as well as shortcomings of the revisionist literature, see the introduction to my monograph, *Ladinos with Ladinos, Indians with Indians,* esp. 2–4.

4. Stephens, *Incidents of Travel,* 1:231–32. The word *alforgas* should be spelled *alforjas.*

5. See Carey's illuminating discussion of the issues involved in interviewing Kaqchikel Maya women in Guatemala in *Engendering Mayan History,* esp. 2–27.

6. The phrase comes from the title of Rodríguez Sáenz's edited volume, *Entre silencios y voces.*

7. AMSJO, Procesos Judiciales (Criminales), 1860–85; AMSJO, Correspondencia, Bultos 1864–70, 1875, 1877–80, 1886. The years with missing data are 1863, 1871, 1876, and 1883–85.

8. The literature on the public-private sphere is vast, but a pioneering formulation of the concept is Rosaldo, "Woman, Culture, and Society."

9. Lacoste, "Wine and Women," 390.

10. Wolfe, *Everyday Nation State,* 63.

11. Hames, "Maize-Beer, Gossip, and Slander," 352–53. Chicha is made from corn. See Hames, but also Eber, *Women and Alcohol,* 22–23. Wolfe describes *chicha fuerte* as "an alcohol made from fermented corn," i.e., an alcohol made from chicha, in *Everyday Nation State,* 61.

12. Taylor, *Drinking, Homicide, and Rebellion,* 53. Pulque is a fermented beverage made from the agave or maguey cactus.

13. Scardaville, "Alcohol Abuse and Tavern Reform," 653.

14. There could have been many reasons that information regarding clandestine aguardiente arrests did not make it to Ostuncalco from these towns during this short period. All three towns are relatively distant from Ostuncalco, and all three were almost

entirely indigenous at the time. Not only did they probably receive less scrutiny from Ostuncalco's ladino officials, and the higher-level state authorities based therein, but they were likely also more lax in cooperating with them. The Mam Maya officials of these three towns may have put less effort into rooting out local Maya clandestinistas, and they probably were less careful about reporting arrests to Ostuncalco's ladinos.

15. Scardaville, "Alcohol Abuse and Tavern Reform," 645–46.

16. AMSJO, Correspondencia, Bulto 1863, "Corregimiento del Departamento de Quezaltenango. Al Publico," September 9, 1863.

17. Woodward estimates Guatemala's national budget at 1,109,000 pesos in 1863. See his *Rafael Carrera*, table 23, p. 410. The figure of 600,000 comes from table 3 (gráfica 3) of Pompejano's *La crisis de antiguo régimen*, 16. Note that table 3 does not give precise figures, and thus the number 600,000 is only approximate. With this in mind, Pompejano shows the combined monopoly revenues fluctuating from around 200,000 to 1,200,000 pesos between the years 1855 and 1869, during which time the national budget fluctuated between 775,000 and 1,963,000 pesos per Woodward, *Rafael Carrera*, table 23, p. 410.

18. McCreery, *Rural Guatemala*, 177.

19. Wolfe, *Everyday Nation State*, 48. As with Pompejano, the percentages from Wolfe derive from figure 1 on p. 48 and thus are only approximate. Akyeampong estimates that in Ghana "by the early twentieth century, liquor revenue had established itself as the single, leading contributor to the colonial government's finances." See his *Drink, Power, and Cultural Change*, 72.

20. Gálvez is quoted in Wortman, *Government and Society*, 256.

21. Wolfe, *Everyday Nation State*, 63; Hames, "Maize-Beer, Gossip, and Slander," 352; Eber, *Women and Alcohol*, 7–8, 22; Taylor, *Drinking, Homicide, and Rebellion*, 38, 53; Scardaville, "Alcohol Abuse and Tavern Reform," 646–47, 653; Lacoste, "Wine and Women," 371–72, 383–91.

22. Pompejano provides insight into this relationship in *La crisis de antiguo régimen*, 40.

23. See Scardaville's comments on the vertical integration of Mexico's pulque industry in "Alcohol Abuse and Tavern Reform," 650; and Hayashida on how Lima's *chicheras*, or female brewers of corn beer, utilized their husbands' harvests in "*Chicha* Histories," 246.

24. AMSJO, Correspondencia, Bulto 1850, "Admon. de Rentas de Quezaltenango. Sr. Alcalde 1º. de Ostuncalco. Quezalto. Eno. 1º. de 850," January 1, 1850; AMSJO, Correspondencia, Bulto 1853, "Sor. Alce. 1ro. de la Municipl. de Sn. Juan Ostuncalco," March 17, 1853; AMSJO, Correspondencia, Bulto 1855, "Juzgado Preventivo y Militar de Sija. Señor Juez Preventivo del Distrito de Ostuncalco," November 24, 1855; Archivo de Gobernación de Quezaltenango (hereafter AQG), Legajo No. 96, "Criminales año de 1854," "Jues de 1ª. Ynsta. del Departo. de Quesalto," August 7, 1854.

25. The following is a short list of planters or planters and spouses who simultaneously cultivated sugarcane on the coast and distilled illegal aguardiente in the highlands: Gregorio Castillo; Máximo Castillo; Cayetano Espinosa; Paulina García and José Pascual Monroy; Ygnacía Molina and Luciano Lópes; Juana Monterrosa and Juan José Galindo; Aniseto Lópes; and Silvería Solís and Marcos Monroy. These names were culled from AMSJO, Correspondencia, various bultos: "Sor. Corregdor," March 11, 1820; "Co. Jues

Politico Antonio Corso," June 27, 1829; "C. Alce. de la Municipld. de Sn. Juan Ostuncalco Bernabe Monterroso," 1830; "Administon. de Rentas de Quesaltengo. Estado de Guatemala. Al Cno. Aniseto Lopes Alce. Constitucional; y Dueño del Estanco de Ostuncalco," November 6, 1833; "De el Alcald. 1º. de Ostuncalco. Al Señor Sesilio Garsia Alcald. de La Costa del Sur en el Asintal," 1841; "Jusgo. 1º. de Ostuncalco. Enero 9 de 1852," January 9, 1852; "Admon. de Rentas de Quesaltenango. Señor Juez Prebentivo de San Juan Ostuncalco. Quezalto. Mayo 10 de 59," May 10, 1859; and Archivo de Gobernación de Quezaltenango (AGQ), "Denuncias," 1836; Legajo No. 155, "Año de 1841. La Municipd. de San Martin Sacatepequez sobre avances en sus ejidos," "Nuestro Mui ylustrisimo Señor presidente del Estado de Guatemala," May 24, 1841. They were cross-referenced with AMSJO, Correspondencia, Bulto 1830, "Padrón General. Departamento de Quesaltenango. Municipalidad de Ostuncalco," August 1, 1830.

26. Akyeampong writes that as "sellers of cooked food, retailers of alcoholic drinks, and prostitutes, women lubricated the engines of capitalist production and urban social formation" in colonial Ghana. See his *Drink, Power, and Cultural Change*, 48.

27. AMSJO, Correspondencia, Bulto 1834–36, "Viernes 11 de Julio de 1834," July 11, 1834.

28. Ibid.

29. See Dunn's chapter in this volume.

30. AMSJO, Correspondencia, Bulto 1834–36, "Viernes 11 de Julio de 1834," July 11, 1834.

31. The sources on which I based the preceding two paragraphs are myriad and moreover often contain small inconsistencies and exceptions. I list the most pertinent here in chronological order: AMSJO, Correspondencia, Bulto 1826–29, "Ciuds. Alcaldes de Ostuncalco," June 10, 1826, and "Co. Jues Politico Antonio Corso," June 27, 1829; AGQ, Legajo No. 68, "Gobierno Departml. de Quesaltenango. Libro Copiador de Municipalidades en San Marcos á diez de Octubre de 1832," "C. Alcalde 1º. de Obstuncalco," November 8, 1832; "N. 878. Ley 5ª," June 10, 1833, in Pineda de Mont, *Recopilación de las leyes de Guatemala*, 2:471–72; AMSJO, Correspondencia, Bulto 1831–33, "Aministon. de Rentas de Quesaltengo. Estado de Guatemala. Al Con. Aniseto Lopes Alce. Constitucional y Dueño del Estanco de Ostuncalco," November 6, 1833; "N. 881. Ley 8ª," May 28, 1834, in Pineda de Mont, *Recopilación de las leyes de Guatemala*, 2:474; AMSJO, Correspondencia, Bulto 1834–36, "Viernes 11 de Julio de 1834," June 11, 1834; "N. 882. Ley 9ª," October 29, 1834, "N. 883. Ley 10ª," December 31, 1834, "N. 884. Ley 11ª," May 7, 1835, and "N. 886. Ley 13ª," August 16, 1835, in Pineda de Mont, *Recopilación de las leyes de Guatemala*, 474–80; AGQ, Legajo No. 112, "Año de 1836," "Departamto. de Quezaltenango," February 29, 1836; "Ministerio general del Supremo Gobierno del Estado de Guatemala. Departamento de Gobernacion. El Gefe Supremo del Estado de Guatemala," April 21, 1837, in *Boletín de noticias de la colera morbo*, 1; AGQ, "Con. Gefe Politico departaml. de la Ciudad de Quesalto.," June 1838; November 25, 1839, in Skinner-Klee, *Legislación indigenista de Guatemala*, 24; "N. 888. Ley 15ª," December 10, 1839, and "N. 348. Ley 15ª," December 14, 1839, in Pineda de Mont, *Recopilación de las leyes de Guatemala*, 480–81 and 605–6; AMSJO, Correspondencia, Bulto 1840–41, "Admon. de Rentas del Departamto. de Quezalteno. Sr. Alce. 1º. de Ostuncalco," March 1, 1841; AGQ, Legajo No. 164,

"Segunda Representación de las mujeres del común del Quezaltenango solicitando se suprima el sistema del Estancos en aquella ciudad, y se restablezca el de Patentes del Aguardiente del país," May 1841; AMSJO, Correspondencia, Bulto 1849, "Corregimiento del Departamento de Quezaltenango y Superintenda. y Comandancia Gral. de los Departams. de los Altos. Al Sr. Alcalde 1º. de Sn. Juan Ostuncalco," October 13, 1849, and Bulto 1850, "Admon. de Rentas de Quezaltenango. Al Sr. Alcalde 1º. de Ostuncalco. Quezalto. Junio 23 de 850," June 23, 1850; "N. 903. Ley 30ª," August 21, 1851, and "N. 904. Ley 31ª," March 10, 1852, in Pineda de Mont, *Recopilación de las leyes de Guatemala,* 499–503; AMSJO, Correspondencia, Bulto 1853, "Comunicaciones de la Cámera de representantes," May 19, 1853, and "Corregimiento del Departamento de Quezaltenango. Quesalto. Julio 20/853. A la municipalidad de Ladinos de Ostuncalco," July 20, 1853; May 8, 1871, in Burgess, *Justo Rufino Barrios,* 75n4–78; "Decreto Num. 19," October 16, 1871, and unnamed decree, February 21, 1872, in Pineda de Mont, *Recopilación de las leyes emitidas,* 1:15–23, 81; "Decreto Número 236," March 2, 1879, and "Reglamento complementario del decreto numero 236," April 4, 1879, in Pineda de Mont, *Recopilación de las leyes emitidas,* 2:253–75.

32. See Opie's chapter in this volume.

33. Skinner-Klee, *Legislación indigenista de Guatemala,* 24; Pineda de Mont, *Recopilación de las leyes de Guatemala,* "N. 888. Ley 15ª," December 10, 1839, and "N. 348. Ley 15ª," December 14, 1839, 480–81, 605–6.

34. AMSJO, Correspondencia, Bulto 1840–41, "Admon. de Rentas del Departamto. de Quezalteno. Sr. Alce. 1º. de Ostuncalco," March 1, 1841.

35. Ibid.

36. Ibid.

37. Ibid.

38. Ibid.

39. AMSJO, Correspondencia, Bulto 1834–36, "Viernes 11 de Julio de 1834," July 11, 1834.

40. AMSJO, Correspondencia, Bulto 1840–41, "Admon. de Rentas del Departamto. de Quezalteno. Sr. Alce. 1º. de Ostuncalco," March 1, 1841.

41. Wolfe, *Everyday Nation State,* 62. See Carey's chapter in this volume.

42. AMSJO, Correspondencia, Bulto 1840–41, "Admon. de Rentas del Departamto. de Quezalteno. Sr. Alce. 1º. de Ostuncalco," March 1, 1841.

43. Aniseto Lópes's positions in the *municipalidad* are documented in AMSJO, Correspondencia, Bulto 1831–33, "Elección de ayuntamiento," December 21, 1811, and "Sn. Juan Ostuncalco. Sbre. 27 de 1833," September 27, 1833, and in AMSJO, Correspondencia, Bulto 1822–25, "Sor. Alc. Pr. Otco. Aniseto Lopes," October 29, 1822. Both Gregorio and Máximo Castillo, for example, owned coastal sugar properties, as described in AMSJO, Correspondencia, Bulto 1855, "En el pueblo de Sn. Juan Ostuncalco á veintiseis de Octubre de mil ochocientos cincuenta y cinco, anti me el Juez Preventivo de este Distrito, compareció el Sr. Gregorio Castillo," October 26, 1855.

44. AMSJO, Correspondencia, Bulto 1834–36, "Viernes 11 de Julio de 1834," July 11, 1834.

45. AGQ, Legajo No. 164, "Segunda Representación," May 1841.

46. Ibid.
47. Ibid.
48. Ibid.; AGQ, Legajo No. 164, "Sr. Superyntendte. de Hacienda, Correjidor de este Departamto," May 1841.
49. Akyeampong notes that poverty likewise drove Gold Coast women to traffic in illegal alcohol. See his *Drink, Power, and Cultural Change*, 101, 104, 109.
50. AGQ, Legajo No. 164, "Segunda Representación," May 1841.
51. Ibid.
52. Ibid.
53. See Carey's chapter in this volume.
54. AGQ, Legajo No. 164, "Segunda Representación," May 1841.
55. Ibid.
56. AMSJO, Correspondencia, Bulto 1849, "Corregimiento del Departamento de Quezaltenango y Superintenda. y Comandancia Gral. de los Departams. de los Altos. Al Sr. Alcalde 1º. de Sn. Juan Ostuncalco," October 13, 1849, and Bulto 1850, "Admon. de Rentas de Quezaltenango. Al Sr. Alcalde 1º. de Ostuncalco. Quezalto. Junio 23 de 850," June 23, 1850.
57. The establishment of the juez preventivo in Ostuncalco is covered in AMSJO, Correspondencia, Bulto 1853, "Corregimiento del Departamento de Quezaltenango. Quesalto. Julio 20/853. A la municipalidad de Ladinos de Ostuncalco," July 20, 1853. The legal foundations of the resguardo de aguardiente are provided in "N. 903. Ley 30ª," August 21, 1851, and "N. 904. Ley 31ª," March 10, 1852, in Pineda de Mont, *Recopilación de las leyes de Guatemala*, 2:499–503. AMSJO, Correspondencia, Bulto 1853, "Comunicaciones de la Cámera de representantes," May 19, 1853, also discusses the establishment of the resguardo. Schwartzkopf covers the establishment of a juez preventivo in Huehuetenango in the preceding chapter.
58. AGQ, "Sor. Corregr. de el Departto. Juzgado Prevento. del Distrito de S. Juan Ostuncalco," December 26, 1856.
59. AMSJO, Correspondencia, Bulto 1857–58, "Gobernatura y Municipalidad de Ostuncalco. Señor Corregidor Superintendente de Hacienda, y Comandante General de los Departamentos de los Altos," October 15, 1858. Pompejano describes the alcohol resguardo as "half public functionaries and half guardians of the private interests of the monopolists." See his *La crisis de antiguo régimen*, 35.
60. AMSJO, Correspondencia, Bulto 1854, "Admon. de Rentas de Quezaltenango. Manuel Carrascal Admon. de este Departamto.," May 24, 1854; AMSJO, Correspondencia, Bulto 1856, "Corregimiento del Departamento de Quezaltenango. Sor. Juez Preventivo del Distrito de Ostuncalco," February 14, 1856, and "Admon. de Rentas de Quesaltenango. Sr. Juez Prebentibo de San Juan Ostuncalco. Quesalto. Octe. 26 de 856," October 26, 1856; AGQ, Legajo No. 96, "Criminales año de 1854," "Sr. Jues de primera Ynsta. del Depto. de Quesalto. Jusgdo. Prev. del Disto. de Ostunco.," October 24, 1854.
61. AMSJO, Correspondencia, Bulto 1854, "Corregimiento del Departamento de Quezaltenango. Sor. Juez Preventivo del Distrito de Ostuncalco," July 31, 1854; AGQ, Legajo No. 96, "Criminales año de 1854," "Sr. Jues de primera Ynsta. del Depto. de Quesalto. Jusgdo. Prev. del Disto. de Ostunco.," October 24, 1854.

62. AMSJO, Correspondencia, Bulto 1855, "Libro de Actas en que la Municipalidad del Pueblo de Ostuncalco deberá continuar asentando las actas de sus respectivos acuerdos en el año de 1854 (hasta 1862)," fols. 42b–43, "En la Sala Municipal del Pueblo de San Juan Ostuncalco reunida la Municipd. en ceccion estraordinaria de este dia veinte y seis de Agosto de mil ochocientos cincuenta y cinco," August 26, 1855, and fols. 48b–49, "En la Sala Municipal del Pueblo de San Juan Ostuncalco el dia primero de Octubre de mil ochcs. cincuenta y cinco. Reunidas la Municipalidades de Ladino he indigenas en ceccion extraordinaria," October 1, 1855; AMSJO, Correspondencia, Bulto 1855, "Juzgdo. Preventivo del Distrito de Ostuncalco. A los Gobernadores y Municipalidades de los Pueblos que al margen se espresan," October 1, 1855.

63. Archivo General de Centro América (hereafter AGCA), Sección B, Leg. 28582, Exp. 195, "Señor Corregidor del departamento de Quesaltenango," June 23, 1855; AMSJO, Correspondencia, Bulto 1855, "Corregimiento del Departamento de Quezaltenango. Sor. Juez Preventivo Comicionado Politico del Distrito de Ostuncalco," November 28, 1855. Ostuncalco's ladino municipal government was not resurrected until January 1862: AGCA, Sección B, Leg. 28586, Exp. 218, "Palacio de Gobierno, Guatemala Octubre 19 de 1861," October 19, 1861.

64. AGQ, "Sor. Corregidor del Depto. Juzgado Prevento. del Distrito de S. Juan Ostuncalco," November 3, 1855.

65. Liberal insurgents pledged to abolish the alcohol monopoly at least as early as 1867. See Ingersoll, "War of the Mountain," 337. Miguel García Granados and his cohorts (including Barrios) formally promised to put an end to it on May 8, 1871. An English translation of their manifesto is published in Burgess, *Justo Rufino Barrios*, 75n4–78. On subaltern opposition to the Conservative alcohol monopoly and its political consequences more broadly, see Pompejano, *La crisis del antiguo régimen*, 40, 207–10.

66. For broader historiographical discussion of popular antipathy toward the Conservative monopoly in the city of Quezaltenango, see González Alzate, "History of Los Altos," 545–47, 554–59; Taracena Arriola, *Invención criolla*, 404; Burgess, *Justo Rufino Barrios*, 81; and AGQ, Legajo No. 164, "Segunda Representación de las mujeres del comun del Quezaltenango solicitando se suprima el sistema del Estancos en aquella ciudad, y se restablesca el de Patentes del Aguardiente del país," May 1841. For Guatemala more generally, see McCreery, *Rural Guatemala*, 176–77; Woodward, *Rafael Carrera*, 343; and the commentary of Manuel Pineda de Mont, in the footnote dated April 1, 1872, related to "N. 915. Ley 42ª," January 31, 1865, in his edited *Recopilación de las leyes de Guatemala*, 520–24.

67. See my *Ladinos with Ladinos, Indians with Indians* for more detail on the Conservatives' land and labor policies.

68. For more on the Liberal insurgents' promise to abolish the alcohol monopoly and how it was received, see Ingersoll, "War of the Mountain," 337; Clegern, *Origins of Liberal Dictatorship*, 112, 116; Burgess, *Justo Rufino Barrios*, 75–78n4, 80–81; Woodward, *Rafael Carrera*, 436; "Decreto Num. 3," June 11, 1871, in Pineda de Mont, *Recopiliación de las leyes emitidas*, 1:3; and the proclamation of Ostuncalco's ladino and indigenous officials in support of this and other Liberal measures in AMSJO, Bulto 1871, Libro de Actas, "En la Sala Municipal de Sn. Juan Ostuncalco," June 18, 1871.

69. See the chapters by Carey and Schwartzkopf in this volume.

70. Akyeampong, *Drink, Power, and Cultural Change*, esp. chaps. 3–6.

71. See Taylor, *Drinking, Homicide, and Rebellion*, esp. chap. 2, entitled "Drinking," on the predominance of women as pulque vendors in Mexico City and its environs. Scardaville also refers to the importance of women as illegal pulque sellers and tavern proprietors in "Alcohol Abuse and Tavern Reform," esp. 646.

72. Hames, "Maize-Beer, Gossip, and Slander"; Lacoste, "Wine and Women." The following sources are in Jennings and Bowser's *Drink, Power, and Society in the Andes:* Perlov, "Working through Daughters," 49–74; Goodman-Elgar, "Places to Partake," 75–107; Jennings and Chatfield, "Pots, Brewers, and Hosts," 200–231; Hayashida, "*Chicha* Histories," 232–56; and Weismantel, "Have a Drink," 257–77. Although the following sources are less concerned with the specific nexus of women and alcohol, see also Scardaville, "Alcohol Abuse and Tavern Reform"; and Rosenbaum, *With Our Heads Bowed.*

73. Hames, "Maize-Beer, Gossip, and Slander," 352; Goodman-Elgar, "Places to Partake," 75; Jennings and Chatfield, "Pots, Brewers, and Hosts," 202, 218–19; Hayashida, "*Chicha* Histories," 234, 236, 238, 244–49; Eber, *Women and Alcohol,* 22.

74. Hayashida, "*Chicha* Histories," 236, 238, 240–41, 244–49. See also Jennings and Chatfield, "Pots, Brewers, and Hosts."

75. Wolfe, *Everyday Nation State*, 63.

3

◇◇◇◇◇◇◇◇◇◇◇◇◇◇◇

"A Sponge Soaking up All the Money"

Alcohol, Taverns, Vinaterías, and the Bourbon Reforms in Mid-Eighteenth-Century Santiago de los Caballeros, Guatemala

ALVIS E. DUNN

Eighteenth-century Santiago de los Caballeros, Guatemala, "ranked behind only Mexico City and Lima in size and importance"[1] as a center of Spanish culture. A visitor in the mid-1700s could have enjoyed a city boasting new university and town hall structures, an impressive palace for the captain general, cobblestone streets, and a dynamic plaza mayor.[2] A system of aqueducts had been delivering fresh water to selected neighborhoods in the city since the sixteenth century.[3] In addition to these secular features, throughout the classic urban gridiron layout were "churches, basilicas, monasteries, and charitable institutions."[4] All of this combined to make "Santiago into one of America's loveliest cities."[5] Along with these positive elements also came typical challenges to metropolitan living. Foremost among elite concerns was the role of alcohol in daily life.[6] While the local government worked to rein in misbehaving townspeople, the Crown also had its own ideas on addressing public health and safety. Across colonial society, benefiting financially from the region's fondness for spirits was a goal often at cross-purposes with the common welfare. Because of the conflicting interests of segments of that society, in Central America the urban culture of drink was one of the earliest contexts where Bourbon policy and the home rule impulse clashed.[7]

Alcohol's availability cut across racial and class lines and was a gauge of the nature of the relationship between the Crown, local government, and the population. In the pursuit of access to aguardiente and wine, the Santiago government and citizenry might find common ground. By the

mid-eighteenth century the inhabitants of Santiago were approaching accord that access to aguardiente and wine should be locally decided. Indeed, merchant and consumer voices increasingly joined those of elites on
the town council to assert local control of alcohol manufacture, sale, and
consumption. Revenues, public and private, were potentially too lucrative
to escape local coffers and flow into imperial ones. The Crown, however,
had other ideas.

As public health and safety issues surrounding alcohol grew progressively more acute in the colony, so too did the realization of the profits possible from the commodity. Both colonists and the Crown sought
avenues by which they might reach the delicate balance between profit-
ably supplying demand and keeping the peace in the streets. The voices
of merchants and some consumers were heeded on this matter, and the
responsiveness of local government broadened. A confluence had been
reached by 1750, and as Bourbon reform efforts began to operate across
the empire, alcohol in Santiago did not go unnoticed.

Accordingly, in 1754, presented with the possibility that a single private
citizen would be awarded a royal monopoly to produce and sell distilled
aguardiente, the attorney for Santiago declared, "[I]f this monopoly passes
to an individual it will be the ruin of all the kingdom: The owner of the
monopoly and distiller could set the price and would be a sponge soaking
up all the money in circulation, moreover, the subsequent introduction
of more alcohol to more places would inevitably result in a significant
increase in drunkenness."[8] The argument was that by granting a single
individual the exclusive right to manufacture and sell aguardiente, the
increase in available supply would capture all the coin in the region as well
as produce an unprecedented degree of insobriety. In truth, specie was
always scarce in Central America during the colonial period,[9] and while
there was likely some exaggeration in the attorney's assertion, alcohol was
indeed significant to both economic and social life in mid-eighteenth-
century Central America.[10] Merchants, importers eyeing the colony's
market, tavern keepers, drinkers, bootleggers, Crown agents, even teetotalers, all harbored interests in the degree of convenience with which
alcohol could be bought, sold, and consumed in the Captaincy-General
of Guatemala. The words and deeds of the town council regarding these
matters reveal strong concerns in regard to not only the economy but also
public health.

The battle waged by the Santiago Town Council over the administration of alcohol was a bellwether of regional efforts to respond to the first signs of Bourbon belt-tightening and reorganization. Local concepts and ideals of fairness as well as rights and privileges vis-à-vis government, informed in specific and historical ways by race, class, gender, and status, were revealed by the wrangle over alcohol. Indeed, in this matter the Santiago Town Council appears to have attempted to harmonize the voices of a broader segment of society than was normal. On a much more mundane plane in the modernizing world of Bourbon Reform, who drank, where they did it, and how drunk they got, along with the overall "organization of public space,"[11] was of increasing import for the ruling class.

Since at least the late seventeenth century, alcohol supply had been an indicator of the colony's economic integration into the empire.[12] In Santiago, anxiety also surrounded the actual composition of alcoholic beverages available as well as the character and organization of the places where it was sold. Systemic reorganization of the regulation of alcohol production and distribution at the midpoint of the eighteenth century accompanied the earliest manifestations of the Bourbon Reforms in the colonies. So pervasive were both supply and demand networks in Guatemala that in 1752 the captain general, José Vásquez Prego, informed the Crown that from his experience attempting to eradicate the clandestine manufacture of alcohol in the colony, the only recourse he could recommend was the creation of a government monopoly. No other method of managing production or demand would be successful.[13] Vásquez Prego's assertion was followed by the announcement of the establishment of the Alcohol Monopoly. In response, Santiago's attorney laid out the unhappy sponge analogy. The issues of contraband production and regulation of aguardiente sales were secondary to concerns about money supply and public comportment.

The argument against privatization won the day, and instead the town council was granted management of the monopoly. Subsequently, from 1755 until 1765 it controlled the production and sale of distilled sugarcane spirits in the Captaincy-General of Guatemala, a subunit of the viceroyalty of New Spain. Presumably, council management of the alcohol market would assure purity, protect propriety, and safeguard public health. Monopolies were also farmed out to eligible municipalities throughout the region. For the city of Santiago the town council created distinct categories and moved to license two types of drinking establishments: (1) vinaterías (wine and liquor shops), where along with sundry items necessary for daily life, only imported wines and alcohols were available; and (2) monopoly taverns, where the state blend was sold in addition to foreign spirits. Close scrutiny of the town council's tenure as monopolist, so near the beginning of the Bourbon Reforms, makes possible a deeper understanding of the relationship between the government and the governed. A fruitful and intriguing aside, such a careful look at the culture of drink permits glimpses of daily life in an eighteenth-century urban setting. Ultimately, local control of alcohol proved a cross-societal nexus of concerns cultural and economic that briefly united colonial elites, merchants, and consumers in the face of Crown policy.

Mixing in Peruvian and Spanish Spirits

Wrangling on alcohol issues was not new in the captaincy-general. Throughout the eighteenth century, deliberation, even dispute, over the status of alcohol was constant. Often intertwined with the subject of local consumption and price was the question of the nature of commerce with Peru, a significant producer of both distilled spirits and wine.[14] Spain had been a source of wine and liquor from the beginning of the colonial period, but Peru had also become a supplier to Central America by late in the sixteenth century. This Pacific traffic went on whether sanctioned or not. Illegal between 1615 and 1685,[15] limited trade was permitted with Central America until 1713.[16] Banned again from 1713 until 1774,[17] the record clearly shows that *frascos* (flasks) of Peruvian wine and aguardiente reached tables and tankards in Central America in great quantities throughout those years just the same.

The reality was that while Spanish liquor and wine maintained their favored position, the demand for alcohol was such that the government looked the other way when scarcities (the norm) required that unsanctioned wine and liquor enter the colony in order to fulfill the needs of drinkers, and perhaps less problematically, the ritual requirements of the Church. Despite consistent violations of restricted trade throughout the eighteenth century, Iberian merchants clung to "illusory monopolies" that outlined on paper their position as favored and exclusive trading partners.[18] The reality was that contraband trade likely rivaled or surpassed legitimate trade.[19] Throughout this period the town council of Santiago regularly discussed the contraband trade and petitioned the imperial government to drop proscriptions on the importation of foreign, especially Peruvian, blends.[20] Even with the prohibitions and restrictions on trade, both distilled spirits and wine from Peru, as well as Spain, appear to have been quite available in Guatemala.

A good example of the open discussion of Peruvian products and their availability in Guatemala is the case of Alonso Gutiérrez. On September 23, 1760, Gutiérrez petitioned Santiago's town council for a license to open a "tavern where wine and brandies of Castille [*Caldos de Castilla*] are sold."[21] In addition to eight hundred bottles of Spanish wine, Gutiérrez also had acquired some Peruvian aguardiente. Unable to sell it wholesale locally, he was seeking permission to do so retail in a "vinatería *pública*." Gutiérrez identified the Spanish wine as having come from a Barcelona firm and himself as a local businessman.[22]

Gutiérrez acknowledged his understanding that there already existed the legal limit of establishments selling imported spirits in Santiago. He was also aware that the town had its share of drunkenness. He promised that if he aggravated this situation then the council would be welcome to take his license. Gutiérrez asserted that his merchandise was not the sort that caused drunkenness but rather that it was very "*espirituoso*" (high proof) and of a higher quality than was normally sold in Santiago. He added that only Spaniards would drink this stock and that common drunks would not be interested because they spent their money on the cheap illegal alcohol. Therefore, the sale of these wines and liquors would be beneficial to the empire. He expressed his hope that the holders of other licenses would not be influential in this matter. Ostensibly referring to import prohibitions, in particular the ban on Peruvian liquor, Gutiérrez noted that if these beverages were not to be sold in the kingdom then they should have been stopped at the port of entry.

The council attorney's response was terse, noting that there existed avenues for the sale of this product and that the state had placed no undue obstructions to the petitioner's attempts to sell the wine or liquor. Nor was Gutiérrez blocked from plying his wares in another part of the colony. Indeed, there were still many unexhausted and untried remedies to this dilemma. The attorney added that while aguardiente was more commonly associated with inebriation, such fine blends still could cause drunkenness.[23] Clearly such an open discussion of Peruvian alcohol by the governing authorities demonstrates the prevalence of the product and the acceptance of its presence despite prohibitions.

There are a number of such emergency requests for licensing like Gutiérrez's throughout this period. One particularly noteworthy example appeared two years later, in 1762, when Don Antonio Joseph Orejuela, a Peruvian captain of the sailing ship *Señor San Joseph*, was granted a six-month license to open two vinaterías in order to sell "Peruvian wine and aguardiente."[24] Similar petitions scattered throughout the records for the 1760s serve as additional indications of the commonness of this officially banned commodity in the region.[25]

Managing Monopolies and Public Houses

Beginning in the 1730s, debate in the Santiago Town Council would range back and forth over the appropriate number of public houses.[26] In 1732 a maximum was set at twelve,[27] only to rise precipitously to thirty-six in 1739, at which time the council communicated with the *audiencia* (court of appeals that also had administrative duties) its wishes to reduce the number to sixteen.[28] Interestingly, just five years later the council moved to set the number of establishments permitted at twenty-four, ostensibly in order to influence tax revenues.[29] Perhaps indicative of several years of rather robust overindulgence, in 1746 the town council again moved to lower the number to fourteen, citing "the well developed state of drunkenness" that had befallen the town.[30]

Some members of the town council were convinced that much of this problem could be traced to the selling of "all class[es] of blended and adulterated drinks."[31] This suspicion regarding the purity of alcoholic beverages was a very persistent issue over the course of the century. Since the town council held the power to issue individual licenses to brew and distill in the early decades of the eighteenth century, petitions for start-up operations were regularly submitted. The prospects for the successful marketing of more than an acrid shot of pungent 100 proof alcohol must have seemed promising enough, as in 1726 Manuel Jurado submitted an application to the town council for a license to sell *mistelas*,[32] as well as to distill "aguardiente anis" (anise-flavored rum).[33] All was not in accord, however, as three years later the owners of the town's vinaterías stood in opposition to Jurado's proposition to sell his more complex blends.[34]

Drinks Available in Eighteenth-Century Public Houses, Santiago, Guatemala

Aguardiente Anis: Locally distilled (from sugarcane) alcohol flavored with anise.
Aguardiente de España: Import distilled from grapes.
Aguardiente de la Tierra: Locally distilled cane alcohol. Usually contraband.
Aguardiente de Peru: Import distilled from grapes; prohibited but openly traded.
Aguardiente de Uva Silvestre: Locally distilled from wild grapes.
Aguadulces: Sugar and fruit juices. Nonalcoholic but could serve as mixers.
Beer: Fermented brew.
Caldo de Castilla: Distilled or fermented alcohols imported from Spain.
Chicha: A fermented drink made of corn, sugarcane, and fruit.
Mistela: A grape-based and aromatic alcoholic beverage with a slightly higher potency and a sweeter taste than wine; used as an ingredient or sold as liqueur.
Mistela Alambicada: A highly refined/distilled mistela and thus of a higher alcohol content, approaching that of brandy.
Rosolios Medicinales: A cordial composed of water, rice, toasted garbanzos, barley, ground cinnamon, and the meat of the citron. This mixture is put into infusion for fifteen days and then distilled.
Vino de España: Wine of Spain.
Vino de Peru: Wine of Peru; prohibited but openly traded.

Fruit and anise-based concoctions were not the only possibility envisioned in Santiago, as in the same year that Jurado proposed his elaborate flavored mixtures, Carlos Antonio Valdio solicited permission for a license to brew beer.[35] Though Valdio's request was apparently denied, in 1731 Pedro Lujan de Escovar submitted essentially the same petition. He too was rebuffed.[36] The following year the door was shut on Jurado's operations when he was prohibited from preparing "mistelas *alambicadas*,"[37] because of the perceived ill effects they produced.[38] A petition for a license to distill yet another variety of alcohol came to the town council from the aptly named Ambrosio de Pasos, who asked for permission to utilize wild grapes in preparing aguardiente.[39] De Pasos also asked for permission to prepare "*rosolios medicinales*."[40] In this case the town council attorney asked for the city's chief medical officer to inspect these blends for "their virtue, quality, purity, effects, and if they were damaging to the human body."[41]

In that same vein, and indicating with more specificity the nature of the problems caused by increasing alcohol consumption in the town, at that same council meeting a motion was passed that ordered public houses to be located no more than two or three blocks from the main plaza and to shut their doors with the final tolling of the evening bell.[42] These restrictions appear to have gone mainly unheeded, as two years later, in 1748, enough sales were taking place after the "authorized hours" that a motion was made that the council itself should take control of the leasing and administration of those accounts because private individuals had "sacrificed the public morality in covering their personal interests."[43] Felipe Manrique de Guzmán was appointed to oversee the public houses, to ensure that the number did not exceed fourteen and that none were located in the periphery of the city.[44] A sentiment is suggested in these proceedings that considerations of community health and security in this matter should rise above those of the individual. This is the same attitude echoed in the quotation that opens this chapter, regarding the granting of the aguardiente monopoly to a single person. The town council would also soon come to take a rather large role in the operation of the town's vinaterías, as well as the taverns attached to the monopoly itself.

In 1749 the town council proclaimed that, not just in the back alleys but in the main streets, there was rampant drunkenness and that throughout the town, murders, robberies, and assaults were increasingly common. This deterioration of the public morality was attributed to the numerous illegal bars and tent taverns (*tiendas de capote*), even in the main plaza, which under the pretext of serving sweet flavored nonalcoholic beverages (*aguadulces*) and beer were also actually vending bootleg liquor.[45] In 1751, Captain General José de Araujo y Rio, speaking for imperial interests, reiterated the prohibition of the sale of aguardiente to the indigenous population under penalty of stiff fines and confiscation of property. Interestingly, the captain general assented to selling Peruvian and Spanish wine to the indigenous population, "because it would cause less damage."[46] Two months later, Araujo y Rio asked the permission of the audiencia to round up the lazy and idle that "in the public plaza dedicate themselves to playing dice and other games of chance," and transport them to the island of Roatán![47] Whether this was actually done is not known. Santiago of the 1740s and 1750s seems to have become a relatively unmanageable haven for the drunk, the rowdy, and the slovenly.

While an accurate comprehension of the character of the city is challenging, alcohol sales were clearly an integral part of the urban economy and culture. Tavern keeping also appears to have been at least perceived as lucrative enough that someone was always ready and eager to open a bar. The number of public houses in the city did fluctuate, and whether such variations in the count were due to economics or politics is not entirely clear. Most likely both considerations were crucial. Of course, not all liquor was consumed in legal public houses or subject to such scrutiny. In addition, not all alcohol drunk in legal establishments was legitimately manufactured.

The regulation of public houses in Santiago prior to the establishment of the Royal Alcohol Monopoly and the town council's acquisition of it appears to have been rather haphazard, at least when viewed across the seventeenth and eighteenth centuries. Over that time, statutes aimed at managing alcohol production, sale, and consumption seem to have been only partially obeyed as attention paid them crested and waned. Consumers and vendors vied with the government constantly over the nature of access, including the issues of where sales could be made, what sales could be made, and to whom sales could be made.[48] It appears that not until the awarding of the monopoly to the town council in 1754 did a truly concerted effort to regulate the manufacture, sale, and consumption of the range of alcohol available materialize with the establishment of two distinct types of public house: the vinatería and the monopoly tavern. Even this attempt ultimately proved an experiment with mixed results and hardly one over which full agreement could be reached.[49] Highlighting the tenacity of clandestine manufacture, in 1762, after seven years of the town council–run monopoly, Manuel de Mello, *el comisario del real estanco* (commissioner of the royal alcohol monopoly), reported that between February and April he had uncovered ninety-four stills and eight illegal taverns in Santiago and peripheral pueblos.[50]

While there were most assuredly economic considerations driving the establishment of the Alcohol Monopoly, questions of morality also appear to have played a role in government decisions related to alcohol. Certainly, concerns of this sort had been voiced. These issues were also intertwined with those of both public health and safety. The captain general's observation on the virulence of bootlegging neatly foreshadowed the Crown's decision to take a larger role in supplying local distilled alcohol.

Changes in the economic and political dynamic underpinned the town council's reaction to the Alcohol Monopoly. Entrepreneurs and merchants were certainly not pleased by the new arrangement, because it limited their range of purchasing possibilities and thus was likely to raise prices and diminish profits. Doubtless bootleggers also were not pleased. From the point of view of most, this increased regulation was a violation of their commercial autonomy and was greeted with disapproval and protest. To what degree the worry was also about perceptions of growing impropriety is unknown. As the eighteenth century unfolded, Bourbons were concerned that the streets were too poorly controlled and that at the heart of this loss of control often lay the consumption of alcohol.[51] At the end of May 1754, the town's attorney warned that there were two persons preparing to vie to win the proposed bidding for the monopoly and if either did so they would visit much misery upon the town, especially the indigenous population.[52]

Unwilling to accept the Crown edict quietly, the town council attorney made his observation that the establishment of the Alcohol Monopoly would not only soak up all the coin but also be the ruin of the colony, resulting in an increase in crime and vice that would overburden colonial forces of public safety.[53] In a victory for local over imperial interests, instead of awarding the monopoly to an individual, the Crown granted it to the town council for a five-year period. The town council–managed Alcohol Monopoly went into effect on February 18, 1755, with the opening of four city saloons, or monopoly taverns, selling the local distillate as well as imported beverages. The same Don Felipe Manrique de Guzmán hired to keep watch over all public houses in 1749 was appointed the distiller.[54] A commissioner was hired to oversee the manufacture as well as the operation of the four monopoly taverns specifically designated as the only vendors of the locally distilled royal liquor. Perhaps the most important task of all fell to Manuel de Mello. As el comisario del real estanco, he enforced laws designating when, where, and how the alcohol could be sold.[55]

Measuring Colonial American Drink Settings

For colonial Guatemala the descriptions of public houses, elite or working class, are few. What sketches we do have, mainly penned by visitors, portray disturbing details about these spaces. No doubt foreign prejudices and unfamiliarities entered into both the vision and the choice of which subjects observers chose to depict, as the Protestant preacher-schoolteacher Henry Dunn's 1828 description of San Pedro El Martyr demonstrates: "We tied our horses to a tree, and entered the *estanco* or spirit shop to get some refreshment, but a scene of misery presented itself too great to be endured. In the middle of the hut was a large fire, on which was boiling a cauldron of fermented sugar. The heat at this time of day was eighty-five in the shade:—three or four dirty children were sitting on the ground, and two women, nearly naked, stretched on a mat, were singing, or rather howling in an advanced state of madness."[56] John L. Stephens painted a similar picture in the 1830s. Like Dunn, traveling the dusty roads of early nineteenth-century Guatemala, Stephens also sought refreshment and company when, "Hearing the sound of a drum and violin, I walked to the house whence it issued, and found it crowded with men and women, smoking, lounging in hammocks, dancing, and drinking aguardiente, in celebration of a marriage. . . . Before me now was an exhibition of disgusting revelry: when a prominent vagabond seemed disposed to pick a quarrel with me, I quietly walked back to the *cabildo* [town council], shut the door, and betook myself to my hammock."[57] These are hardly inviting descriptions. The reader must understand the context of these troubled musings from Anglo-Protestant travelers regarding alcohol consumption and the comportment of locals. Although Stephens wrote in the early nineteenth century, such scenes could be found virtually the world over in the eighteenth century, and certainly some taverns in Spanish colonial America were comfortable and welcoming. Nevertheless, for Guatemala no in-depth account of such a setting has come down to us.

Foreign observers were not the only ones to express their alarm in those days. In *Propriety and Permissiveness in Bourbon Mexico*, Juan Pedro Viqueira Albán suggests that Enlightenment ideas held by colonial elites in New Spain prompted them to perceive a decline in morality (which may or may not have actually been occurring) and thus react to it with new laws aimed at controlling public behavior, including drinking culture.[58] The authors writing on British America also propose that economics played a role in motivating the effort to control and regulate alcohol and its consumption.[59] Thus, economics, through class concerns and jousts over imperial policy, combined with alarm over ethics were salient issues in both Mexico City and the British colonies to the north. These matters appear also to have been intertwined in the story of the initial stages of the management of the Alcohol Monopoly in the Captaincy-General of Guatemala.

Christopher Lutz's *Santiago de Guatemala, 1541–1773: City, Caste, and the Colonial Experience* provides a rich bank of information on urban life and alcohol in the capital of the captaincy-general.[60] Interestingly, Lutz suggests that self-identity, so drenched in economics and disquiet over decency in eighteenth-century Santiago, could be revealed by one's choice of drink. "Knowing which alcoholic beverage a person customarily drank was as good a way to identify economic and socioracial status in Spanish Guatemala as knowing whether he or she regularly ate bread or tortillas."[61] In particular, race was ever a consideration when the manufacture, sale, and consumption of alcohol was under consideration. Spaniards, *negros*, mestizos, and mulattos tended to be treated reasonably similarly, though the Spaniard was always the more privileged by law and custom. At the bottom of the socioracial scale, Indians were generally forbidden distilled spirits, and the law generally restricted them to more traditional indigenous blends, such as the fermented chicha. Of course, the rule and the reality were often far from one another in colonial Guatemala; Indians often drank the more potent distilled beverages.

Lutz also provides pertinent information on tavern ownership, finding that in the late 1600s and early 1700s, as hard economic times befell Santiago, ever more licenses were granted to sell alcohol. Regulations were lessened and mulattos and mestizos were permitted to own and operate public houses during those times. He states that in 1689–90, twenty-one permits were issued, three of which were held by mulattas.[62] Still, he stops short of thick description of their ownership or location, especially for later in the colonial period.

The Dunn and Stephens descriptions of drinking houses in Guatemala reveal little of furnishings: the first mentions a fire, a cauldron, and a floor mat; the second, a hammock. Of the patrons we learn of contentiousness, inebriation, and affinity for smoke. Using the ideal of ordinances in the capital of New Spain we can perhaps get an idea of reality in Santiago.

Louis E. Bumgartner's biography of the celebrated thinker and Central American Founder José Cecelio del Valle yields at least a clue to the public house's place in the daily lives of colonial Central America's elites: "For relaxation he might have read Alexander Pope's translation of *Homer* or *Pensamientos de Pascal sobre la religión* rather than say, have a drink with the 'boys' at the 'Lucretia.'"[63] Here a footnote states that the Lucretia was a tavern in Guatemala City. Although Bumgartner refrains from labeling Del Valle a tippler, there is the suggestion of a culture of public drinking among his peers: "Valle . . . kept *aguardiente* and wine within arm's reach, but he used in the manner suggested by Goicoechea, who declared: 'Aguardiente, wine, chicha, pulque, and other beverages made by fermentation are susceptible to abuse; however, used with moderation, are positively good.'"[64]

Michael Scardaville outlines the ideal and the reality related to the design of taverns in eighteenth-century Mexico City:

[They were] much more than places to buy and consume alcoholic beverages on the premises. They were an integral part of the social and financial life of the lower classes, serving as places of recreation where leisure hours could be spent dancing, singing, gambling, and drinking with family, friends, and lovers. They provided lodging for the homeless poor who, for free or for a nominal fee, could sleep in a back room or under the bar. They were places where the poor could easily pawn their own or stolen goods in return for money, credit, or drink. The drinking house functioned as a reassuring institution in a society subject to the anxieties of accelerating corn prices, periodic epidemics, and job insecurity.[65]

Mapping the Vinatería and the Tavern

Vinaterías were popular in Bourbon Mexico as well as Guatemala. In Mexico, according to John Kicza, "They served both men and women; the customers could drink on the premises (the shops were popular gathering spots in the evenings) or take their purchases with them."[66] In Mexico,

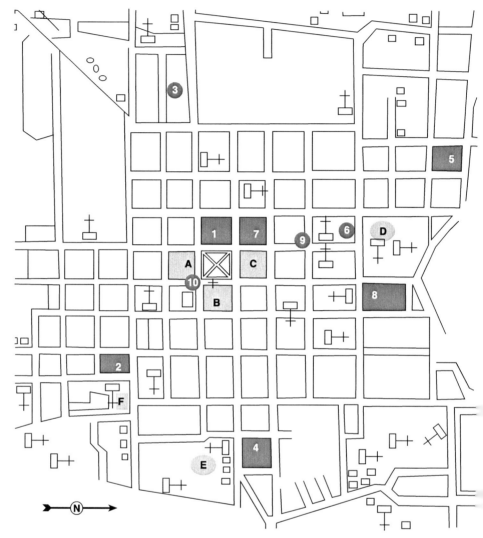

Map 3.1. Map of Santiago showing locations of vinaterías, 1768. Sources: AGCA, A1.2–7, Leg. 4008, Ex. 30547 & A3.4, Leg. 2375, Ex. 35076. Alvis Dunn created the map with graphic artist Jesse Davis.

Legend

A. Palace of the Captains-General
B. Cathedral
C. Cabildo
D. La Merced
E. Convent of La Concepción
F. Church of San Francisco

Vinaterías

1. *El Portal de los Panaderos* (on the main plaza)
2. In the vicinity of the Church and Monastery of San Francisco

3. In *Plazuela de San Pedro* (2 establishments)
4. In *Plazuela del convento de Monjas de Nuestra Senora de la Concepción*
5. In *Plaza de San Sebastian*
6. In front of the *Iglesia de Nuestra Senora de la Merced*
7. Beside the town council building also known as the *Ayuntamiento* (on the main plaza)
8. Near the *Iglesia de Nuestra Senora de la Merced* in the house where Tadeo Ramírez once lived
9. In front of the *Iglesia de Santa Catarina* (2 establishments)
10. In front of the *Casa de Moneda*

Vinatería Rules

◇◇

1. The aguardientes and wines of Spain and those of Peru can be sold only to Españoles, mestizos, negroes, and mulattos and not to Indians.
2. The vinatería must be within a four-block radius of the *plaza pública*, and the stock must be made available for inspection by *alcaldes* and other judges.
3. The establishment must not serve after the evening bells and must not reopen for anyone.
4. In no way can this license be transferred.
5. At the end of the six months of the license, the holder must return to the town council immediately and, if they so desire, request another for six months.

Source: Archivo General de Centro América, Sección A1.2–7, 1767, Leg. 4008, Exp. 30548.

vinaterías were "omnipresent" and, in addition to foreign and domestic alcohol, offered "glassware, containers, and such food items as sugar and dried fish."[67] They also seemed to have often operated as pawnshops. By comparison, Santiago vinaterías offered oils, vinegar, and fruits for sale.[68] The vinatería was oriented to serve an upper-crust clientele, at least ideally.

The Santiago Town Council worked to control the character of the vinatería from the initial establishment of the monopoly in 1755. In order to obtain and keep a license, five rules were outlined that addressed clientele, location, and hours. Strict licensing also prohibited subleasing, and operators were required to renew their contracts regularly. Although vinaterías were required to be within four blocks of the main plaza of Santiago, this encompassed a large area (see map 3.1). In regard to the vinaterías and taverns in Santiago, exact locations are difficult to pinpoint, and sadly, no pithy names have come down. Still, a 1768 vinatería inventory can help us envision the culture of drink in eighteenth-century Santiago.

If we step back from street-level in order to focus on colony-wide matters and the overall impact of the creation of the Alcohol Monopoly on the Captaincy-General of Guatemala, the successful struggle of the town council to wrest control of aguardiente production and sale, and thus to a degree consumption, appears to be one of the more visible indicators of adjustments being made across the empire. Miles Wortman depicts this time at midcentury as one during which the new Spanish commercial class moved to overpower the old oligarchy and expand Guatemalan commerce throughout Central America and into regular international markets. In turn, however, the Crown was also mounting its own offensive against that emerging merchant clique through the efforts of the *visitador* (colonial inspector) to New Spain, José de Gálvez. Seeing the town council in the 1750s as representing this new merchant class and not the old oligarchy, Wortman finds "three distinct, antagonistic factions . . . the state, the merchant, and the producer, with the church now a vestige of the past and under the control of the government. The tensions between these groups continued until the independence period, causing much of the friction that led to freedom from Spain and the later dissolution of Central America."[69] This merchant class had managed to best royal wishes and gain control of the Alcohol Monopoly via the Santiago Town Council, not only for Santiago but also for all of Central America. Wortman notes, "The opposition of the *cabildo* was strong enough—or the resolution of the crown weak enough—so that the liquor monopoly was established, but it was awarded to the cabildo."[70] While this free market in alcohol was not the ideal, it did make the town council essentially a strong voice for the new merchants, players in the system rather than mute actors and recipients of royal edicts.

Christophe Belaubre and Jordana Dym take Wortman's assertion a step further, arguing,

[F]or Central America, the most important consequence of the reform processes was not success or failure in achieving the monarchy's goals but success in providing opportunities for visible and subtle shifts in the relationship of government and society and for increased opportunities for those sidelined by Hapsburg institutions—the *castas* (persons of mixed race) and professional classes—who were able to maneuver within the interstices provided in Church finance and marriage reform, implantation of new monopolies and taxes, changing trade rules and regulations, dispersion of political power to *intendants* (Spanish governor) and municipal officials, and other innovations introduced in the name of greater control.[71]

That the town council had managed to secure the grant to administer the distillation and sale of aguardiente in the face of the Crown imposition of the Alcohol Monopoly indicates a successful effort on the part of colonials, in particular a new merchant class, to carve out space within the changing power relations of reform.

For her part, Dym asserts that the creation of the two-branch system of alcohol sales (and consumption) in Santiago, the monopoly taverns and the vinaterías, was a move by the town council calculated to weaken the liquor monopoly while strengthening its own political role by increasing "the council's sense of representing all socioeconomic groups rather than just the elite creole and the Spanish merchant class."[72] This appearance of standing for a freer access to alcohol, albeit a compartmentalized and class-based one, across the socioeconomic landscape of Santiago, when coupled with the town council's hold-the-line response to new taxes, especially the *alcabala* (sales tax), another looming reform measure, enhanced that body's standing as more broadly representative.[73]

The Dym and Belaubre volume deepens our understanding of the local response to reform, finding the bottom line important but not to the exclusion of desires to "redefine the relationship of institutions and subjects to the state," not only in "matters of finance" but also in "the administration of justice."[74] These relationships between people and the state were certainly flavored by the manner in which justice was defined and applied. A return to the baseline function and operation of the vinatería in Santiago proves illuminating. This tighter focus provides further insight into the town council's goals as it maneuvered to negotiate that relationship between people, the state, and justice. Justice was wound tightly into the fabric of the right to manufacture, sell, and consume alcohol and was so for segments of the colonial population divided quite starkly by race, class, and status.

Minding the Stores and Overseeing Inventories

The Alcohol Monopoly remained under the control of the town council of Santiago until 1766, when the Crown made it a wholly royal operation by nullifying the grant and sending in its own administrator to take over. Nevertheless, the first five-year period of town council management of the monopoly (1755–60) appears to have been relatively uneventful. The second five years, however, generated controversy and the accompanying documentation. From July 1761 to January 1762 the town council ran a weekly inventory of the sales of each vinatería in the city. This inventory consisted of four beverage categories: Peruvian aguardiente, Spanish aguardiente, Peruvian wine, and Spanish wine. The counts appear to have been prompted by strong suspicions that the operators of some of the vinaterías were selling locally made alcohol, either bootleg or the monopoly's locally distilled version.[75] Either action would have been illegal, as vinaterías were licensed to sell only the imported alcohol.

There were two ways in which this type of sale might be made: selling it outright and with full disclosure to the buyer, or using it secretly to stretch the more expensive imported product. Clearly, either method would result in a greater number of tax-free sales. Bottle counts were kept by the management of each vinatería, and when matched against inventory, sales were calculated. Using the illicit liquor to supplement would at least mean that a percentage, if not all, of the sale was not taxed.

This tactic would also make the general overhead for the outlet lower than for those not cheating, meaning that where making enough sales to keep one's doors open is a question, those abiding by the law were at a distinct disadvantage. Of course, lower prices on alcohol and other goods could also be offered for the same reasons in the defrauding taverns. More nuanced reasons for adulteration might prompt these practices. A customer could be given a cheaper price for a blend of Peruvian and Santiago aguardiente, for example. Perhaps the taste might even be preferable.

In order to more accurately scrutinize alcohol sales, the town council required the twelve vinaterías in Santiago to submit to inventory inspections for a period of thirty-seven weeks, from May 16, 1761, until January 30, 1762. Theoretically, such a review would catch irregularities in purchases and sales. The closer scrutiny given these establishments would also, ideally at least, result in state agents uncovering other violations of the local alcohol law.

In mid-eighteenth-century Central America, large quantities of alcohol, particularly wine and brandy, were measured most commonly in *frascos*. One colonial frasco contained roughly the amount of three modern 750 milliliter bottles of wine. The archives yielded weekly inventories for three periods encompassing four and one-half months, or 126 days. Period one runs from mid-May until mid-June 1761, while the second runs from July to mid-September that same year. A third inventory period encompasses the month of January 1762. These records cover twenty-one weeks of sales out of the thirty-seven monitored (57 percent of the period). For all vinaterías combined during the times reviewed, there were eight, nine, or ten vinaterías operating. During the entire period, sales of aguardiente from Peru averaged 8.5 frascos daily. Aguardiente from Spain, a pricier blend, was consumed at a rate of one-half frasco a day. Cheaper wine from Peru averaged six and one-half frascos, and finally, fine Spanish wine registered at four-fifths of a frasco per day. Over the twenty-one weeks where inventories are available, aguardiente de Peru outsold the same product from Spain by 1,065 frascos to 62. Likewise, Peruvian also bested Spanish wine, 814 frascos to 108. All of these numbers were steady rather than spiked. Sales were, of course, not uniform from public house to public house, and several locales far outsold others.[76]

In representative weeks, the most popular vinatería, run by the lone female operator, the widow Manuela Guerra, might sell fourteen frascos of Peruvian aguardiente but only one of the Spanish brand.[77] As for wine, fourteen frascos of Peruvian and two Spanish was a normal week's business for Guerra. The steadiness of sales across time in these vinaterías is remarkable. There is, for whatever reason, little to no fluctuation from week to week in most of the establishments. One can imagine a stable clientele, family and business networks, specialty retail offerings, even tailored hours as contributing to consistent business, for good or ill. One can also imagine all manner of book- and tavern-keeping tricks of the trade.

We know little about the license holders. Don Juan de Luque, operator of the vinatería that offered the most competition for Manuela Guerra, was also the royal armorer. Luque contracted a manager to run his vinatería, and this appears to have been the most common practice. For example, in February 1762 when there were thirteen vinaterías in operation, over half (seven) were clearly run by administrators rather than the license holders. In only three cases was it clear beyond a doubt that the owner was also the operator.[78]

The investigation into whether vinaterías were illegally pouring monopoly aguardiente proved fruitful. Of thirteen establishments (one holder, Don Francisco Benitez, operated two establishments by dint of one license), only four had no inventory irregularities. This finding coincided with the time for renewal of licenses. The town council decreed that by virtue of the evidence gathered, nine vinaterías should be fined. Working with Commissioner Manuel de Mello, Don Diego Solís, the *aforado*, or official examiner/taster of liquors, had corroborated the audit.

Matching the list of fiscal offenders, he found that all but five vinaterías mixed aguardiente with Peruvian liquor as well as other ingredients that added color.[79] Each of the offending operations was notified to shut down immediately. Luque and Guerra, who was most successful in sales, were among the *vinateros* (owners of vinaterías) whose operations were found to be in compliance with the laws. By adding cheaper spirits to stretch their product, the offending vinaterías sold more and cheaper liquor. They were not, however, according to the numbers, operating sustainable businesses. Inventory numbers actually indicated that the establishments found guilty were selling too little alcohol to make their overhead and expenses. Clearly, this was not the actual case. Profit had just been cleverly hidden. The monopoly taverns also noted that their sales had been adversely affected by this development as well.[80] All but four vinaterías were shut down on February 19, 1762. In the end it appears that fines were soon paid, licenses were reissued in most cases, and the long-time tavern keepers continued to ply their trade.[81]

As the Bourbon fiscal reforms were applied to the colony, the town council in Santiago expanded its role from an advocate solely for elite creole interests to represent other socioeconomic groups.[82] For the period 1755–65, roughly the two terms that the town council controlled the Alcohol Monopoly, as it tried to extend its reach across the alcohol market it also took on the role of arbiter and enforcer of alcohol legislation among competing sectors of the economy. Vinateros, monopoly tavern operators, and consumers across the social hierarchy all became to some degree constituents of the town council. There was a conflict of interest built into this scenario, as the town council was itself a producer and seller of alcohol. The bottom line dictated that the more alcohol sold legally, the better the fortunes of the town council (at least, the fuller the coffers). This arrangement created tension, especially if considerations of morality or public safety were brought to bear. No doubt a web of commercial and social relations bound together town council members and the public sellers, buyers, and consumers, complicating the situation.

The town council did manage to keep itself relevant to local Santiago politics. As long as it was actively engaged in the arbitration of the alcohol culture in Santiago, it was germane to the daily lives of the people of the city. Of course, quite clearly the town council had thrust itself into the middle of the local economy by serving simultaneously as a producer, seller, and government regulatory agent. Those concerned or invested in a safe, calm, and prosperous city also found cause with the actions of the town council. Indeed, the institution proved that it could still wield power regarding how and to what degree reform was implemented. The town council managed to stall the complete implementation of the monopoly in the beginning by maneuvering itself into the position of monopolist and then attempted to orchestrate into place a system that minimized the effects of that change. These machinations were successful for close to a decade. Set against a backdrop of perceived growing urban decadence, the interplay of competing actors in the local market drew too much attention from the Crown. The imperial reaction was to complete the takeover of the alcohol economy while at the same time working to bring greater control over the daily lives of the Crown subjects in the region.

After 1762 the number of vinaterías increased and violations of the law regarding the nature of sales and the character of the alcohol sold rose.[83] Of course, the Crown revoked the town council's control over the Alcohol Monopoly in 1766 and from then on operated it through royal agents. This maneuver by the monarchy was extremely unpopular and, combined with other reform measures, resulted in the primary representative in the captaincy-general, *subvisitador* Sebastian Calvo de la Puerta, fleeing the region.[84]

Conclusions: Maintaining the Flow

The Santiago Town Council worked to manage the business of alcohol manufacture and sale as well as the drinking culture of the city for over a decade. The right to manufacture, sell, and consume alcohol was judged fundamental by a good portion of the colonial population, and the town council represented that sentiment for most of the period. In the face of the increasing encroachment of the imperial state on the economic matters of the colony, this governing body, traditionally quite narrow in its responsiveness, broadened its outlook as never before to encompass the concerns of a wider range of the local population. As the years passed, the council-run monopoly struggled to maintain its hold on the market. Corruption grew, consumption increased, and eventually the Crown moved to take control.

As Bourbon Reforms played out in the isthmus, alcohol and economics were often center stage. Across society, no matter the individual's demographic profile, the convenience by which alcohol could be made, obtained, or traded was important. Communities of drinkers, elite and plebeian, accustomed to downing an espirituoso Spanish wine, a harsh aguardiente de la tierra, or even a sweet blended but illegal mistela might find common ground, as could merchants and town councils when a threat to availability arose. Here the patrons of the taverns and vinaterías of Guatemala met and overlapped with the town council in the juncture between politics, economics, and culture, and briefly and tentatively a unity of voices was heard.

Notes

1. Woodward, *Central America*, 41.
2. Markman, *Colonial Architecture of Antigua Guatemala*, 14–15; Webre, "Water and Society," 59–60.
3. Webre, "Water and Society," 59.
4. Woodward, *Central America*, 41. In *Colonial Architecture of Antigua Guatemala*, Markman has little good to say in description of Santiago's design. In contrast, Woodward envisions an eighteenth-century Santiago of sublime beauty.
5. Woodward, *Central America*, 41.
6. For a discussion of this issue and perceptions, see Viqueira Albán, *Propriety and Permissiveness*, esp. 129–63.
7. This is an intentional allusion to the famous assertion by historian Carl Becker regarding the sentiment guiding the war for independence among the British colonies to the north: "The first was the question of home rule; the second was the question . . . of who should rule at home." See Becker, "History of the Political Parties," 22.
8. Pardo, *Efemérides para escribir la historia*, 210. Also see García Peláez, *Memorias del antiguo reino*, 3:8.
9. Wortman, *Government and Society*, 21.
10. Ibid.
11. Viqueira Albán, *Propriety and Permissiveness,* esp. chap. 3.
12. MacLeod, *Spanish Central America*, chap. 14; Wortman, *Government and Society,* 20–24.
13. Pardo, *Efemérides para escribir la historia*, 210.
14. We cannot be certain whether or not this aguardiente was of the type today known as *pisco*, a viscous, distilled blend created from the residue, stems, hulls, and juice of winemaking. This distillate often has an anise or licorice-like flavor. Interestingly, *anis* is several times mentioned in the documentation discovered in the Archivo General de Centro América (hereafter AGCA). The following article suggests that the blend reaching Guatemala may very well have been pisco: Huertos Vallejos, "Historia de la producción de vinos y piscos en el Perú."
15. MacLeod, *Spanish Central America,* 266.
16. Pardo, *Efemérides para escribir la historia,* 140.

17. MacLeod, *Spanish Central America*, 268; also see Pardo, *Efemérides para escribir la historia*, 140.

18. MacLeod, *Spanish Central America*, 268.

19. Wortman, *Government and Society*, 21–22.

20. Again, see Pardo, *Efemérides para escribir la historia*. Between 1713 and 1773, the discussion of trade with Peru appears no less than on ten occasions. This tally does not take into account the times the issue was but ancillary.

21. AGCA, Sección A1.2–7, Leg. 4008, Exp. 30531.

22. Gutiérrez did figure prominently in the alcohol trade in the city. He had been sold a license to open a vinatería in 1760; see AGCA, Sección A1.14.10, Leg. 4067, Exp. 31962. The following year he was listed as an owner and operator of a vinatería; see AGCA, Sección A1.2, Leg. 2375, Exp. 35076.

23. AGCA, Sección A1.2–7, Leg. 4008, Exp. 30531.

24. AGCA, Sección A1.2–15, Leg. 5917, Exp. 51036.

25. See, for example, AGCA, Sección A1.3, Leg. 2375, Exp. 35083.

26. The term *public houses* is borrowed from the English and yields the more familiar term in modern parlance, *pub*, i.e., a retail drinking establishment. To avoid confusion, this term is employed throughout the chapter to mean all legal establishments selling alcohol. After 1755, the terms *vinatería* and *tavern* came to have very specific meanings in Santiago. Not until the creation of the Royal Alcohol Monopoly and the subsequent town council management of it in 1755 did public houses come to be officially designated as either vinaterías or monopoly taverns.

27. Pardo, *Efemérides para escribir la historia*, 173.

28. Ibid., 185; García Peláez, *Memorias del antiguo reino*, 2:608. García Peláez notes that this was a time of "*escasez de caldos puros*" (scarcity of pure alcoholic beverages), during which the taverns had branched out into the barrios, attracting large crowds of people, often many of them indigenous.

29. Pardo, *Efemérides para escribir la historia*, 196.

30. Ibid.; García Peláez, *Memorias del antiguo reino*, 2:609. The suggestion here is that the town council saw the presence of beer and chicha as well as bootleg and legal aguardiente for sale in Santiago as contributory to this state.

31. García Peláez, *Memorias del antiguo reino*, 2:609, "*todo género de caldos hechizos y adulterados*."

32. Mistela is a grape-based and aromatic alcoholic beverage with a slightly higher potency and sweeter taste than wine. Domine, *Ultimate Guide to Spirits*, 799.

33. García Peláez, *Memorias del antiguo reino*, 2:608; also see Pardo, *Efemérides para escribir la historia*, 162.

34. Pardo, *Efemérides para escribir la historia*, 166.

35. Ibid. According to Pardo, this solicitation was opposed by the town council's attorney. García Peláez also mentions this in *Memorias del antiguo reino* (2:608). For a colonial Latin American recipe for beer, see Wilson, "Pineda's Report," 82.

36. Pardo, *Efemérides para escribir la historia*, 171. Beer was evidently eventually brewed in Santiago, as the town council complained about its presence in 1749. See García Peláez, *Memorias del antiguo reino*, 2:609.

37. *Mistela por alambique* is listed in Wilson, "Pineda's Report" (84), where it is identified as being derived from the mescal plant. This is not likely for a beverage mentioned in Guatemala, where the plant does not grow. Here the concoction was probably a highly refined/distilled mistela (see note 32, above) and thus of a higher alcohol content, approaching that of brandy. The term *alambique* means a still or alembic.

38. Pardo, *Efemérides para escribir la historia*, 173.

39. Wilson, "Pineda's Report" (81) contains an entry for *aguardiente de uba silvestre*, or distilled liquor made from wild grapes.

40. Pardo, *Efemérides para escribir la historia*, 177. Also see García Peláez, *Memorias del antiguo reino*, 2:608. When rosolios contained alcohol, they were identified as liqueurs. *Resoli* is defined as a "liquor composed of water, rice, toasted garbanzos, barley, ground cinnamon, and the meat of the citron. This mixture is put into infusion for fifteen days and is afterwards distilled in the *alambique* [still]." Wilson, "Pineda's Report," 86.

41. Pardo, *Efemérides para escribir la historia*, 178. Interestingly there is very little mention in the records at this time of the more strictly indigenous beverages. Nevertheless, such brews were part of the culture of drink of the time. While chicha has more in common with beer than a distilled beverage such as aguardiente, in most cases the Maya consumed *chicha* and *aguardiente* interchangeably, employing the one most available in either ceremonies or recreational drinking. Other terms used are *guaro*, usually distilled rather than fermented; *balché*, fermented; *pulque*, fermented; *chinguirito*, distilled; and *kuxa*, fermented. In the case of some of the older documents, the term *vino*, for wine, is used to describe a range of alcoholic drinks.

42. Ibid., 198.

43. Ibid., 200.

44. García Peláez, *Memorias del antiguo reino*, 2:609.

45. Ibid.

46. Pardo, *Efemérides para escribir la historia*, 205. Whether questions of purity were concerned is unknown, but regarding potency, most certainly wine is a drink significantly weaker in alcoholic content than is liquor.

47. Ibid., 206. Located off the Caribbean coast, Roatán was a prison colony.

48. García Peláez, *Memorias del antiguo reino*, 2:608–11.

49. Meneray, "Kingdom of Guatemala," 261–62. Evidently the audiencia was dissatisfied with the state of town council record keeping regarding the monopoly. The two governing bodies apparently were never able to reach accord on this matter.

50. AGCA, Sección A1.2, Leg. 5917, Exp. 51038.

51. See Viqueira Albán, *Propriety and Permissiveness*.

52. García Peláez, *Memorias del antiguo reino*, 2:8; Pardo, *Efemérides para escribir la historia*, 210.

53. García Peláez, *Memorias del antiguo reino*, 2:8.

54. Pardo, *Efemérides para escribir la historia*, 211.

55. García Peláez, *Memorias del antiguo reino*, 2:8.

56. Dunn, *Guatimala*, 304.

57. Stephens, *Incidents of Travel*, 1:145.

58. Viqueira Albán, *Propriety and Permissiveness*.

59. See Conroy, *In Public Houses*; Thompson, *Rum Punch and Revolution*; Salinger, *Taverns and Drinking*; Thorpe, "Taverns and Tavern Culture."

60. Lutz, *Santiago de Guatemala*.

61. Ibid., 152.

62. Ibid., 153, 306n64.

63. Bumgartner, *José del Valle*, 44.

64. Del Valle did pay careful attention to the role of alcohol in the world around him, as Bumgartner reveals in excerpts from the Central American Founder's diary of a journey to Mexico in which he notes the number of *estanquillas de chicha* (small shops selling chicha) in the towns through which he passed. Bumgartner, "José del Valle's Unfinished 'Diario.'"

65. Scardaville, "Alcohol Abuse and Tavern Reform," 656–57.

66. Kicza, *Colonial Entrepreneurs*, 118.

67. Ibid., 120.

68. Pardo, *Efemérides para escribir la historia*, 211. Also see AGCA, Sección A1.2, Leg. 2375, Exp. 35076, "*otros efectos que en las tiendas expenden que no son licores sino comestibles*."

69. Wortman, *Government and Society*, 145.

70. Ibid., 140.

71. Belaubre and Dym, "Introduction," 7.

72. Dym, "Bourbon Reforms," 85.

73. Ibid.

74. Webre, "Conclusion," 268.

75. AGCA, Sección A1.2, Leg. 5917, Exp. 51037.

76. AGCA, Sección A3.4, Leg. 2375, Exp. 35076.

77. Ibid.

78. Ibid.

79. AGCA, Sección A1.2, Leg. 5917, Exp. 51038. Presumably these five matched with the four found not to have been cheating on their inventories.

80. AGCA, Sección A1.2, Leg. 5917, Exp. 51037. There is mention in this document of "*cargadores, cosecheros*" (long-distance merchants, wine growers) who were granted temporary licenses, perhaps at this time three of them. They are also pointed to as having been little invested in obeying local regulations regarding proper sales procedures. See AGCA, Sección A1.2, Leg. 5917, Exp. 51036.

81. Six years later, six of the eighteen taverns licensed in Santiago were listed with owners among the thirteen operating in 1762.

82. Dym, "Bourbon Reforms," 85.

83. AGCA, Sección A1.2-7, Leg. 4008, Exp. 30547. This 1768 document numbers the vinaterías at twenty-one.

84. Wortman, *Government and Society*, 144.

4

⬦⬦⬦⬦⬦⬦⬦⬦⬦⬦⬦⬦⬦⬦

Alcohol and Lowdown Culture in Caribbean Guatemala and Honduras, 1898–1922

FREDERICK DOUGLASS OPIE

In 1922, Eugene Cunningham and his companion, both white travelers from the United States, entered a combination bar and grocery store in Zacapa on the Caribbean coast of Guatemala. The store was operated by a white American expatriate. An African American customer, also an expatriate, invited the travelers to have a drink with him. When they ignored this request, the man ordered the two white men to join him, after which a violent altercation ensued. In the course of his travels, Cunningham also heard of a white bar operator who warned a racist Irish American expatriate that if he continued to call blacks "nigger," "his end would come suddenly from a knife between the ribs."[1]

What do anecdotes like these—anecdotes in which white men of European ancestry are threatened by black Americans in Guatemala—tell us about the relationship between alcohol and culture, class, and race on the Caribbean coast of Guatemala in the late nineteenth and early twentieth centuries? Black immigrants went to Guatemala in the hope of finding better economic opportunities than were available to them in their home region. The labor market in lowland Guatemala was good because Guatemalan nationals refused jobs in malaria-infested regions where railroad track was laid. Black immigrants were willing to go there and work long hours for higher wages. Eventually, some workers seized opportunities to become small-scale entrepreneurs. Because of the labor scarcity in the railroad industry and their status as U.S. citizens abroad, they were able to exercise some latitude in confronting would-be exploiters in Guatemala.

At the turn of the century, black laborers in Guatemala had a greater degree of freedom and rights as U.S. citizens than did blacks in the Jim Crow U.S. South, because the U.S. State Department was determined to protect U.S. nationals and capital in Central America. When they could, workers sought the aid of U.S. diplomats in struggles with contractors and racist and repressive Guatemalan officials. But dealing with racist U.S. diplomats was difficult, and the majority of workers maintained a shaky existence, hoping one day to return home, to purchase a profitable piece of property, or to start a successful business. The most successful immigrants married Guatemalan women and acculturated into Guatemalan society. Their stories, so often ignored by scholars, suggest both the opportunities that the oppressed black laborers of the U.S. South found outside the country and the degree to which their struggle for just treatment had a foreign and diplomatic dimension.[2]

By 1922, large numbers of black immigrants from the United States and the West Indies had settled in places like Zacapa and Izabal, which also hosted a population of native Garifunas, known at the time as "black Caribs" in Livingston (see figures 4.1 and 4.2). The settlement's leisure culture included integrated bars with live music and gambling houses. According to the Nicaraguan revolutionary Augusto César Sandino, who worked on banana plantations in Honduras, the same could be said for that country's Caribbean coast. On paydays, it was common to see laborers in banana and railroad towns on the coasts of both countries drunk on aguardiente, their pockets filled with U.S. greenbacks. Considering such evidence through the lens of cultural history, I argue that enjoying liquor, food, gambling, sexual contact, and jazz music in juke joints and rum shops represented a continuation of the salient cultural traditions of the black immigrants who came from the U.S. South and the Caribbean and resided on the Caribbean coast of Guatemala and Honduras.

* * *

This chapter focuses on the Guatemalan departments of Izabal and Zacapa, where two Caribbean coast African diaspora communities developed, as well as on the bordering coastal region of Honduras, which had a similar demographic makeup.[3] In contrast to the other contributions in this volume, this chapter focuses on foreigners not nationals, the lowland instead of the highland region, and black subjects instead of indigenous people. Like Alvis Dunn's contribution, this chapter focuses on the places where

Figure 4.1. Black stevedores loading bananas on a railroad car in Costa Rica, circa 1920. From the 1870s until the start of the Great Depression, black roustabouts frequently migrated, seeking jobs in the railroad and banana industries, high wages, and liquor-laden leisure throughout the modern Atlantic world. The United Fruit Company of Boston had operations like this one in Costa Rica and port cities including Mobile, Alabama, New Orleans and others throughout the Caribbean. Scanned image courtesy of the Latin American Library, Tulane University, New Orleans.

alcohol was consumed. Whereas Dunn looks at mid-eighteenth-century taverns and vinaterías, I examine three foreign institutions introduced to Guatemala during the national period: juke joints (sometimes spelled "jukejoint"), honky-tonks, and rum shops. For largely working-class im-migrant groups, these institutions served as ethnic clubs, social outlets, and getaways and havens from employers and state officials. These places functioned as what I call entertainment maroons that provided escape from the harsh realities of work in the railroad and later banana industries on the Caribbean coast.

Enslaved Africans from the Wolof (Senegal and Gambia) and Bam-bara (Mali) empires introduced the term *juke* (sometimes spelled "jook") meaning wicked or disorderly to the colonial South: in Wolof the word is *dzug*, and in Bambara it is *dzugu*. Over time, African Americans used the term to describe wicked places or moves. As southern blacks linked juke with shacks, houses, barns, makeshift nightclubs, and dancing, it became

Figure 4.2. Black stevedores unloading bananas from a railroad car in Mobile, Alabama, 1937. Image is reproduced courtesy of the Prints and Photograph Division, Library of Congress, Washington, D.C.

closely associated with more formal structures serving liquor, food, and producing live or recorded dance music (see figure 4.3). Recorded music they said came from a juke, or jook, box.[4] Southern African Americans also coined the term *honky-tonk*, which literally meant a segregated white shack (or juke joint) where rural whites likewise drank liquor but listened to country music instead of African American jazz.[5]

In contrast to juke joints and honky-tonks, rum shops had their antecedents in the Caribbean rather than the U.S. South. There are other differences as well between these three alcohol-driven institutions. Based on anthropological fieldwork on the Colombian island of Providencia, in the Caribbean Sea, anthropologist Peter J. Wilson describes rum shops as "no more than a room in a private house, or perhaps a special addition to the house. In a few instances it is a separate small hut."[6] He goes on to say that they are "crudely furnished with a few rough-hewn wooden tables and chairs or benches, a dirt floor if it is a separate hut."[7] As simple structures,

Figure 4.3. Juke joint in Melrose, Natchitoches Parish, Louisiana, 1940. Image is reproduced courtesy of the Prints and Photograph Division, Library of Congress, Washington, D.C.

rum shops required less startup capital to build or rent than juke joints or honky-tonks. A second difference is the rum shops' function and the gender of its customers. Historically, rum shops, like Guatemala's taverns and vinaterías and Argentina's pulperías, served as places for male socializing and refuge from women.[8] Wilson insists that rum shops were spaces where "men gather and women enter only in cases of emergency and at the risk of embarrassment to themselves."[9] Similarly, historian Frederick H. Smith maintains that rum shops served as male sanctuaries where men resolved the problems they encountered at home with women and on the job. They also functioned as social welfare centers where unemployed men went to obtain loans and free food.[10]

What is most useful is understanding how spaces like juke joints, honky-tonks, and rum shops have historically constructed themselves to cater to specific occupations, classes, ethnicities, and nationalities.[11] On the Caribbean coast, foreign nationals developed a common working-class identity rooted in a shared language, migrant experience, occupations, company housing, and conflicts with Guatemalan officials prejudiced against immigrants, especially blacks, and set on exploiting them. Like the multiethnic maroon communities of the colonial period, juke joints and rum shops in Caribbean Guatemala and Honduras served as multiethnic, egalitarian, working-class spaces of refuge for black immigrants and the few working-class white immigrants and Guatemalan nationals who lived among them, as the opening bar scene in this chapter suggests.[12] As this historian and, most recently, historians Lara Putnam and Ronald Harpelle have documented, race- and class-based Jim Crow hierarchies existed on the Caribbean coast of Central America. Putnam and Harpelle aptly call them "White Zones."[13] White zones included the U.S.-controlled Panama Canal Zone and the United Fruit Company (UFCO) and International Railroad of Central America (IRCA) compounds. However, the black majority immigrant population in the same region created maroon-like societies in which blacks showed little to no deference to whites or Guatemalan nationals, particularly those of a similar or lesser socioeconomic status. They drank, ate, gambled, and caroused with them as equals in juke joints, rum shops, and honky-tonks. As the black working-class immigrants and their culture dominated the Caribbean coast, they radically changed the racial politics of white-owned honky-tonks. In Caribbean Guatemala, honky-tonks outside of white zones became black spaces or, at the least, Jim Crow–free spaces.

In addition to being about the spaces where Caribbean residents consumed alcohol, this chapter, like that by David Carey Jr., is about the lucrative entrepreneurial aspects of alcohol. I argue that for black laborers in first the railroad and later the banana industry, engaging in the alcohol trade served as one of the quickest routes to capital accumulation and thus to upward mobility. An itinerant laborer's decision to start up a juke joint also signaled his decision to settle on the Caribbean coast and, more than likely, marry a local woman. In the same way René Reeves's and Carey's chapters highlight the role of women in the alcohol economy, this chapter shows that the majority of black proprietors of bars in Caribbean Guatemala had Guatemalan girlfriends and wives as business partners.

This chapter is also about the role of alcohol (and gambling) as a temporary means of escape from the challenges of daily life on the Caribbean coast. As mentioned, this part of the immigrant experience in Caribbean Guatemala had antecedents in the U.S. South and the Caribbean. As Smith found in his social and economic history of rum, "alcohol use was widespread in the Caribbean and the enormous amounts of alcohol available contributed to a climate of excessive drinking."[14] Similar findings exist to describe the consumption of moonshine in the rural U.S. South.[15] I argue that hard drinking and gambling had been an integral part of the cultural identity of the Caribbean coast workforce before they arrived in Guatemala. Although the Caribbean coast became the site of a largely male African diaspora, cultural identities cut across race, class, and gender with migrant workers from North America, Latin America, and the West Indies participating in similar activities in similar leisure spaces.

A sampling of U.S. and Guatemalan government correspondence and travel accounts support my conclusions. Although out-migration to Guatemala is often interpreted from the perspective of middle- and upper-class whites, this chapter draws on these sources to illuminate the leisure culture of migrant laborers on the Caribbean coast of Guatemala and Honduras, considering what we might call the alcoholic drinkways of Caribbean coast workers.

Lowdown Culture in Guatemala and Beyond

Agents representing the railroad and banana industries promised workers lucrative wages and better opportunities if they migrated to Guatemala. Persuaded by the sales pitches of recruiters, workers traveled to the Caribbean coast of Guatemala from important port cities, such as New Orleans, Mobile, and Kingston.[16] Between 1899 and 1900, one railroad contractor brought in from seventy to eighty workers on a weekly boat from New Orleans. Although it is unclear how many returned to New Orleans, the evidence suggests that at least seventy-eight hundred consigned laborers arrived at railroad camps throughout Guatemala, other parts of Central America, and Mexico. One work camp in Guatemala had a hundred or more men, some with their wives; an observer described the camp as a small village.[17] In 1902, Frank Dennis wrote, "[T]he most irksome part of my duties as Consular Agent is defending and protecting the Afro American; numbers of whom were brought from the U.S. to work on the Rail Road and are now stranded here."[18]

In the Guatemalan context, most of the migrants worked for U.S. railroad contractor Minor Keith's UFCO or his IRCA. Established in 1899 by Keith, UFCO began its banana plantation operations in Guatemala in 1901. By 1904, Keith had gained control of various railroad lines in Guatemala, and he operated UFCO and the railroads virtually as a single entity. That same year, he consolidated many of the railroads around Guatemala to form the IRCA.[19] In 1909, consular agent Edward Reed informed representatives of the Galveston, Texas, chamber of commerce that UFCO had some "1200 laborers at work on her banana fields in this Republic."[20] Within a year, Reed said, UFCO would need to import additional workers "to handle the output of bananas from her plantations in Guatemala alone."[21] He stated that Puerto Barrios had "a population of about 500, who save for a few Guatemalan officials and foreigners, are mostly colored laborers who are employed by the Guatemala R. R. in handling the freight of the in-coming and outgoing steamers."[22] Greater openings and opportunities for advancement in Guatemala came to those workers with an education, knowledge of Spanish and English, and a well-connected benefactor. Foreign workers had to cope with the problem of communicating with non-English speakers, who constituted the majority of local officials in Guatemala. In a report to the Guatemalan minister of development, a Northern Railroad official claimed that as late as 1895, one could "calculate that 75% of the [North American] employees cannot speak Spanish."[23] By 1912, UFCO labor agents had imported "large numbers of new laborers for the greatly increased banana plantations near Quiriguá and Virginia."[24] Many black laborers also lived and worked for the railroad and banana industries in Cayuga, Dartmouth, Puerto Barrios, Livingston, and Zacapa. The new immigrants transformed the bordering departments of Izabal and Zacapa into a provincial African diaspora occupied by blacks of various nationalities.

When UFCO established plantations in Guatemala, it enforced a strict Jim Crow social hierarchy in which the company refused to treat blacks as equal to whites.[25] But aguardiente became part of an integrated, itinerant, wild working-class milieu in which elements of the culture of the U.S. South and the English-speaking Caribbean mixed with those of Latin America on the Caribbean coast of Guatemala. Historian Pete Daniel describes this kind of pleasure-seeking culture practiced by relatively autonomous single men and women—roustabouts, as it were—as "lowdown culture."[26] These men and women entered and left the Caribbean coast in search of high wages and plenty of time for lowdown culture, which became synonymous with drinking, gambling, and sexual activity.

The working-class culture on the Caribbean coast is reminiscent of other black and migrant labor cultures of the nineteenth and twentieth centuries. A case in point is Langston Hughes's description of junk joints in his novel *Not Without Laughter*, set in the small town of Stanton, Kansas, between 1912 and 1918. Speaking about the black section of town, he writes, "At night in the Bottoms victrolas moaned and banjos cried ecstatically in the darkness . . . and dice rattled with the staccato gaiety of jazz music on long tables in rear rooms. Pimps played pool; bootleggers lounged in big red cars . . . young blacks fought like cocks and enjoyed it."[27] He goes on to say, "White boys walked through the streets winking at colored girls; men came in autos; old women ate pigs' feet and watermelon and drank beer; whisky flowed; gin was like water; soft indolent laughter didn't care about anything; and deep nigger-throated voices that had long ago stopped rebelling against the ways of this world rose in song."[28]

Similar is ethnographer Zora Neale Hurston's description of lowdown culture among black southern, West Indian, and Native American field hands in the Florida Everglades. As on the Caribbean coast of Guatemala and Honduras, on paydays workers in the Everglades drank, gambled, and listened to music in black districts. "Saturday afternoon when the work tickets were turned into cash," writes Hurston, "everybody buy coon-dick and get drunk."[29] She adds, "By dusk dark Belle Glade was full of loud-talking, staggering men. Plenty of women had gotten their knots charged too. The police chief in his speedy Ford was rushing from jook to jook and eating house trying to keep order, but making few arrests. Not enough jail space for all the drunks so why bother with a few? All he could do to keep down fights and get the white men out of colored town by nine o'clock."[30] Black entrepreneurs accustomed to white customers owned these jooks (juke joints) and eating houses in the segregated South.

Interpreting the dual role of these spaces in the rural South, anthropologist Anne Yentsch insists that in the Mississippi Delta, juke joints also served as places where laborers ate their daily meals: "The grilled chicken, spare ribs, spicy pork, and whole range of smoky barbecued meat cooked so well in these places . . . are a continuum of the cooking that males did, beginning with those on plantations."[31] She adds, "In an odd reversal of southern apartheid, throughout the first half of the twentieth century white men sneaked in [juke joints] quietly and cautiously to pick up food and liquor in plain paper bags."[32]

The Caribbean coast, similarly, had "color towns," described as "jazz-crashing" black districts where blacks and whites went to drink, eat, dance, and gamble.[33] One found both black and white entrepreneurs operating bars, restaurants, and gambling houses in these black working-class districts.

Yentsch found that people who migrated out of the South "wanted familiar homegrown" institutions and cuisine once they arrived in their new destinations. Entrepreneurs capitalized on this by opening informal businesses catering to the alcohol and food demand needs of newcomers.[34] Similarly, in Caribbean Guatemala, some black entrepreneurs began as illegal moonshine operators and then mushroomed into formal legitimate juke joints with music and food. Others started with the purchase of a liquor license and blossomed from there. Either way, these legal and illegal businesses could most often be found in close proximity to railroad labor camps, train stations, banana plantations, and immigrant neighborhoods, where they formed an important part of workers' culture of leisure.[35] Steamboat and railroad camp cooks brought these foods with them wherever they traveled. "Juke joints had urban alter egos," argues Yentsch, "and whether sited on an alley or by a cotton field their down-home food was but one focus. Music [and alcohol were] another. The cooks had southern roots, and the food was simple yet complexly layered."[36]

Contraband and Legal Liquor Sales

Sources dating to 1897 indicate that "individuals of bad law," as one railroad contractor described them, participated in the trade in contraband liquor. Contraband aguardiente—untaxed liquor sold by unlicensed individuals—represented a profitable commodity, with many eager customers among UFCO laborers.[37] Bootleggers selling contraband aguardiente converged on railroad work camps and in the UFCO-controlled Quiriguá region on the Caribbean coast. As Stacey Schwartzkopf and Carey demonstrate in this volume, illegal sellers and workers alike supported the sale of contraband alcohol because the sale of tax-free liquor provided prosperity to entrepreneurs while giving consumers a cheap source of alcohol.[38]

Railroad, UFCO, and Guatemalan officials, in contrast, vehemently opposed the illegal sale of liquor. Contraband aguardiente commerce effectively robbed the Guatemalan treasury of revenue gained from the sale of spirits to retailers and ordinary consumers alike. The turn-of-the-century Guatemalan state, under the Liberal dictatorship of Manuel Estrada Cabrera (1898–1920), spent the lion's share of state revenues on constructing the Northern Railroad and a deep-sea Caribbean port at Puerto Barrios in the department of Izabal. Estrada Cabrera also spent a large percentage of state revenues on a repressive military apparatus that included his appointed departmental jefes políticos, commandants with garrisons full of soldiers, and local police who carried out his orders. As Carey shows, alcohol taxes represented the regime's greatest source of revenue to pay for these initiatives in modernization and political repression.[39]

The Guatemalan state both taxed the sale of alcohol and issued gambling licenses. In Zacapa, for example, officials charged $82.50 per month for the right to sell alcohol until 9:00 p.m. and an additional $10.00 per month to sell liquor until 11:00 p.m. A gambling license cost $700 a month; the hours that having a license enabled an establishment to be open are not clear from the available records. Jefes políticos strictly enforced the proper use of the licenses. In 1897, Judge Mario E. Orellana of Zacapa "ordered the detention of various individuals found playing Rolet in a liquor establishment" at one o'clock in the morning. The jefe político of Zacapa violently and permanently shut down Simon Shine's barroom/gambling house after finding it open after 9:00 p.m., because he suspected Shine did not have authorization to keep the bar open until 11:00.[40] Similarly, in 1913, the jefe político in Izabal arrested African American Wilfred Brown, the co-owner of a Puerto Barrios cantina, for "selling liquor after 9:00 p.m. without a license."[41] According to Simon Shine, the possession of a liquor license guaranteed one a "profitable business," but this was predicated upon state officials policing unlicensed liquor sales in bars and cantinas. As Reeves presents in an earlier chapter, the state had to prevent the illegal sale of liquor if officials hoped to encourage the purchase of liquor licenses and thus the sale of legal alcohol in bars and liquor stores that would ensure the continued flow of revenue to government coffers. So, for instance, in Puerto Barrios, police arrested several men for selling aguardiente illegally. In a letter to W. F. Sands of the American legation in Guatemala, UFCO manager Victor Cutter delighted that local authorities in Izabal had "vigorously . . . suppress[ed] . . . illegal liquor sales and as a result" helped put down a banana plantation strike in 1910. Both UFCO and IRCA officials insisted that heavy drinking emboldened some usually more docile laborers to become militant strike organizers.[42]

The railroad and banana industries had their own reasons for opposing the sale of illegal liquor. Since the 1880s, railroad construction companies had operated company commissaries in railroad camps and railroad towns.[43] In 1901, UFCO built a huge commissary in Puerto Barrios, the largest in the republic. The gigantic commissary had smaller branches in UFCO plantation towns throughout the Quiriguá region, all of which sold alcohol at monopoly prices.[44] Though the precise markup at which the commissaries sold alcohol is unknown, we do know that the UFCO commissary in Puerto Barrios sold tobacco for twenty cents that would have cost five cents in the United States.[45] Railroad and UFCO officials, like planters and merchants throughout other parts of the Americas, operated debt peonage systems, giving advances on commissary goods like alcohol as a way to encourage their employees to contract debt and thereby to control them.[46] As on the Caribbean coast of Costa Rica, in Guatemala, high commissary prices for spirits legally purchased with company scrip (a payday proof of company wages), quetzales (Guatemalan currency), U.S. dollars, or credit made the purchase of cheaper contraband aguardiente very attractive to workers.[47]

One railroad construction manager complained that the sale of contraband liquor resulted in workers getting drunk, not fulfilling their labor contracts, and thus delaying the completion of railroad construction.[48] Company officials in both the railroad and the banana industries wanted control over their workers' access to alcohol because they wished to ensure the availability of a sober, docile, and productive workforce. So they controlled when company commissaries sold alcohol and pressured local officials to stamp out the sale of contraband aguardiente in and around company property. This was a legitimate concern: there is evidence to indicate that violence regularly accompanied the abuse of alcohol in UFCO's Quiriguá region, for example. "Every Sunday, every fiesta, every payday is marked by the machete in red," wrote traveler Morley Roberts.[49]

Two cases, one in Guatemala and the other in Honduras, lend support to the theory that UFCO and IRCA officials attempted to repress alcohol abuse to ensure worker dependability on the job. On about October 3, 1901, Richard Barthel, manager of the Central American Improvement Company, wrote a letter to F. C. García, the Guatemalan minister of development, complaining about the negative effects that drinking had on his railroad workforce. Liquor stores located in close proximity to various work camps threatened "the conservation of good order in the camps and the progress of the work," said Barthel.[50] The problem of worker abuse of alcohol escalated to the point that company officials fired five skilled workers with North American surnames—a mechanic/machinist, master mechanic/machinist, an agent/conductor, and two conductors—for coming to work drunk and therefore not properly performing their duties. As a result of the dismissals, the fired workers organized a strike on about October 26, 1901. "Everything revolves itself around the fact that certain employees under the influence of alcohol . . . have been discharged, and these, not only did not want to work, but they are instigating the others to declare a strike, to disobey the orders of the superiors, to refuse to work, [and] to leave their jobs," Barthel told García.[51] "These men excited by the effect of the liquor . . . declared that the rest of the employees will help them in their goal of avoiding the movement of the trains," he warned.[52]

Similarly, we know that abuse of alcohol caused at least one train wreck, thanks to a detailed account of a 1904 train crash in Honduras involving several North American engineers who reported to work intoxicated. In the fall of 1904, officials in San Pedro, Honduras, arrested, tried, and convicted African American brakeman Abe Jones on charges of causing a train wreck due to intoxication. Eyewitnesses claimed that Jones gave the wrong start signal, which led to the train crash. An American consulate investigation into the case provides interesting details about the drinking habits of some train engineers. According to Albert W. Brickwood Jr., who wrote the report, "The crew of both trains [involved in the wreck] had been drinking, and . . . the engineer, Hicks Robinson, was undoubtedly drunk."[53] The report continued, "Jones' general reputation with reference to the use of liquor is not bad; in fact, it does not appear that he drank to excess at any time. . . . In placing the blame for the collision upon Jones, the general belief is that the other members of the train crews were simply seeking to exonerate themselves, and that their testimony given against Jones was collusive, and there appears to be justification for this view."[54] As in the U.S. railroad industry, the white North Americans who ran IRCA favored white U.S. employees in hiring and promotion to higher-paying positions like locomotive engineer and conductor, relegating jobs like brakeman and fireman to black workers. Thus, it is certainly plausible that Jones faced a racist conspiracy to frame him as just another drunken Negro. The plot against Jones almost worked because of the common stereotype that U.S. and Central American elites held that black immigrants were "frequently drunk and disorderly," while white workers were sober and respectable.[55]

While employers used company security forces and pressured state officials to curb the drinking habits of rank-and-file workers, this goal contradicted that of the Guatemalan state, which granted liquor licenses to anyone who could pay the fee, encouraging liquor sales as a source of state revenue. Sources show that entrepreneurs of all stripes went into business selling legally purchased and taxed alcohol. The first bars can best be described as makeshift rum shops or crude juke joints constructed in the vicinity of work camps during the construction phase of the Central American railroad system. After construction crews completed IRCA in 1901, very often IRCA workers branched off to open more formal juke joints and honky-tonks at important hubs on the railroad, such as the provincial capitals of the departments of Zacapa and Izabal.[56] "Jukes are never built from scratch. . . . Instead, proprietors and patrons reappropriate almost any available building and transform the space to a jukejoint with complex yet subtle gestures," argues historian Jennifer Nardone in her research on juke joints in the Mississippi Delta.[57]

She found that juke joints in the Delta never generated a significant amount of income for the proprietors she studied. Most operated their juke joints part time—Thursday through Sunday evenings—while they had a full-time job. In the Delta, juke joints served as "gathering spaces for particular communities" and spaces for "listening to blues and having a certain amount of freedom to drink, dance, smoke, and celebrate without real threat of being stifled or stopped."[58] Juke joints played a similar social role in Guatemala, but this role differed economically in part because of the strict enforcement of the state liquor monopoly. In addition, black immigrants found greater economic opportunity in Caribbean Guatemala than in their home regions. As we see in the next section, Guatemalan juke joints with state liquor licenses and multiple businesses made lucrative profits. Most proprietors operated them full time after years of saving enough capital to do so as employees working in the railroad or banana industries.

Bar Ownership in Zacapa and Puerto Barrios

For the shrewd, aggressive, and hard-working black immigrant with a Spanish-speaking wife, Guatemala had its benefits. Despite its corruption and dictators, it was a much easier place for a black immigrant to become a business owner than the Jim Crow South or the British colonial West Indies. Juke joints housed in elaborate structures represented both a source and an indicator of social mobility for immigrants. Most are best described as a combination of bar, restaurant, gambling house, bank, and barbershop. In other words, bar owners focused on generating multiple sales on payday, when workers with pockets bulging with money wanted to indulge in maximum amounts of pleasure—which meant some form of drinking, gambling, music, and eating.

According to one source, in Zacapa, there were various juke joints a "stone's throw" from the railroad station in a bustling black neighborhood.[59] Traveler Arthur Ruhl referred to the Guatemalan Caribbean coast city of Zacapa as a "dreary outpost of Industrialism" inhabited by West Indian, Guatemalan, Honduran, and North American railroad workers.[60] Political instability in Guatemala in 1897 exacerbated the country's economic woes, creating large numbers of unpaid and unemployed workers. This situation resulted in social unrest in Zacapa, where unemployed black workers turned to crime to acquire basic necessities.[61] That year, Zacapa's jefe político, Elias Estrada, described members of Zacapa's black immigrant community as violent and lawless. A municipal judge in Zacapa told the minister of government and justice that before him came black men whom Zacapa police arrested for robbery, homicide, and attempted rape.[62]

Under Estrada Cabrera, the departments of Izabal and Zacapa each had strategically placed fortified garrisons manned by poorly paid soldiers and military officers. The soldiers had the responsibility of enforcing liquor laws and arresting those charged with drunken and disorderly conduct.[63] Most often, the line between civic and military officials was blurred, and jefes políticos and their subordinates customarily used a multitude of methods to illegally supplement their meager government salaries. Authorities did their best to financially exploit subaltern groups, arresting drunken workers often for the explicit purpose of robbing them of their money while in custody, for example.[64] In September 1898, U.S. consular agent Dennis reported a number of "robberies and abuses . . . mostly if not entirely confined to the Zacapa section," where "there are about 350 to 400 American citizens, more or less in destitute conditions."[65]

But not all immigrants ended up in dire economic situations. In fact, the available evidence suggests that some immigrants transitioned out of jobs on the railroad once they had saved enough money to move on. In fact, some would be described as "well dressed and very pompous" blacks.[66] A November 1897 source tells us that John H. Ulyses operated a bar and gambling house at El Rancho, located in the highland department of Alta Verapaz and on the same rail line as the department of Zacapa. The crowd that frequented the honky-tonk seemed to be made up of black immigrant workers who freely traveled between both departments as employees of the railroad. They proved so disreputable that the owner of the property took "legal measures to eject" his tenant, Ulyses. A fight ensued between the two over the matter, resulting in Ulyses shooting his landlord twice.[67] The need for a strong police presence remained serious in Zacapa, a city where, according to one worker, "numerous killing affairs [were] common."[68] Zacapa police arrested Ulyses, and the municipal judge in the city sentenced him to jail time for the crime.

We know more about other proprietors in Zacapa, such as the aforementioned African American Simon Shine.[69] Born in 1880 in Montgomery, Alabama, Shine set out alone for Guatemala at the age of fourteen. He came to Guatemala under contract with the Northern Railroad. During his thirteen-year stint with the Northern Railroad, he lived in Zacapa. He worked his way up on the railroad from water boy to brakeman to fireman and eventually to section foreman. In 1907, he still lived in Zacapa, and by the age of twenty-seven he had managed to save approximately fourteen thousand dollars. Shine and his Guatemalan wife earned enough money to pay all the required monthly municipal fees to operate several small but profitable businesses, including a boardinghouse, barbershop, and juke joint with games of chance, all in the same building. The business did well enough to pay the additional state fees for the right to close at 11:00 p.m. instead of Zacapa's designated 9:00 p.m. closing time.[70] Only a month after it opened, however, Zacapa jefe político General Enrique Aris decided to shut Shine down despite the fact that he ran a legal liquor business. Aris probably did so because he did not like the fact that Shine was American, black, and quickly becoming wealthy. Aris also had a reputation in Zacapa and elsewhere for being a violent despot who regularly assaulted those he disliked.[71]

Economic opportunities on the Caribbean coast attracted immigrants from around the world (see figure 4.4). A Serbian named Tomas Arankosky operated an all-night "canteen" in the same neighborhood as Shine. In 1907 and 1908, respectively, Shine and Arankosky managed establishments that catered to the neighborhood's working-class black immigrants.[72] Another source describes a white American named Charley Swanson who "ran a combination bar and grocery store in Zacapa." At one time, Swanson worked as a cook on a schooner on the Gulf of Mexico.[73]

In addition to the department of Zacapa, immigrants also settled in the port community in and around Puerto Barrios. Starting in the 1890s, the

Figure 4.4. Bodega that sold food and alcohol in Panama. Similar ones are described in records on Guatemala, circa 1905. Scanned image courtesy of the Latin American Library, Tulane University, New Orleans.

population of Puerto Barrios boomed as a result of renewed efforts by Estrada Cabrera's predecessor, José María Reyna Barrios (1892–97), to complete the Northern Railroad.[74] The railroad facilitated the construction of hotels, restaurants, jails, juke joints, and honky-tonks. The construction boom provided additional job opportunities for unskilled laborers. In addition to construction, immigrant workers controlled many of the waterfront jobs at the turn of the century.[75] Highly skilled artisans, such as cooks, blacksmiths, boilermakers, carpenters, plumbers, electricians, and mechanics, also found work in Puerto Barrios as a result of labor agents

who took out attractive advertisements in U.S. and West Indian newspapers. Several black U.S. nationals in Puerto Barrios became juke joint
owners. Both unskilled and skilled workers found plenty of aguardiente
and jazz music at local clubs. The documented evidence shows that juke
joints on the Caribbean coast served a mixed clientele in terms of both
class and color.[76]

Employment opportunities in Puerto Barrios attracted workers from
around the world who spoke many different languages. When traveler
Nevin O. Winter visited the Caribbean port, he heard "Spanish, German,
French, English, Chinese, and the unintelligible gibberish of the Carib
[the Garifuna]" spoken by members of the port's small population.[77]
"Drunkenness is quite common" in the area, Winter noted. He regularly
observed people "in a drunken stupor" and unable to walk.[78] Miguel Angel Asturias, a Guatemalan Nobel laureate in literature, described Puerto
Barrios as being like the Florida Everglades, a place with the "mystery of
languages" and the "confusion of the Tower of Babel."[79] By the early 1900s,
African Americans who had first come to the port in the 1880s as railroad
workers had, like Simon Shine, saved up their money and started small
businesses, including bars and restaurants.

Like Shine, black immigrant Sam Lee operated a juke joint in Puerto
Barrios with his Guatemalan wife. Lee was born in 1878 in Mississippi. In
1895, at the age of seventeen, he departed for Guatemala. Those who knew
him in Guatemala described him as "quite a shrewd fellow," and he was
well-known throughout the "towns, farms, and camps along the railway"
in the department of Izabal.[80] After marrying Guatemalan national Josefa Guzmán, Lee became a successful juke joint operator who sold food
in Puerto Barrios, as well as a merchant. As members of a marginalized
group, English-speaking immigrants like Lee obtained socioeconomic
advantages and thus social mobility by courting and marrying nationals. Such advantages included kinship relations, access to local populations, and assistance in learning the native language and customs; this
more than likely provided them with competitive advantages over other
immigrants who lacked these connections and skills. Co-ownership of
alcohol-related businesses may have been common. For example, black
immigrants Hedley Ward and Wilfred Brown co-owned a juke joint in
Puerto Barrios that had a license to sell liquor until 9:00 p.m. Municipal
judges' records from Izabal describe Brown as single, a machinist, illiterate, and employed as an "Urban Police Agent" in Puerto Barrios.[81]

While the existing records about immigrant bar owners on the Caribbean coast are patchy at best, they do make it clear that places like Zacapa and Puerto Barrios offered migrant workers an opportunity to pursue upward mobility by catering to the needs of other workers. More important, they served as important indicators that a given immigrant had put down roots on the Caribbean coast. Juke joint ownership meant that a person had decided to become an expatriate.

Consumption Habits and the Culture of Alcohol

IRCA and UFCO workers, the majority of them immigrants, spent many leisure hours in juke joints and honky-tonks like the ones described above. As mentioned earlier, juke joints served as social outlets and entertainment maroons that allowed men and women to escape and relax with friends. The drinking that happened in juke joints provided what Smith calls "an alcoholic marronage, a temporary relief from social inequalities, which probably hindered organized efforts to resist" labor exploitation.[82] Historically, U.S. railroad workers made drinking an important part of their working-class culture. Drinking provided them with a temporary escape from the hazards of the job, as well as a fraternal activity that fostered worker solidarity. They would drink to share industry news, to forget mishaps on the job, and to cope with tormenting supervisors and company officials.[83] As in the rural Caribbean and southern United States, the spirit of the juke joint and the drinking that occurred there permeated black immigrant culture on the Caribbean coast of Central America. In these maroons, friends and coworkers could eat, talk, gossip, hear music, dance, gamble, and drink.[84]

Several scholars have discussed the meaning of excessive drinking. Smith argues that poor working and living conditions, frustrations, anxieties, and a lack of occupational fulfillment led to excessive drinking in the Caribbean.[85] Historian Ronald Takaki interprets excessive drinking among Asian immigrant workers on plantations in Hawaii around the same time as this study. He argues that excessive drinking enabled immigrant workers to escape the reality of years of separation from family and community.[86] One sees similar trends in Caribbean Guatemala. Virginia Garrard-Burnett aptly points out in the conclusion to this volume that as a Catholic nation Guatemala did not have the same restraints on alcohol as did the immigrants' Protestant home communities. Similarly, prior to

World War II the Caribbean coast had a largely working-class male milieu with few familiar restraints on drinking, such as Protestant women in one's kinship network.

Another interpretation of the role of alcohol among Caribbean coast immigrants comes from anthropologist Stanley Brandes's work on drinking and working-class male identity politics across the Guatemalan border in Mexico. He contends that "Mexican men demonstrate friendship through drink."[87] Manhood and drinking are so closely related that "most men in the Mexican laboring classes—come to associate imbibing and inebriation with male identity."[88] One observes similar male ideology and behavior in Caribbean Guatemala. A final interpretation of the role of excessive drinking comes from Smith, who found that drinking emboldened the marginalized to challenge "social-structural inequalities" and their bosses. In short, excessive drinking encouraged the less powerful to attack the more powerful.[89] In Caribbean Guatemala, excessive drinking played a decisive role in causing labor strikes and confrontations between workers and company and government officials.

An unknown state department official in Honduras told assistant secretary of state Robert Bacon, "Since I have been in charge of this Consulate . . . almost the entire number of arrests of Americans here, are of negroes who are frequently drunk and disorderly, and almost invariably resist arrest, and it is almost impossible to convince them that they should submit and go quietly, when arrested."[90] Similar disrespect of those in authority occurred across the border in Guatemala among banana plantation workers in Quiriguá. V. M Peralta, an agent of the Northern Railroad, reported, "[O]ne of the many [drunkards] ran over me at my office" in the Puerto Barrios train station, adding, "This morning the drunkenness was horrible, station employees see this regularly."[91]

It would be foolish to argue here that excessive drinking generally advanced the interest of workers. Historian Aviva Chomsky argues, for example, that the abuse of alcohol and violence against other workers seemed "to be a way of turning dissatisfaction and resentment inward, or onto other workers, instead of organizing for any kind of effective change in the unsatisfactory situation."[92] Railroad officials, banana producers, and government officials on the Caribbean coast expressed an aversion to paydays because they often became times of disorderly conduct and bloody fights similar to the fights Langston Hughes describes in the juke joint section of Stanton, Kansas, and Zora Neale Hurston describes in

Jacksonville and the Everglades of Florida. Former UFCO foreman John Williams recalled that on payday, several fights were likely to "occur due to the vicious native liquor that is cheap and as powerful as T.N.T." He went on to say that on payday, gambling and the "terrible native liquor" caused "the racial feelings [to] break out."[93] In the final analysis, when workers drank too much and fought each other, their behavior undermined worker solidarity and attempts to improve working and living conditions.

Conclusion

Analyzing the trade in and consumption of aguardiente provides interesting insights into culture, class, and race on the Caribbean coast of Guatemala and Honduras. By 1922, the UFCO and IRCA frontier towns and port communities of the region had reputations as places full of bars, saloons, and raggedy Louisiana- and Mississippi-style juke joints and honky-tonks catering to quick-tempered immigrants. Here, as in other places around the world where migrant workers congregated, the immigrant workforce exhibited the characteristics of "lowdown" cultural identity: these were men who turned to gambling, drinking, and womanizing as a source of escape, solace, and entertainment.[94] For black migrant workers who decided to put down roots and stay, the sale of aguardiente, whether legal or illegal, provided a pathway to better opportunities.

Notes

1. Cunningham, *Gypsying through Central America*, 40.
2. Opie, "Black Americans and the State," 608–9.
3. Opie, *Black Labor Migration*, 14.
4. Hurt, *African American Life*, 123; Nardone, "Roomful of Blues," 167, 169, 173.
5. Arnold, "'Which way to the honky-tonk?'" 19.
6. Wilson, *Crab Antics*, 166.
7. Ibid.
8. Lacoste, "Wine and Women," 363.
9. Wilson, *Crab Antics*, 166.
10. Smith, *Caribbean Rum*, 244.
11. Ibid., 17; Peiss, *Cheap Amusements*, 17.
12. Opie, *Black Labor Migration*, 11.
13. Ibid., 41, 54; Putnam, "Eventually Alien," 284–85, 288; Harpelle, "Whites Zones," 307–12.
14. Smith, *Caribbean Rum*, 125.

15. Hurt, *African American Life*, 12; Nardone, "Roomful of Blues," 169.

16. Opie, *Black Labor Migration*, 16–21.

17. Ibid., 21.

18. U.S. National Archives II, College Park, Maryland (hereafter USNA), Records Group (hereafter RG) 84, vol. 18, Frank C. Dennis, Livingston U.S. Consular Agent, to N. G. Hunter Jr., Vice and Deputy Consular General, Guatemala City, June 1, 1901.

19. Opie, "Adios Jim Crow," 109.

20. USNA, RG 84, vol. 13, p. 230, Edward Reed, Livingston U.S. Consular Agent, to the Galveston Chamber of Commerce, Galveston, Texas, May 11, 1908.

21. Ibid.

22. USNA, RG 84, vol. 26, Edward Reed, Livingston U.S. Consular Agent, to C. C. Hoard, Celeste, Texas, December 15, 1909.

23. Archivo General de Centro América (hereafter AGCA), Ministerio de Fomento (hereafter MF), Leg. 15813, José M. Amerlinck, Technical Director Engineer of the Northern Railroad, to F. C. García, General Superintendent of the Northern Railroad, Puerto Barrios, December 4, 1895.

24. USNA, RG 59, box 3838, Hugh R. Wilson, American Chargé d'Affaires Guatemala, Guatemala City, to the Secretary of State, Washington, D.C., June 17, 1912.

25. Opie, "Adios Jim Crow," 118–19.

26. Daniel, *Lost Revolutions*, 121–25.

27. Hughes, *Not Without Laughter*, 218.

28. Ibid.

29. Hurston, *Their Eyes Were Watching God*, 149.

30. Ibid.

31. Yentsch, "Excavating the South's," 84.

32. Ibid., 85.

33. Opie, "Afro-North American Migration," 12.

34. Yentsch, "Excavating the South's," 85.

35. Opie, "Adios Jim Crow," 137.

36. Yentsch, "Excavating the South's," 85.

37. AGCA, MF, International Railroad of Central America (hereafter IRCA), Leg. 15872, V. M. Peralta, Agente del Ferrocarril a Comandante de Armas, Puerto Barrios; Admor de Rentas, Gerente General, Estación de Quiriguá, Izabal, May 9, 1922.

38. Opie, "Adios Jim Crow," 20–21.

39. Ibid., 141–43.

40. USNA, RG 84, vol. 40, Affidavit de Simon Shine, Livingston, September 20, 1907.

41. AGCA, Jefatura Política de Izabal (hereafter JPI) records, 1913, Juzgado Municipal de Puerto Barrios a Jefatura Política y Nominas de Izabal, "Criminal contra el presente reo de asesinated Wilfred Brown, en la persona de Jorge Morrison agente de Policia," September 1913.

42. USNA, RG 59, box 3838, Victor M. Cutter UFCO Guatemala Division Manager, Puerto Barrios to W. F. Sands American Legation to Guatemala, March 24, 1910, Guatemala City.

43. Opie, "Adios Jim Crow," 119.

44. Ibid.

45. Williams, "Rise of the Banana Industry," 36.

46. Opie, "Foreign Workers, Debt Peonage," 42.

47. Chomsky, *West Indian Workers*, 175.

48. AGCA, MF, Correspondencia de Los Contratistas del Ferrocarriles 1897, Leg. 15819, H. Boiault, Foreign Railroad Contractor, Puerto de Iztapa to Minister of Development, Guatemala City, February 20, 1897.

49. Roberts, *On the Earthquake Line,* 44.

50. AGCA, MF, Correspondencia de Los Contratistas del Ferrocarriles, Leg. B106-1, Ricardo Barthel, General Manager, Central American Improvement Company, speaking about Barranquilo, Department of Guatemala, in a letter to the Ministro de Fomento, Guatemala City, October 3, 1901.

51. AGCA, MF, Correspondencia de Los Contratistas del Ferrocarriles, Leg. B106-1, Ricardo Barthel, General Manager, Central American Improvement Company, to Minister of Development, October 26, 1901.

52. Ibid.

53. USNA, RG 84, vol. 38, pp. 1–5, Albert W. Brickwood Jr., American Consulate, Puerto Cortes, to Hugh S. Gibson, Secretary, American Legation Tegucigalpa, Puerto Cortes, Honduras, January 19, 1909.

54. Ibid.

55. USNA, RG 84, vol. 3, Vice and Deputy Consul, Puerto Cortes, Honduras, to Robert Bacon, Assistant Secretary of State, American Legation Tegucigalpa, Washington, D.C., February 22, 1907.

56. Foster, *Gringo in Mañana-Land,* 211.

57. Nardone, "Roomful of Blues," 167.

58. Ibid., 169.

59. Winter, *Guatemala and Her People*, 147–48.

60. Ruhl, *Central Americans,* 222–23.

61. AGCA, Ministro de Gobernación y Justicia (hereafter MGJ), Leg. 28964, Exp. 1787, Juan Paz Tomas to the Secretaria de Fomento a Ministro de Gobernación y Justicia, Guatemala City, July 11, 1898.

62. AGCA, MGJ, Leg. 28935, Exp. 1897, Elias Estrada, Jefatura Política de Zacapa al Ministerio de Gobernación y Justicia, February 2, 1897, Zacapa; AGCA, MGJ, Leg. 28935, Exp. 1897, Juzgado de la Instancia del Dept de Zacapa a MGJ, February 4, 1897.

63. USNA, RG 84, vol. 93, Collin C. W. Owen, Manager, Agencias del Norte, to Frank C. Dennis, U.S. Consul Agent at Livingston, February 10, 1897.

64. USNA, RG 59, roll 5, no. 41, Whitehouse to James B. Porter, Assistant Srcetary of State, May 24, 1885.

65. USNA, RG 84, vol. 76, Frank C. Dennis, U.S. Consul Agent at Livingston, to Arthur M. Beaupré, U.S. Secretary of the Legation and Consul-General at Guatemala, Guatemala City September 2, 1898.

66. Cunningham, *Gypsying through Central America*, 237.

67. USNA, RG 84, vol. 72, Frank C. Dennis, U.S. Consul Agent at Livingston, to D. Lynch Pringle, U.S. Consul General to Guatemala, Guatemala City, November 5, 1897.

68. USNA, RG 84, vol. 171, Affidavit of James Wilson, May 11, 1910, Guatemala City; USNA, RG 84, vol. 153, P. L. Moore, Zacapa, to Edward Reed, U.S. Consular Agent, Livingston, August 21, 1913.

69. USNA, RG 84, vol. 72, Frank C. Dennis, U.S. Consul Agent at Livingston, to D. Lynch Pringle, U.S. Consul General to Guatemala, Guatemala City, November 5, 1897.

70. USNA, RG 84, vol. 40, Affidavit of George Walters, Livingston, September 16, 1907.

71. Opie, "Black Americans and the State," 604.

72. USNA, RG 84, vol. 126, Edward Kanlson, Zacapa, to American Minister, Guatemala City, Zacapa, June 19, 1908.

73. Cunningham, *Gypsying through Central America*, 239–40.

74. Opie, *Black Labor Migration*, 13–14.

75. *El Norte*, April 20, 1893; AGCA, MF, Leg. 15813, Amerlinck to García, December 4, 1895.

76. Latin American Library, Tulane University, Rare Book and Manuscript Department, New Orleans, Louisiana, William T. Penny, "Notes and Comments on Travels through Mexico and Central America, being the personal happenings to and experiences of yours sincerely" (Guatemala City, 1913), 68; AGCA, MF, Leg. 15819, L. P. Pennypacker, Inspector Engineer Ferrocarril del Norte, Zacapa, to Jose M. Amerlinck, Director Engineer Ferrocarril Central del Norte, November 11, 1897; AGCA, MF, Leg. 15821, p. 1, R. H. May and Pennypacker to Amerlinck, September 21, 1898.

77. Winter, *Guatemala and Her People*, 146.

78. Ibid., 129.

79. Asturias, *Strong Wind*, 30.

80. USNA, RG 84, vol. 184, Edward Reed, Livingston U.S. Consular Agent, to Collin C. W. Owen, Manager, Agencias del Norte, January 20, 1910 (and enclosure no. 1).

81. AGCA, JPI, 1913, Juzgado Municipal de Puerto Barrios a Jefatura Política y Nominas de Izabal, "Criminal contra el presente reo de asesinated Wilfred Brown, en la persona de Jorge Morrison agente de Policia," September 1913.

82. Smith, *Caribbean Rum*, 167.

83. Licht, *Working for the Railroad*, 238.

84. Hurt, *African American Life*, 123; Yentsch, "Excavating the South," 84.

85. Smith, *Caribbean Rum*, 140.

86. Takaki, *Strangers from a Different Shore*, 145.

87. Brandes, "Drink, Abstinence, and Male Identity," 155.

88. Ibid., 156.

89. Smith, *Caribbean Rum*, 118, 158–59, quotation from 118.

90. USNA, RG 84, vol. 3, Vice and Deputy Consul to Bacon, February 22, 1907.

91. AGCA, MF, IRCA, Leg. 15872, V. M. Peralta to Admor de Rentas, May 9, 1922.

92. Chomsky, *West Indian Workers*, 175.

93. Williams, "Rise of the Banana Industry," 34, 121.

94. Opie, "Adios Jim Crow," 120–21.

5

◇◇◇◇◇◇◇◇◇◇◇◇◇◇◇

Distilling Perceptions of Crime

Maya Moonshiners and the State, 1898–1944

DAVID CAREY JR.

On December 3, 1932, authorities in Quezaltenango discovered a clandestine still that was producing 250 bottles of aguardiente a day in the Administración de Rentas (Treasury Administration) building. Remarkably, this was not the first such offense. Previous moonshiners also had set up shop in the building, perhaps surmising that such production was best disguised in the entrails of the very institution that was most concerned with stamping it out. Maybe their instincts were right; this latest distillery had remained hidden in plain sight for over a month before authorities found "a great quantity" of fermenting sugar "destined for distillation."[1]

In an effort to downplay this scandal, less than a week after the director of Quezaltenango's Administración de Rentas confirmed rumors of the operation, his office along with the Jefatura Política (Governor's Office) reported that the war against *clandestinismo* (bootlegging) was going well. They explained, "The Treasury Police with the support of the department's military authorities makes daily raids into different places in the region, inspecting with prudence and circumspection the houses that have had or have stills. . . . The telegrams that the press publishes daily about the capture [of moonshiners] in Quetzaltenango best demonstrate the actions of the Treasury Police and Jefatura Política."[2] As images from *La Gaceta: Revista de Policía y Variedades* (the *Police Gazette*, henceforth *La Gaceta*) such as figure 5.1 suggest, authorities also published photographs to convey their apparent success. Yet the telegram that reported the distillery in the Treasury building did just the opposite. If the Treasury Ministry did not even know what was going on in its own back storeroom, authorities

Figure 5.1. Four Treasury agents pose with a captured clandestinista (Demetrio Sigüenza Morales) and the implements of his trade. *La Gaceta: Revista de Policía y Variedades*, April 19, 1942. Image is reproduced courtesy of Hemeroteca Nacional de Guatemala.

were not likely to be able to curtail the moonshine trade throughout the countryside.

During the first half of the twentieth century, the proceeds from alcohol sales filled government coffers, fueled local economies, and fortified family livelihoods. Because its sale, production, and consumption were steady throughout the year (excepting spikes during fiestas), alcohol, more than any other commodity—including coffee (which generally involved Mayas only during the harvest season)—was at the center of relations between Mayas, ladinos, Creoles, and local and national authorities. Despite national rhetoric decrying excessive alcohol production and consumption and Maya rhetoric lamenting the deleterious effects of alcoholism, neither the state nor local denizens had the political will to eradicate *aguardiente clandestino*. Although bootleggers did not consider themselves guilty by their own definitions of crime, neither did they claim innocence. Since ladino legal constructs deemed their actions criminal, Maya moonshiners shifted the debate outside the confines of the law to consider the broader injustices of ethnic, gender, and class discrimination.

By pointing out that aguardiente was produced clandestinely to escape penury, some defendants advanced thinly veiled critiques of (and warnings about) the government's inability to provide for its citizens. They let judges, police, and scribes know that the state's failure to provide the conditions for subaltern survival let alone success was a greater affront than selling moonshine to feed one's family. Poor indigenous defendants were painfully aware that ladino elites established alcohol laws to both impose their moralistic musings and enrich themselves. Since the alcohol tax was regressive, it affected the poor more than other groups and therefore encouraged them to look for ways to circumvent it.

Because the state lost money to bootleggers, financial concerns drove public policy. By the turn of the twentieth century, as in Mexico, the Guatemalan government was dependent on alcohol income, particularly to finance such agencies of repression as the military and police. In 1899, for example, alcohol tax was the largest source of revenue for Estrada Cabrera's government (1898–1920).[3] Coffee crises like the one set off when Brazil's 1897 record harvests depressed international prices underscored the advantage of alcohol revenue. Since alcohol consumption was relatively inelastic (even during economic downturns, both Maya and ladino drinkers prioritized their drinking habits), its revenue was spared the volatility of other commodity markets. Like Estrada Cabrera's regime, General Jorge Ubico's government (1931–44) depended on alcohol income. From 1931 to 1935, for example, liquor revenues provided over 46 million quetzales. Though nearly 40 percent of this income was from import taxes, the state could count on 200,000 quetzales annually from taxes on the sale of hard liquor, including legally produced aguardiente.[4] As the Guatemalan intellectual J. Fernando Juárez Muñoz noted when Ubico assumed office, "Alcohol! Alcohol is the vice that stimulates the state" and "maintains a great part of the bureaucratic machine of Guatemala."[5] Perhaps for that reason, National Police reports concerning the battle against extralegal alcohol production reveal an obsession with filling state coffers. After boasting about decommissioning "the best and most productive" stills in Santiago Sacatepéquez in June 1931, for example, the police explained, "We are auguring a formidable advance in the department's revenue. . . . [B]y diminishing this fraud, the sanctioned distilleries necessarily will sell more liquor and greater will be the taxes paid by them."[6]

To a certain extent, the state's alcohol policies also encouraged Maya integration into the national economy. By shutting down clandestine production, the state hoped bootleggers would either purchase licenses to continue their business or pursue other (presumably licit) endeavors. In turn, by shutting down illegal vendors, the state hoped to compel poor drinkers to pay the higher prices at state-sanctioned venues. At those prices, indigenous consumers would have to engage more fully in the cash economy to support their habit.[7]

Alcohol facilitated this integration in other ways too. Many Mayas emerged from their drunken binges only to realize they owed their labor to a plantation whose representative had posted their bail or floated a loan so they could keep drinking. Because of unscrupulous *enganchadores* or *contratistas* (labor brokers) and exploitative *finca* (large landed estates) managers, many laborers never escaped these debts.[8] Even though they can be construed as openly defying the national economy and society, in their own way, Maya moonshiners and clandestine vendors contributed to campesino indebtedness, which in turn helped to fuel the coffee economy. Yet through their court testimonies, clandestinistas informed authorities that if good jobs were available to them, they would participate in the (legal) national economy. As long as they remained mired in poverty and victims of exploitation, poor indigenous people had little choice but to break the law to support and entertain themselves.

Although the costs were prohibitive for most indigenous people, for ladinos who could afford it, the freedom to operate in plain view of the authorities increased their access to clients. As María Rogelia Gálvez Roca, Paula Hernández, Beatriz Álvarez, Roselía Ruano de Roca (whose ages ranged from twenty-nine to seventy-four), and other ladinas learned on the eve of Ubico's overthrow, it was not difficult to get a liquor license as long as one paid the fees.[9] At times such state-sanctioned operations seemed brazen by local standards. For example, Kaqchikel-Mayas (henceforth Kaqchikel) of San Juan Comalapa (henceforth Comalapa) decried ladinas who set up their stalls in front of the Catholic church on Sundays to offer libations to congregants as soon as they filed out of the church.[10] Seldom did clandestine vendors have such a captive audience. Of course the state's pursuit of bootleggers made getting a license more desirable (and lucrative).

To sustain their dictatorships and maintain an image of order and modernity, Estrada Cabrera and Ubico had to balance the need for alcohol's revenue with the demand to eradicate alcohol's social ills. Both despots sought to eradicate the illegal production and distribution of alcohol, particularly homebrewed chicha and *k'uxa* (moonshine); as occurred elsewhere in Latin America, newspapers celebrated these efforts.[11] As the Ubico dictatorship wore on, even those who were not seeking to turn a profit became targets. In 1940, for example, the Ministry of Agriculture and Hacienda outlawed the fermentation of chicha, even for personal consumption. Since popular images and intellectual discourse associated "indios" with alcohol and its clandestine production, the government focused its efforts in the highlands.[12] By 1940, the National Police had claimed success. David Ordóñez, the director of the National Police, boasted that his corps had decommissioned 243 stills between 1937 and 1940.[13] As further proof that illegal alcohol production was down, he asserted that in "the departments of Guatemala, El Progreso, Sacatepéquez, Escuintla, Santa Rosa, Suchitepéquez, Retalhuleu, Izabal, Zacapa, Chiquimula, Jalapa and Jutiapa . . . during 1940 NOT EVEN ONE clandestine aguardiente distillery was confiscated. And those departments that for their extension, topography, or whatever other circumstance are propitious for committing these crimes, remain as orientation bases to reinforce future police action."[14]

In truth, thinly veiled racism informed the state's approach to alcohol. For example, the departments listed in Ordóñez's report were predominantly ladino areas, whereas those where the focus of police efforts would be reinforced were predominantly indigenous areas. Although the police were vague about what constituted "other circumstance[s] . . . propitious for" producing aguardiente illegally, clearly ethnicity was a salient factor. These findings resonate with historian Virginia Garrard-Burnett's study of alcohol-related crimes in the departments of Quezaltenango, El Quiché, and Jutiapa, where the latter ladino department had far fewer arrests than the two former indigenous departments despite being a transshipment point for contraband, including alcohol, from El Salvador. As Garrard-Burnett points out, these figures speak more to a lax enforcement of the law in ladino areas than a Maya propensity for alcohol production.[15] As the individuals named in figure 5.2 demonstrate, the state's campaign against bootlegging often pitted such ladino Treasury Police as Pedro Francisco Corzo and José Hernán Flores Monzón against such indigenous moonshiners as Leonso Tahom and María Baquiax (numbers 2 and 3, respectively).

By pursuing indigenous bootleggers and turning a blind eye to ladino violations, the police were both influenced by and perpetuated discourse that associated indios with alcohol and crime. But these efforts also reflect the state's growing strength, which allowed it to expand its reach and shift its focus. With its small and constrained institutions during the

Figure 5.2. Treasury
Police with clandestinis-
tas and their wares. In
photograph number 2,
agent Pedro Francisco
Corzo (*right*) poses with
clandestinista Leonso
Tohom. In photograph
number 3, agent José
Hernán Flores Monzón
(*right*) appears with
clandestinista María
Baquiax, who has a
baby strapped to her
back. *La Gaceta: Revista
de Policía y Variedades,*
June 1, 1941. Image is
reproduced courtesy of
Hemeroteca Nacional
de Guatemala.

nineteenth century, the Conservative and even early Liberal state struggled to control the ladino populations and their municipalities, let alone
indigenous people.[16] As the twentieth century progressed and the state
apparatus gained power, the state could increasingly turn its attention to
the municipal and regional institutions and affairs of Mayas.

Based on judicial records, aguardiente was an equal opportunity commodity and vice; neither ladino, Maya, male, nor female were excluded
from the production, sale, or consumption of alcohol in Guatemala. Although the extent of their involvement varied depending on the region
and time, like their counterparts in other areas of Latin America (and
the world), Guatemalan women played a prominent role in the alcohol
economy.[17] As Stacey Schwartzkopf and René Reeves document in their
chapters in this volume, Guatemalan women played a prominent and at
times dominant role in the nineteenth-century alcohol economy. Like
Chilenas and Bolivianas who produced and sold wine and chicha, respectively, Guatemaltecas used the alcohol economy to showcase their entrepreneurial, managerial, and commercial skills.[18] Legal or not, the sale and
production of alcohol was one of the few ways lower-class, particularly
single or widowed, women could generate a modest income and shape
national identity.

Although they risked losing their livelihoods, entrepreneurs who
avoided the licensing fees and taxes (mainly because they could not afford
them) offered their drinks at lower prices than licensed taverns. Naturally,
this savings appealed to lower-class drinkers who may not have been able
to afford (or have been willing to pay) the sanctioned prices.[19] When the
state cracked down on poor indigenous clandestinistas, it was responding
to economic as well as class, gender, and ethnic biases. When clandestinistas appeared in court, they often used it to advance their own claims by
pointing out the injustices and practical implications of these prejudices.

State agents and Maya moonshiners were like awkward dance partners
who both believed they were leading. As the opposing strategies of deception and detection reveal, neither group dominated. These clashes continued in the courtroom, where defendants confronted judicial authorities.
More than any other commodity in Guatemala, aguardiente compelled
disparate groups to interact. These interactions ranged from cordial to
confrontational. Whether it was as the focus of policies designed to enrich
state coffers, the fuel for local black markets and the export coffee economy, or the product whose consumption both reified and broke gender,

ethnic, and class hierarchies, alcohol was paramount to Guatemala's nation formation.

Establishing State Control

Throughout the nineteenth century, the national government looked to the alcohol monopoly system as a primary source of income even as district governors, local officials, cofrades (members of a cofradía, or religious confraternity), and indigenous and ladino denizens circumvented the state's mandate.[20] Guatemala was not unique in this regard; other Latin American nations such as Colombia and Mexico too relied on alcohol revenue and taxes.[21] But the Guatemalan government's dependence on alcohol revenue often undermined its stability. Widespread resentment against the aguardiente police and broad opposition to the Conservative government's alcohol monopolies, which favored elites and eventually granted exclusive rights to produce and sell aguardiente to the Compañía Anónima de Aguardiente, helped to bring down the regime in 1871, as Reeves elaborates on in his chapter.[22] Yet almost immediately after their victory in June 1871, Liberals broke the spirit of their promise to abolish the monopoly and established aguardiente licensing regulations, fees, and taxes that ultimately turned most small producers and vendors into criminals. Even had they learned from recent history, Liberals had little choice: they needed alcohol income to govern the country.

Since local economies depended on this cottage industry and local officials were complicit with it, clandestinismo thrived. The Liberals failed to eradicate the aguardiente clandestino trade largely because it was both ubiquitous and elusive. Even when they called upon the military to support its police forces, the government's efforts seemed futile. At times, private individuals and institutions, such as landowners and haciendas, took it upon themselves to suppress bootlegging.[23] Even though the government looked to the alcohol monopoly system as a primary source of income throughout the nineteenth century, not until the early 1880s did the Liberal state earnestly resume the enforcement of alcohol laws, which in effect altered the definition of crime in ways that contravened indigenous conceptions of legality.[24] By that century's end, Estrada Cabrera used alcohol revenue to help create the first Guatemalan police state. True to his paternalistic rule, he granted exceptions and pardons to some bootleggers to earn their loyalty.[25] This leniency notwithstanding, if criminal records from Chimaltenango are any indication, punishing those who defrauded the Treasury in the liquors sector consumed an inordinate amount of the judicial system's time during the first five years of Estrada Cabrera's regime.

By the 1930s, the state increasingly used jefes políticos to convey the importance of this campaign. Some enticed local authorities by pointing out that arresting illegal alcohol production would enrich municipalities. In one such exhortation on the eve of Ubico's rule, Chimaltenango's jefe político reminded mayors in his jurisdiction of "the obligation you have to impose the liquor law to pursue actively and without rest contraband and fraud against the Treasury. Remembering at the same time, that the Municipality should interest itself in the disappearance of this fraud. The more aguardiente consumed from [official] depositories, the greater the income the Municipality will receive from the taxes. For each bottle sold . . . its tax is evidence of the investment in works of progress and utility."[26] Although such enticements did not ring hollow—the San Martín Jilotepeque (henceforth San Martín) *alcalde* (mayor) learned on October 31, 1931, that his municipality's account in the Banco Central had surpassed two thousand quetzales thanks to *fondos de aguardiente*[27]—plying local officials with promises of improved infrastructure and other public works highlighted the state's contradictory, if not hypocritical, stance. While the memorandum explicitly encouraged authorities to crack down on bootleggers, it also implicitly encouraged leniency with drunks; after all, each bottle they purchased contributed to national income. The National Police too framed their hunt for moonshine in economic terms. When the Sololá police confiscated three stills and arrested their owners in 1931, *La Gaceta* hailed it as "one of the great . . . accomplishments by the police against the delinquents that hurt [the government's] fiscal interests."[28] Two years later the jefe político of Jalapa, General Serapio Cuyun, notified local leaders in his department that all government employees should "cooperate in the persecution of *aguardiente clandestino*."[29]

Some locals too saw the wisdom in regulated liquor sales. Drawing attention to Sololá's chronically empty coffers that stifled public works projects, in 1937 one licensed vendor, Antonio Ralón, proposed that the municipality take over the regulatory process and offer the National Treasury 20 percent of all license fees and "a donation" of fifteen cents for every eighteen-liter *garrafón* (vessel) of aguardiente sold. Although the *intendente* (intendant) said he would bring it up with the jefe político, the silence on the issue thereafter in the municipal record suggests the proposal fell on deaf ears.[30]

The Art of Deception

Despite authorities' increased efforts, contraband alcohol was never in danger of extinction. At the same time, its very nature constrained entrepreneurs.[31] The threat of arrest, incarceration, fines, and having their goods confiscated compelled most producers and vendors to keep their operations (and capital invested in them) small. Even the most successful ones seldom expanded their business beyond a cottage industry, unless local authorities protected them, as was the case with the "famous great still" in Tecpán dubbed "La Municipalidad." As the nickname suggests, the owners were members of Tecpán's town council. In fact, the still was on the alcalde's property. Although this operation was well known throughout Chimaltenango, so adept were the owners at shielding it from their superiors that ministry officials and the police believed its existence to be a rumor. When police finally discovered it in May 1931, they considered the operation to be "one of the largest that to this day has been decommissioned."[32]

Clearly, Tecpán's municipal authorities could not have duped their superiors without the collusion of laconic locals. That national authorities believed the story to be a rumor underscores just how large the chasm between local and official knowledge could be. Remaining silent in the face of hegemonic inquiry and ignorance is akin to what James Scott calls "hidden transcripts," where marginalized populations build an oppositional culture without overtly confronting or challenging authorities.[33] By acting obtuse and withholding information, locals could maintain a certain degree of autonomy. Knowledge was power, and neither was necessarily in the hands of national authorities.

La Municipalidad and other stills intimately linked to the state's chain of command point to the complex, contradictory, and complicit nature of the state. If the very authorities charged with eradicating moonshine were producing it, how could the government ever hope to advance its campaign? If the national government could not effectively police such urban centers as Quezaltenango and Tecpán, how could it stamp out moonshine in rural villages and hinterlands where its power of surveillance was stretched so thin as to be nonexistent in some cases? Such challenges shed light on the theatre of rule in Guatemala, where the national government lacked the resources to effectively govern and control the nation. If the state did not at least attempt to impose its rule and intermittently make its presence known, however, subjects and citizens—particularly indigenous people in rural areas—would be unaware they were ruled at all and behave all the more autonomously.

Despite (or perhaps because of) the presence of various police forces charged by the Ministerio de Hacienda (Treasury Ministry) to suppress the aguardiente clandestino trade and assistance from the military, complicity between officials and producers was not uncommon.[34] As Reeves demonstrates for nineteenth-century western Guatemala in chapter 2, local leaders were often involved in the alcohol business.[35] Although they did not reach the extremes of using alcohol to buy votes and lubricate machine politics like their counterparts in early twentieth-century Yucatán, Mexico, many local Guatemalan authorities too were corrupted by alcohol and its profits.[36] In an attempt to curb the tendencies of complicitous officials, Estrada Cabrera brought in outside personnel. During his dictatorship, the *comandantes del resguardo de hacienda* (commanders of the Treasury's Rural Guard) in Chimaltenango tended to be from other departments and linguistic regions. Because they did not speak Kaqchikel or know the area or local population well, comandantes such as Valentino Gramajo, who moved from the K'ichee'- and Mam-speaking area of Quezaltenango to patrol the Kaqchikel town of San Martín, were dependent on their assistants (both indigenous and ladino) and the local population to guide their searches.[37] Ubico too employed a strategy of bringing in outsiders to reduce corruption. The official Guatemalan daily *Diario de Centro América* praised his treasury secretary for replacing personnel in charge of combating clandestinismo with "honorable and capable" men who improved the fiscal interests of "*nuestra patria*" (our nation).[38] Armed and organized, the Treasury's Rural Guard could be an intimidating force, as images from *La Gaceta* sought to convey (see figures 5.1 and 5.3 for examples).

Bringing in outsiders had its costs, though. If vendors did not produce aguardiente where they sold it, finding the source could be difficult. Often authorities only discovered stills because they received a *denuncia* (denunciation) from a community member.[39] Yet just as often as individuals pointed authorities to private homes or farms (where authorities had a greater arrest rate), witnesses denied knowing who owned stills

Figure 5.3. Stills decommissioned by the Treasury's Rural Guard in December 1932. The headline reads, "Totonicapan: Treasury Police's labor in benefit of the interests of the nation, vulnerable to contraband." *La Gaceta: Revista de Policía y Variedades,* January 15, 1933. Image is reproduced courtesy of the Latin American Library, Tulane University, New Orleans.

discovered on communal land.[40] By setting up their operations on communal lands, moonshiners made it virtually impossible for authorities to trace the stills back to them.[41] In a typical scenario, the assistant Julian Catú only further frustrated Comalapa officials who discovered one such operation in 1902 when he explained, "According to what you hear, the owner of the still is an individual from San Martín, but no one knows his name."[42] According to Catú's recounting of community rumor, the only

leads were based on geography and gender, and perhaps both were designed to derail rather than aid the search. Not surprisingly, officials never
found the owner. Geographical dispersion impeded the state's campaign
against bootlegging. Taking advantage of the central highlands' mountainous topography, sparsely populated rural areas, and comandantes'
lack of familiarity with the region, many moonshiners avoided detection.

In a reflection of the geography of power and the importance place
played in helping moonshiners hide from authorities, one Kaqchikel word
for aguardiente is *siwan ya*,' or canyon water.[43] When the *policia montada*
(a small mounted troop) found three stills in one of the most remote areas
of Zacapa in 1933, they observed that the stills had been operating for quite
some time. On that occasion they arrested just one owner.[44] Judging from
the paucity of arrests in such remote settings, the conditions overwhelmingly favored distillers. As such, it was with reserved celebration that the
authorities from Santiago Sacatepéquez reported that they had broken the
record for confiscated stills. "The bad part is," they conceded, "we cannot
capture the owners."[45] When authorities found a still that could produce
one hundred bottles a day in one of Comalapa's deep canyons, they admitted, "It was not possible to locate [the owner] because of the rough and
thorny terrain."[46] At the same time, the tips that most often led authorities
to these operations indicate an inherent risk in bootleggers' operations.
They established their distilleries remote enough to avoid detection by
authorities but close enough to access the local population; at times the
latter collaborated with the former.[47]

When considering the location of stills, gender emerges as a salient
factor. Whereas men tended to set up their operations in ravines, mountains, or forests far from the traveled routes of authorities, women often
produced and sold moonshine in or around their homes.[48] Men's use of
the most remote areas to establish their businesses speaks to a broader indigenous resistance to state incursions into their daily lives. For ladino authorities, it provided a metaphor of barbarous indios fleeing civilization.[49]
In contrast, thanks to propriety and the notion that women's activities in
the home were beyond the purview of state officials, some clandestinistas
remained hidden in plain sight. To cite one particularly noteworthy example, in 1933 a widow and three men operated a still that produced over
six hundred bottles in the city of Quezaltenango without arousing the
"least suspicion" of authorities.[50] Even more so than the frequent raids
of smaller stills that yielded twenty-five to fifty bottles, the quantity of

aguardiente produced in this Quezaltenango home speaks to the magnitude of the illicit economy operating alongside the formal one. Like the textile industry, the production and sale of alcohol allowed women to work from home. Of course, once they did, female vendors' and producers' homes became public spaces where authorities could readily intrude.

Even when discovered, many women eluded authorities' grasps. Such was the case at the turn of the century when Fermina Fuentes, Lorenza de Mata, María Ochoa, and Trinidad Alemán went missing just as the police discovered that their homes were virtual distilleries.[51] Women who produced aguardiente clandestino on premises they rented were even more mobile.[52]

Fleet-footed clandestinistas notwithstanding, defying the law was risky. Police in Zacapa were on to the eighteen-year-old Adelina Cruz, whom they identified as a "very active *contrabandista*, with her cunning and audacity." In February 1933, they arrested her and three other women who sold aguardiente clandestino in the train station. As the base for the International Railroad of Central America, the Zacapa train station provided ample clientele. The *indígena* (indigene) Martina Boror was similarly brazen in her attempt to sell aguardiente clandestino in the public market. Authorities found four liters of it hidden in her basket of tomatoes.[53]

For those who operated close to home, avoiding detection demanded diverse strategies, particularly since the powerful and pungent smell of their products often betrayed clandestinistas' locations.[54] As mentioned above, some simply fled.[55] In an indication of how highly they valued their products, some refused to leave their goods behind. It was probably this miscalculation that allowed the police, who were alerted by the "strong *chicha* odors," to catch both Julian Sinto and Manuel Marroquín in 1932. Since each bottle was worth fifteen quetzales, Sinto tried to escape with the two he had just purchased and Marroquín tried to escape with his *garrafón*, which contained the equivalent of twenty-five bottles.[56] Others hid or buried their products.[57] One Kaqchikel female elder explains, "A long time ago, over fifty years ago, women made aguardiente and then hid it in the well with the water so when the *guardia* came they had no idea and would not find it. But some women were arrested and taken to jail for making moonshine."[58] Although her location too was eventually detected, María Baquiax (see figure 5.2, bottom image) camouflaged her still in the milpa around her house.[59] Deception by consumption was another option. Fearing that the foreign traveler Aldous Huxley and his party were government officials when they arrived at his home in 1933, the owner, who had been selling liquor without a license, drank his entire stock.[60]

The best scenario was to avoid authorities' gazes altogether. By their very nature, successful deceptions never made it into official documents. For these histories we turn to Kaqchikel historical narratives. Ixsimïl, a Kaqchikel elder, explained how those who escaped detection managed their operations:

> My grandparents prepared aguardiente only at night. They did not do it in the town or houses. They did it in the ravine. It was the same when I was preparing [it]; I would only bring it at night. At the same time, if you wanted to sell, it was always at night. They did everything at night. . . . Very late my grandfather would come down to town with vessels of *guaro* [moonshine]. He was not afraid during that time to walk at night; it was only that it was so late and he had to carry it on his back. . . . My grandparents just dedicated themselves to selling guaro. Their home was in a *callejon* [alley] where they could sell it. Eventually, they prepared it in their home because it was more profitable.[61]

Ironically, the same conditions that discouraged crime protected bootleggers. According to Kaqchikel historical narratives, people felt safe during Ubico's reign because he was tough on crime and particularly harsh with murderers, thieves, bootleggers, and drunkards. So omnipotent was the sense of security, many Kaqchikel did not lock their doors at night.[62] Yet as Ixsimïl's testimony reveals, bootleggers also felt safe moving about at night. In other words, bootleggers took advantage of Ubico's success against crime. Authorities were not always so easily duped, however. Even though he slept during the day and worked from nine p.m. until dawn, the police in Totonicapán caught Juan Macario García, a merchant turned clandestinista.[63]

Evidence of recidivists in the criminal record and Kaqchikel historical narratives intimate that for many moonshiners the business was too lucrative to abandon.[64] B'eleje' Imox, a Kaqchikel raconteur who spoke of the Ubico years as an idyllic time, recalls:

> Men and women both made k'uxa, but it was illegal. One man told me he did it and was caught by the Guardia de Hacienda. The first time he was caught, he got twenty-five lashes on his backside, which

was really fifty lashes because they did not count the ones on the way back. [B'eleje' Imox animatedly reenacted the whipping motion.] He had to walk to Guatemala City to get the punishment because back then they did not have cars. But on his way home, he bought two pounds of sugar and *afrecho* [bran] to make k'uxa again. He was caught a second time and got fifty lashes and a third time and got seventy-five lashes.[65]

Physical punishment, incarceration, and fines did little to dissuade some clandestinistas.

The Art of Detection

That indigenous communities balanced a desire to keep outside interference to a minimum with the occasional need (often coming from an individual) for government officials' assistance to maintain peace, resolve disputes, or seek revenge suggests that community members, more so than authorities, determined which bootleggers were caught. Although a preponderance of arrests in San Martín and Tecpán convinced police that these municipalities were hotbeds of moonshine production, perhaps this perception was exaggerated by rumors such as the aforementioned one recounted by Julian Catú.[66] Kaqchikel from neighboring towns could divert authorities' gaze from their own operations by pointing them toward San Martín. False tips could consume significant amounts of officials' energy and time. In October 1907, for example, when the Chimaltenango jefe político learned that a Tecpán couple was selling moonshine from a hole in the ground behind their store, he sent Treasury Police from two different towns to investigate. None turned up evidence of moonshine (or even a hole).[67] Often cooperation was motivated as much by inter- and intra-communal tensions as by a desire to collaborate with authorities. According to Kaqchikel historical narratives, some informants planted liquor on their enemies' properties to frame them.[68] An incident that occurred a few years after Estrada Cabrera's overthrow intimates the way such denuncias could tear communities apart. After Nicolás and María Atz and Simeona Cuzanero of San Martín had their equipment confiscated, they accused the widow Vicenta Huz of accepting a six-hundred-peso bribe from the municipality to denounce them. Their verbal abuse was so persistent and denigrating that Huz asked the mayor to intervene.[69]

Even during the more relaxed political climate of the 1920s, some local authorities vigorously pursued drunks and bootleggers. For example, "In order to comply with the obligations that the laws impose," Comalapa's municipal officers charged "the Municipality with tirelessly pursuing inebriation, vagrancy, the movement of illegal arms, gambling, [and] fiscal fraud."[70] The latter was largely the result of the aguardiente clandestino trade. Shedding light on the motives of Mayas who supported government intervention in the alcohol trade, the seventy-year-old *texel* (member of a religious sisterhood) Ix'eya' argued that such vigilance was warranted to curtail alcoholism and protect public health: "A long time ago it was prohibited to make k'uxa . . . [so] the vendors went to jail, and in those days, they washed the pot well to make k'uxa. It was clean, but now . . ."[71] Similarly, during her research in the early 1930s, anthropologist Ruth Bunzel found that some K'iche' in Chichicastenango supported "stricter enforcement of the licensing laws."[72]

Some officials became so desperate to stamp out aguardiente clandestino that they entrapped vendors. When in September 1930, the San Martín Rural Guard learned that someone in town was producing aguardiente, they sent an undercover agent to purchase a ten-peso bottle. Although she was grinding corn when the man arrived at her home, *la indígena* Francisca Popol immediately obliged his request. Having lived in town for only eleven days, she already knew that her neighbor Elvira Elías sold aguardiente. Unaware that Popol had purchased the bottle from Elías (at no profit to herself), the agent made the mistake of arresting Popol, whom the judge immediately set free (in part because the twenty-seven-year-old Elías testified on Popol's behalf).[73]

At times, drunks led authorities to vendors. One seventy-year-old texel recalls, "When a man asked for an *octavo* [an eighth], *la señora* [ladina] gave it to him. Then the soldiers arrived at her house to bring her to jail. Many days later the same thing happened to another señora. Later, women would not sell to drunks; they hid it from them and kicked them out of their doorways so they would not cause problems."[74] By using the term *señora*, Ixsub'äl downplayed the role of indigenous vendors. While middle- and upper-class ladinas were more likely to run state-sanctioned operations (because they could afford the licensing fees), as many indigenous as ladina women were arrested for selling aguardiente clandestino.[75] Unlike other areas of Guatemala where ladinos tended to dominate the alcohol trade,[76] in the highlands of Chimaltenango, enough Mayas were

QUEZALTENANGO Y ZACAPA

LA POLICIA NACIONAL EN SU TESONERA LABOR
PRO LOS INTERESES DEL FISCO

(Fotos para "La Gaceta").

Defraudadores a la Hacienda Pública en el Ramo de Licores

ARRIBA.—(A la izquierda). Nº 1, Cleopatra de Egipto Mazariegos, mujer a la que le fué decomisada por la Policía Nacional, de servicio en la ciudad de Quezaltenango, una fábrica de aguardiente clandestina. El decomiso se efectuó en casa de Cleopatra de Egipto, ubicada en el cantón La Democracia, de la ciudad de referencia. Quedó consignada la reo y a disposición de Juez competente. Nº 2, agente FIDEL MUÑOZ y Nº 3, agente ENRIQUE RODRÍGUEZ, quienes laboraron para el buen éxito de la aprehensión.
ARRIBA.—(A la derecha del lector).—ZACAPA.—La reo Rosa Morales, de 20 años de edad, soltera, originaria de Santa Cruz. de esta jurisdicción, hija natural de Cecilia Morales y de Francisco Aldana. Esta mujer, que había descollado como una de las

Figure 5.4. The headline reads, "Quezaltenango and Zacapa: The National Police in Its Tenacious Work in the Interest of the National Treasury." *Clockwise from top left*: officers pose with clandestinista Cleopatra de Egipto Mazariegos; the "cunning" clandestinista Rosa Morales; agents (numbers 4 and 5) stand behind three captured clandestinistas (numbers 1, 2, and 3). *La Gaceta: Revista de Policía y Variedades,* January 22, 1933. Image is reproduced courtesy of the Latin American Library, Tulane University, New Orleans.

producing and selling alcohol in its varied forms that Kaqchikel seldom were compelled to purchase their libations from ladinos, although, of course, many did.

To document their campaign and project an image of success, the National Police regularly used photographs. The January 22, 1933, edition of *La Gaceta* offers one example (see figure 5.4). In the top left photograph, the arresting officers proudly pose with Cleopatra de Egipto Mazariegos, who operated a still out of her home in Quezaltenango. Their colleagues (shown in the back of the lower photograph, numbers 4 and 5) similarly pose with other Quezaltenango bootleggers (standing beside the barrels, numbers 1, 2, and 3) and their decommissioned accoutrements in the photograph below. The photograph on the top right shows the twenty-year-old spinster Rosa Morales, who was "one of the most audacious and dangerous *clandestinistas*" in the area. As the caption explains, despite her "cunning," the police finally caught her. As Susan Sontag and others have observed, photography facilitates an illusion of objectivity, possession, and control. For police departments, photographing criminals and their wares also projected an image of efficacy.[77]

The description of Morales notwithstanding, despite women's prevalent role in the alcohol economy, authorities generally downplayed female infractions. Take, for example, the report by the National Police in the January 15, 1933, edition of *La Gaceta* (see figure 5.3). Photographs of agents posing with two male clandestinistas and their equipment draw the reader's attention to the article. One of the celebrated captives ran "a copper machine capable of producing 75 bottles of *aguardiente* a day." Although *la indígena* María Chan's operation had the same capacity, authorities considered hers "a little machine."[78]

Women's participation in the sale, distribution, and even production of contraband aguardiente belied state-sanctioned economic relations that privileged men. Despite Liberals' assumptions that men were the fundamental drivers of the economy, via their roles in public markets and the informal alcohol industry, women too were crucial contributors to highland economies. Although the state must have been aware of this (authorities constantly arrested and harassed female vendors and moonshiners), it never explicitly recognized the gendered component of Guatemala's economic development.[79] Wise to assumptions about women's diminutive status, female clandestinistas used such impressions to their advantage in the courtroom.

Distilling Perceptions of Crime

In an attempt to absolve themselves or mitigate their punishment, female defendants and their lawyers played on images of women as meek and naïve. Some complemented these images with the gendered language of motherhood. (Note the female clandestinista, María Baquiax, shown at the bottom of figure 5.2 with a baby strapped to her back). Although such rhetoric reinforced women's subordinate status, it also helped to reduce their sentences. In a shift from the late nineteenth century, when women commonly used the gendered defense that being illiterate and living a sequestered life precluded knowledge of the law, as the twentieth century wore on, female defendants increasingly embraced the law and developed narratives around their poverty to explain their transgressions. In this way, they were coyly putting the state on trial. For if defendants were hard working (as evidenced by their very crimes), then who was to blame for their indigence? Through their testimonies and very presence, defendants demonstrated that it was not laziness that led them to poverty but rather a lack of opportunities, resources, and such basic human rights as education. In the same way that clandestinistas who operated out of their homes in urban centers, set up shop in government buildings, or enjoyed the collusion of local officials were defying the laws in plain sight, defendants who voiced (however subtly) their disapproval of the state's hegemonic project in the courts too challenged the state right in the belly of the beast.

Unlike Manuel Escobar de León, who attacked agents with a knife when they arrested his wife on May 14, 1937, once caught most bootleggers went peacefully.[80] In contrast to other areas such as Chiapas, Mexico, where indigenous communities attacked police when they attempted to decommission stills, in Guatemala during the first half of the twentieth century such collective responses are notably absent in the archival record.[81] Not surprisingly, however, a number of bootleggers attempted bribery.[82] When confronted in court, the ladina widow María Coroy initially admitted to trying to bribe the officers, but then in a postmodern reversal she questioned whether it really could be considered bribery since she never indicated how much (or even what) she was offering them. Coroy further explained that she "did it [produced aguardiente] . . . because she believed she had not committed a crime."[83]

Whether Coroy was arguing that manufacturing aguardiente should be legal or that she was ignorant of the law is unclear, but she was not alone in either assertion. When arrested on January 26, 1900, the forty-five-year-old indigenous day laborer Agustín Muj insisted he did not know producing aguardiente was a crime. He added, "Since I saw ladinos doing it, I thought I would make a little."[84] Surely, this was not the form of *ladinoization* national leaders had in mind. In a nation that tended to idealize ladino behavior as the model of citizenship, perhaps Muj was suggesting that who was he, a simple Indian, to suspect that following the example of a ladino would put him in trouble with the law? Did not ladinos epitomize civilization and the rule of law? Of course, he may have been intimating that authorities looked the other way for ladino bootleggers or that because of their socioeconomic positions ladinos could afford the state's licensing fees. Whatever his underlying message(s), Muj drew the judge's attention to injustices.

Echoing the naiveté if not innocence of earlier bootleggers who claimed ignorance of the law, some defendants assured the courts that this was their first attempt to make moonshine; a few went so far as to claim they were not even certain they had done it correctly. No one wanted to convey expertise. When the police arrested Domingo Abac of Momostenango in a house he was renting, he insisted he was "*un Pichón*" (young pigeon/darling) who had just begun learning the trade. The police quipped that now "his wings were clipped."[85] In turn, when asked how many bottles she had produced prior to the Rural Guards' arrival, the thirty-three-year-old widow Maxima Sical responded, "Not even one bottle. The first time I was going to begin, the *resguardo* prevented me."[86]

Some described their first attempt as a last-ditch effort to survive. Since the forty-five-year-old widow Dolores Fiatz was monolingual, she relied on an interpreter to convey her sense of desperation: "Even though she had worked it [the still] one time, because she did not know how, she did not produce any *aguardiente*. Due to her poverty, she dared to do something that she had never attempted before."[87] By insisting that they were first-time offenders, defendants demonstrated that their goal was never to manage a permanent operation but rather a desperate attempt to escape their indigence. As the twenty-one-year-old Adela Barrabute admitted in 1916, "It is true I was making moonshine. It is the first time I have experimented with making it . . . and I did not have the intention of establishing a business, only to succor my needs."[88]

Although they did not abandon the language of domesticity, many female defendants emphasized their poverty.[89] For Mayas and poor ladinos,
the courtroom provided one of the only venues for them to inform the
state of their privations. In truth, the illicit production and sale of alcohol could provide a modest income. By enlightening judges and authorities about the struggles of poor rural denizens, bootleggers pointed out
that their behavior was rational and just. Read this way, defendants were
doing more than just highlighting their inferior status to gain a judge's
sympathy; they were arguing that the law itself was unjust and that the
government's failure to provide for its citizens was criminal. These narratives resonate with Kaqchikel oral histories. Ixkotz'i'j, a female elder, recalled, "My father made k'uxa because we were poor. What else could we
do? And he was taken away by the guardia."[90] Like the many indigenous
defendants and witnesses who mentioned poverty but never explicitly articulated what the consequences of such oppression might be, she rhetori-
cally asked, "What else could we do?" What the state and ladinos feared
was revolt.

A number of Guatemalan intellectuals similarly critiqued the alcohol
laws. In 1931, Flavio Guillén wrote,

> The distillation of intoxicating liquor is no longer a crime when it
> covers the fiscal rights; but the confiscating apparatuses, closing
> down the still and imprisoning the producer, come down without
> mercy when the production takes place without the prior permis-
> sion of the Treasury; this [money] is . . . given to the Treasury for
> official ostentation and waste. Therefore, drinking is not a crime,
> nor the sale of this lethal liquid, nor its distillation. The crime is in
> the government's refusal to part with the earnings from this brutish
> money. That is a despicable crime. . . . That is a crime of the state.[91]

Although Guillén's perspective differed from that of bootleggers in that
he hoped to reduce alcohol production and consumption, both pointed
to the hypocrisy and futility of the state's effort. As an elite male who
was not on trial, Guillén could be more explicit in his critique than indigenous defendants. But Kaqchikel oral histories also indicate that few
Kaqchikel considered producing and selling alcohol a crime. "The seller is
not to blame. The one who looks for it [aguardiente] is to blame," asserted
Ixsub'äl, a seventy-year-old texel.[92]

To underscore their poverty, most offenders and their legal counsel claimed they were simply trying to support their families. In 1901, the Chimaltenango departmental court scribe noted one twenty-year-old woman's reasons for making moonshine in her father's home in Tecpán: "Her necessities are so ominous that they obligate her to produce a little *aguardiente clandestino* to alleviate something. . . . [O]nly in this manner can she earn a living and provide for her family."[93]

Many female defendants and their lawyers combined descriptions of their poverty with the gendered discourse of motherhood. The lawyer for the forty-four-year-old widow Petrona Espanderas noted, "As the defendant is a single woman with ten children all minors and crippled who live off the personal work of the defendant, she saw the need to establish a still to produce *aguardiente clandestino* in her house."[94] Women also appealed to their roles as mothers to get out on bail as did the aforementioned Coroy, for example, when she insisted "the prison that I suffer is great because my poor children, who are minors, are essentially abandoned because today they lack the mother who I am."[95]

In a reflection of poor, indigenous, female plaintiffs' ability to alter penal decisions, judges found their arguments about poverty compelling. After reading the aforementioned *molendera* Dolores Fiatz's testimony about her poverty, the Chimaltenango judge allowed her to commute half of her three-month sentence and waived her legal fees due to her "highly evident poverty."[96] Unlike many of his contemporaries, however, he ignored her plea to be let out on bail, perhaps because unlike some of her counterparts, as a forty-five-year-old widow, Fiatz did not or could not claim she had young children at home who needed her maternal care.

Following the lead of her counsel, Fiatz pursued another strategy to reduce her sentence. "According to the experts," she noted, "the value of the objects that they apprehended from me were only worth seven pesos. The penalty that should be imposed on me would be two months less according to what is laid down in the precept of article 128 of the liquors law."[97]

For an illiterate, monolingual indigenous woman, Fiatz was well versed in the details of the liquor law. Instead of claiming ignorance of it, Fiatz used her knowledge of the law to mount her defense and then negotiate her punishment. She worked closely with her court-appointed lawyer, who argued, "[T]he crime for which you have processed my defendant is of such little importance that I believe that the prison suffered and the express circumstances in the first, third and fourth clauses of article 125 of the liquor law proceed her immediate release."[98] Both Fiatz and her lawyer insisted that the punishment did not fit the crime. Based on the judge's detailed ruling, however, their references to the law did little to change his mind. After paying the commutable rate for half her sentence, Fiatz was released from Chimaltenango's women's jail on January 15, 1908, about a month and a half after she was arrested. By drawing attention to both her poverty and the excessive nature of the punishment, Fiatz and her lawyer pointed out the injustice of a system that imprisoned poor people for trying to improve their lot.

Like Fiatz, other defendants also pointed out the low value of the goods confiscated to emphasize both their poverty and the insignificance of their crime. Even witnesses occasionally made this point. When he testified on behalf of María Coroy, Francisco Ruano implored the court "not to sentence her for the very little that they found, [moreover] she (la Coroy) has cooperated fully."[99]

As subjects of gender, class, and ethnic discrimination, some poor indigenous women indicated that they did not even have access to the resources needed to commit the crime. Lorenza Tuch's lawyer argued as much when he tried to convince the court that the still the police found in her home in June 1901 could not be hers:

It is true they found the apparatus that produces *aguardiente*, but from this you cannot deduce that Tuch is the defrauder, because being *indígena* and a *molendera* [corn miller], it would not make sense for her to do something that was outside of her station. Neither can you conceive that she would have the money to install a still. As you know, one needs many resources and knowledge. For these reasons, I think that Tuch is not guilty and in light of that I ask you to absolve these crimes that have been formulated, and set her free.[100]

In short, how could a person who was ignorant, poor, and lacking social capital establish her own business? The irony, of course, is that according to both the criminal record and oral histories, many poor indigenous women did. Nonetheless, in this case, even though the judge did not reduce the length of Tuch's three-month sentence, he cut the commutable rate in half and waived some of her legal fees due to her "highly evident poverty."[101] Such gestures were not insignificant. In 1909, when authorities arrested Angel María Ruano and Eduardo Estrada for their still, it cost them four hundred pesos each to get out of jail.[102]

Although male defendants like the aforementioned indigenous *jornalero* Agustín Muj too argued that poverty compelled them to produce aguardiente clandestino, they crafted their narratives differently than women.[103] Like nineteenth-century Q'anjob'alan Maya in Schwarztkopf's chapter, early twentieth-century Kaqchikel men often related the production (and consumption) of aguardiente to custom and tradition, as Francisco Calel's case demonstrates. Aware that aguardiente clandestino was illegal, Calel hid his stash under some rags on his bed. When the *regidor* and two *indígenas* searched his house in Comalapa on September 24, 1902, they found it. The notary penned Calel's explanation: "About a month ago *su mujer* [his woman] Rosa Morales bought from an individual from San Martin Jilotepeque a *garafón* [demijohn] containing aguardiente, for the price of fifteen pesos. They used the aguardiente in a wedding *festividad* [festivity] that they had in their house . . . the little that was left over [was] what had been confiscated."[104] In his effort to subtly challenge the alcohol laws by pointing out aguardiente's ceremonial use, Calel was careful to offer some specific details such as the alcohol's price (fifteen pesos) and origin (San Martín) while omitting others such as the individual's name and whether it was produced and sold illegally. Unfortunately for Calel, pointing out that authorities and laws criminalized indigenous customary practices held as little sway in twentieth-century Chimaltenango as it did in nineteenth-century Huehuetenango.

Calel's appeal to be let out on bail demonstrates another way men's narrative strategies differed from women's. Instead of emphasizing the effect their incarceration would have on their families, most men warned of the damage it would do to their business interests. Seldom did they claim their crimes were insignificant, as women often did.[105] Even though patriarchal power diminished as one descended the socioeconomic ladder, poor indigenous men held privileged positions vis-à-vis indigenous women and therefore refrained from presenting themselves as powerless. When asking to be let out on bail, Calel explained to the judge that his imprisonment caused his "small interests to be completely abandoned."[106] Instead of saying he was destitute, the fifty-eight-year-old Guatemalteco pointed out that he had humble yet important matters to attend to.

Asserting that one had important (presumably economic) "interests" had its drawbacks, however, since it generally precluded judges from waiving legal fees or setting low bails. Nonetheless, the judge must have been sufficiently impressed with Calel's testimony; he set the bail at 150 pesos—quite a bit more reasonable than other bails, which were set as high as 400 pesos for moonshining during the Estrada Cabrera years. When the thirty-one-year-old farmer Laureano Mich posted bail on October 15, 1902, Calel was freed three weeks after he had been incarcerated. He was far from absolved, however. Over two years later, on May 2, 1905, the Chimaltenango departmental judge ordered Calel to return to court for further questioning regarding the case. As Calel's bondsman, Mich was responsible for making sure he showed up.[107]

Cantina Perils

Cantina owners and other aguardiente vendors were generally ambivalent toward authorities. Although they turned to the state's police and judicial institutions when they felt affronts against them warranted it, often they preferred to keep the state out of their business. Naturally, their interest in the state's intervention depended on the circumstances involved and power contested. The extent to which their places were damaged, clients endangered, or reputations and safety threatened largely determined how proprietors responded to the crisis at hand. Since one's reputation affected business in small highland towns, cantina owners had to be careful when and why they invited authorities' interventions.

In turn, the police were not eager to be involved in every altercation that took place in these establishments. Upon getting a license to play marimba in her bar, the widow Marcela de Rodríguez learned she was "taking responsibility for any disorder that might occur in her establishment, if not reported to the authorities."[108] Even though officials preferred that owners deal with minor disturbances themselves, if altercations turned violent, police reprimanded owners for not calling them. Salvador Rubio learned as much when he was fined for injuring a rowdy client whom he tried to remove from his cantina on Christmas Eve 1933.[109]

Once women (and men) converted their abodes into drink shops, their homes became public venues.[110] As such, cantina owners could not (and at times did not want to) shield drunks from the police, as Manuel

González learned when he was arrested for scandalous intoxication in "La Selecta."[111] The more violent the incident, the more likely proprietors were to solicit authorities, as was the case when a drunk merchant from Chichicastenango began smashing dishes and destroying the aguardiente dispensary in Francisco Ruiz's home.[112] For Ruiz and others, the knowledge that at times bartenders and aguardiente vendors were attacked and in rare cases even killed must have encouraged them to call for help.[113]

Despite the dangers of their professions, bartenders, vendors, and owners did not necessarily call upon the police to settle altercations, nor did they always offer their cooperation. As the owner of a *chicharía* at the turn of the century, the twenty-seven-year-old bachelorette Juana Lopéz regularly flirted with violence. When an "unknown *indito*" attacked the musician Cayetano Matamba in the entrance of her establishment, Lopéz claimed not to know anything about the aggressor. Whether she was protecting an indigenous patron or simply did not want to get involved in the dispute is unknowable, but her reaction to it disclosed the composure of someone familiar with fights.[114] Since a successful business was dependent on loyal customers, owners often stood by their regulars. When authorities asked Petrona Quiñones, a sixty-year-old widow who sold aguardiente out of her home in Patzicía, if Jesús Mutzutz had been at her cantina the night Valeriano Sisimit attacked him with a machete, she replied, "Jesús Mutzutz came to my house. Well, he always comes."[115] Clearly, she knew her indigenous clients well. The 1907 altercation between Sisimit and Mutzutz also revealed that indigenous residents did not necessarily turn to the police to resolve conflicts. When José Choy witnessed the fight break out, he ran to get his mother for help.[116]

Although cantinas and other alcohol dispensaries were often the sites of violence, owners and clientele understood that in general a certain level of decorum and respect should be maintained in these establishments.[117] When Isaías Higueros Álvarez insulted Josefa de Mata in her cantina, she took him to court. Because the judge agreed with de Mata that neither Higueros Álvarez's inebriation nor amnesia exculpated him, he spent four days in jail.[118] Since highland cantinas tended to be small and their clientele local, maintaining a favorable reputation was crucial for business and partly contingent upon upholding the owner's sense of honor.

In turn, neither did clients take insults from bar owners lightly. Manuel Meses took Nicolasa Corona to court in 1923 because when he arrived at her cantina, Corona spoke "very grave words . . . saying I was [a] *sinvergüenza* (shameless scoundrel)," for taking advantage of the inebriated woman who had accompanied him the night before.[119] Even in the cantina, this "accusation threatens me (in regards to) my behavior and social position."[120] Drunks too were sensitive to insults. When asked why he hit Francisca Xico in the head in front of her husband, Julio Merece told the court, "I hit her because she was making fun of me for being drunk."[121] Despite being held in disdain by some, what was said and done in cantinas, bars, and other alcohol dispensaries mattered especially because news of what transpired in them often spread throughout the community. Since many proprietors preferred to keep the state at bay, the criminal and judicial record provides only a partial view of this crucial aspect of highland social relations.

Conclusion

Distillers and vendors of aguardiente clandestino established a parallel economy. Whether moonshiners simply survived or thrived on their profits, their motives and means mirrored that of the state. Both used the avenue of alcohol production (whether directly or indirectly) to turn a profit. Since the state and its charges approached the alcohol economy with similar strategies, goals, and priorities, the potential for collaboration and cooperation was omnipresent. Only the possession of a license separated licit from illicit activity, and at times authorities were willing to overlook this detail. That the dominant theme in the archival record was conflict did not make such relations inevitable. By its nature, the archival record captures conflict. Because they were neither extraordinary nor sensational, collaborative relations seldom were documented.

Perhaps more than any other type of criminal litigation, bootlegging cases evoke a relatively peaceful, stable, and orderly world that operated both outside and alongside the law-abiding one. Indeed, as Reeves suggests in this volume with his analysis of Ostuncalco's nineteenth-century authorities who opposed legal aguardiente monopolists while tolerating clandestinistas, in the twentieth century too it was the threat of state intervention implied by the physical presence of the legal, licensed aguardiente producers and vendors that held the potential to destabilize the tranquility of rural communities.

Although few Guatemalans might have perceived it as such, the alcohol economy helped to shape the nation by bringing disparate parties together through exchanges that were both confrontational and cooperative. Even through conflict, indigenous subalterns and ladino authorities were getting to know, if not respect, one another. The judicial record indicates that at least a few judges came to empathize with indigenous defendants. For some intellectuals, the state was compromised by its involvement in the alcohol economy. According to Juárez Muñoz, if the state remained dependent on "money that brings with it so much misery," then "we will never be a nation."[122] In contrast, government leaders like Estrada Cabrera and Ubico believed alcohol revenue was essential to creating a nation that could proudly portray itself as modern. Only with those funds could the state build infrastructure that would impress foreign investors. Similarly, historian Lowell Gudmundson argues that moonshine revenues were "central to Guatemala's process of state formation."[123]

For the Estrada Cabrera and Ubico dictatorships, the pursuit of aguardiente clandestino represented an attempt to impose their order in the most remote and isolated parts of the nation. By the early twentieth century the state was becoming strong enough to begin contemplating shifting its focus from ladinos to indígenas even if it was far from doing so with any success. Following the late nineteenth-century Liberal Reforma, this effort coincided with a transformation in the definition of citizenship from the hierarchical caste system followed by the Conservative state to a more universal (and exclusionary) understanding of citizenship based on ladino identities and norms.[124]

To a certain extent, the many police and other personnel who all but admitted the futility of trying to eradicate aguardiente clandestino speak to the weakness of the state in many parts of the country. Bootleggers who established their stills on communal land in "rough and thorny terrain" constantly frustrated authorities. Even in regional centers of state power, moonshiners often held the upper hand. Women used notions of femalehood to operate out of their homes in busy towns and cities. The most brazen offenders established their businesses in government buildings. All these acts helped to shape the nation, by letting authorities know that no matter how powerful or fearful they appeared under brutal dictatorships, resistance or defiance would accompany the hegemonic project.

At the same time, permitting a little resistance goes a long way in letting off steam and preventing the serious challenges to its power that the government wanted to avoid at all costs.[125] Stills are a good example of this lower-level resistance. Certainly the government wanted to collect alcohol revenues, and many individual functionaries pursued convictions with great zeal. In addition, the fines paid by those found guilty enriched government coffers. Yet some officials also understood (through clandestinistas' comments and testimonies) that most indígenas and poor ladinos could not afford to purchase licenses or, for that matter, legal alcohol. Removing aguardiente clandestino entirely would cause upheaval in the countryside and upset the economic system by which enganchadores recruited laborers. The sale of aguardiente clandestino was also an important source of revenue flow in highland villages. Even if the state could not directly access it, this revenue fed into local and regional economic systems through, for example, the purchase of brass bands and rental of horses for fiestas. In short, to cut off aguardiente clandestino completely would have caused a contagion of negative intended and unintended consequences. The local collaboration and complicity that ranged from corrupt officials looking the other way to authorities establishing their own illicit operations was as much driven by personal interest as this knowledge. Nonetheless, this collusion partly stemmed from the state's ambivalence about the efficacy of its alcohol policies, which in turn made enforcement spotty by design. "La Muncipalidad" still in Tecpán and those in the Treasury building in Quezaltenango lend credence to this suggestion.

The government's inability to eradicate aguardiente clandestino parallels its failings in other areas, such as efforts to compel Mayas to abandon their culture for ladino or Western norms. At the same time, the government did make some inroads in these projects. Just as some Mayas took on ladino attributes, so too did the state capture some bootleggers. Yet once captured, moonshiners often further challenged the hegemonic project by pointing out the state's failings and subtly suggesting solutions of social justice. Their testimonies in court and statements to authorities before arriving there can be read as efforts by indígenas and poor ladinos to let the state know they understood the system (and even specifically the laws); they also sought to inform the state about their own lives and ideas of justice. By emphasizing poverty, they drew judges' and other authorities' attention to what they considered to be one of the fundamental ills in Guatemalan society.

The police, judges, and other officials who listened to these perspectives and at times acted in accordance with them helped to maintain social order. For it was through airing their grievances and at times gaining concessions, however limited, that indigenous women and other marginalized Guatemalans enjoyed a sense that they were both part of the nation and held the potential to benefit from its institutions. Even while calling the state's authority into question, defendants used the government's tools to further their own goals and thus buttressed the state's and the legal system's legitimacy. Especially in remote areas where the state's presence was intermittent at best, the legal system's efficacy shored up the state's standing even as it remained weak.

The multiple and varied interactions both inside and outside the courtroom contributed to an increased awareness between marginalized peoples and the state's representatives, some of whom were not so removed from the reality they policed and judged. This growing experiential knowledge among subalterns, interlocutors, and hegemons contributed to the development of a nation that, if not united, was in some areas and at some levels getting to know its distinct features. Nation-state formation seldom reflected what subalterns or hegemons had envisioned. This ongoing process was full of fits and starts and disappointing, even tragic, developments. The different perceptions of what was just and unjust, legal and illegal informed these interactions and shaped the nation. That poor indigenous women were contributing to this process during two of Latin America's harshest dictatorships speaks to the influence of marginalized people during extraordinary times.

Acknowledgments

Research for this essay was made possible by grants from the American Historical Association, John Anson Kittredge Educational Fund, and University of Southern Maine. Comments and critiques on earlier drafts of this chapter from Frederick Smith, René Reeves, Allen Wells, Ginny Garrard-Burnett, and Todd Little-Siebold helped me to sharpen its focus and argument. I also wish to acknowledge the memory of Stephen, Mary, Bob, and Jay O'Brien, whose zest for happy hours first planted the seed that a book of this nature would be worthwhile, enlightening, and engaging.

Notes

1. *Diario de Centro América*, December 8, 1932.

2. *Diario de Centro América*, December 13, 1932. In nineteenth-century documents, Quezaltenango is spelled as such; however, some twentieth-century Guatemalan

newspapers spelled the name as "Quetzaltenango," with a *t* preceding the *z*. In his *Diccionario geografico de Guatemala* (vol. 3), Francis Gall spells both the department and the city without the first *t*. For the sake of consistency in this volume, I follow Gall's and common nineteenth-century spelling. However, when I am quoting a source, I leave the spelling in its original form.

3. McCreery, *Rural Guatemala*, 176–79; Buffington, "Prohibition in the Borderlands," 28. Even before the Liberal revolution, perhaps as much as 25 percent of the government's income was generated by alcohol taxes. See Reeves, *Ladinos with Ladinos*, 116, 227n47. Also see chapter 2, note 17, in the present volume.

4. Garrard-Burnett, "Indians Are Drunks," 350–53. During the Ubico period, the quetzal was pegged to the U.S. dollar.

5. Juárez Muñoz, *El indio Guatemalteco*, 84–85.

6. *La Gaceta*, June 21, 1931.

7. As Peter Mancall shows in *Deadly Medicine,* his fine study of indigenous people and alcohol in the colonial United States, many colonists (excepting religious leaders) lauded the alcohol trade for its ability to draw indigenous peoples into the capitalist marketplace and thus "civilize" them.

8. Bunzel, "Role of Alcoholism," 362–63; Bunzel, *Chichicastenango*, 258, 259; McCreery, *Rural Guatemala*, 176, 293–94; Cambranes, *Coffee and Peasants,* 110; Colby and van de Berghe, *Ixil Country,* 72–73; Stoll, *Between Two Armies,* 33; Eber, *Women and Alcohol,* 28–29; Adams, "Guatemala," 100–101.

9. Archivo General de Centro América (hereafter AGCA), Jefatura Política de Chimaltenango (hereafter JPC), 1944, Legajo (hereafter Leg.) 88A, Sanidad no. 72, María Rogelia Gálvez Roca, March 17; Roselía Ruano de Roca, January 27; Paula Hernández, April 20; Beatriz Álvarez, April 16; AGCA, Indice 116, Chimaltenango 1901, Leg. 2f, Exp. 45; Reeves, *Ladinos with Ladinos*, 124. In the mid-twentieth century, one ladina cantina owner earned enough to make 500-peso ($5.00) loans to local men. See Reina, *Law of the Saints,* 292.

10. For other examples of entrepreneurs establishing their liquor booths (and blasting music) near the church, see La Farge, *Santa Eulalia,* 91, 97.

11. Lewis, "La guerra del posh," 131.

12. Garrard-Burnett, "Indians Are Drunks," 352–54. Recall that *indio* is a pejorative term deployed by nonindigenous Guatemalans to denigrate *indígenas* (indigenous people).

13. *Memoria de la Secretaría de Gobernación y Justicia 1940, presentada 1941* (Guatemala: Tipografía Nacional, 1941), 113.

14. *Memoria de los trabajos realizados por la dirección general de la Policía Nacional durante el año de 1940* (Guatemala: Tipografía Nacional, 1941), 31 (emphasis in the original).

15. Garrard-Burnett, "Indians Are Drunks," 354. In contrast, for the nineteenth century, Reeves argues that since the state had a much greater presence in urban ladino areas, illegal ladino enterprises were much likely to be detected than (rural) Maya ones. See Reeves, *Ladinos with Ladinos,* 121.

16. Reeves, *Ladinos with Ladinos.*

17. Sanders, *Contentious Republicans,* 15, 52, 53; Kennedy, "Role of Beer"; Taylor, *Drinking, Homicide, and Rebellion,* 38, 53, 54; Eber, *Women and Alcohol,* 7, 22, 33; Ericastilla and Jiménez, "Las clandestinistas de aguardiente"; Reeves, *Ladinos with Ladinos,* 106, 111–12, 116–24; Gudmundson, "Firewater, Desire," 257–65; Schwartzkopf, "Maya Power and State Culture"; McCreery, *Rural Guatemala*; Reiche, "Estudio sobre el patrón," 121; Bunzel, *Chichicastenango,* 255; Colson and Scudder, *For Prayer and Profit.*

18. Lacoste, "Wine and Women," 365, 386, 391; Hames, "Maize-Beer, Gossip and Slander"; Rebolledo, "Pícaras y pulperas."

19. Reiche, "Estudio sobre el patrón," 110, 123.

20. McCreery, *Rural Guatemala,* 87–88, 176–77; Reeves, *Ladinos with Ladinos,* 104, 116, 227n47; González Alzate, "History of Los Altos," 141–48; Bunzel, "Role of Alcoholism," 363, 386; Gudmundson, "Firewater, Desire," 254–55n30; Ingersoll, "War of the Mountain"; Schwartzkopf, "Maya Power and State Culture." For evidence of indigenous communities resisting the Mexican state's attempt to impose monopolies in the twentieth century, see Eber, *Women and Alcohol,* 31.

21. Yarrington, "Román Cárdenas"; Márquez, "Stamp Tax on Alcoholic Beverages."

22. Pompejano, *La crisis de antiguo régimen*; Reeves, *Ladinos with Ladinos,* 133, 135; Schwartzkopf, "Maya Power and State Culture."

23. Reeves, *Ladinos with Ladinos,* 116, 122, 123; McCreery, *Rural Guatemala*; Gudmundson, "Firewater, Desire," 261–62; Ericastilla and Jiménez, "Las clandestinistas de aguardiente," 14–15. Interestingly, early Liberals under the Mariano Gálvez government (1831–38) largely conceded the loss of revenue to local distillers by recognizing that most did not pay taxes. See Wortman, *Government and Society,* 254, 256.

24. McCreery, *Rural Guatemala,* 87–88, 176–77; Reeves, *Ladinos with Ladinos,* 104, 116, 227n47; Pompejano, *La crisis de antiguo régimen,* 16; González Alzate, "History of Los Altos," 141–48; Bunzel, "Role of Alcoholism," 363, 386; Gudmundson, "Firewater, Desire," 254–55n30; Ingersoll, "War of the Mountain"; Schwartzkopf, "Maya Power and State Culture." As Reeves points out in this volume, the Conservatives made a similar push to enforce alcohol laws during their rule in the 1850s.

25. In an indication of how differently rural denizens experienced the early twentieth-century state, Estrada Cabrera granted amnesty to clandestinistas in Quetzaltenango. See Ericastilla and Jiménez, "Las clandestinistas de aguardiente," 21.

26. AGCA, JPC, 1930, Leg. 73, carta de Jefe Político de Chimaltenango al alcalde de San Martín Jilotepeque, October 11, 1930. In a marked departure from his colleagues, one departmental governor tried to convince his superiors that drunken behavior ultimately cost the state more money than it made through monopolies and taxes. See Reeves, *Ladinos with Ladinos,* 128.

27. AGCA, JPC, 1931, carta al Señor Alcalde Primero Municipal, October 31, 1931.

28. *La Gaceta,* June 1, 1931. During the nineteenth century, the state used monies from fines and the sale of confiscated property and equipment to reward informants. See Reeves, *Ladinos with Ladinos,* 131.

29. *Diario de Centro América,* April 22, 1933.

30. Archivo Municipal de Sololá, "Libro de actas de sesiones municipales del 1-10-35 al 10-6-43," March 22, 1937 (92–93).

31. Reiche, "Estudio sobre el patrón," 106; McCreery, *Rural Guatemala*, 178–79.

32. *La Gaceta*, May 24, 1931; *La Gaceta*, June 7, 1931.

33. Scott, *Domination*.

34. McCreery, *Rural Guatemala*, 384n79; *Diario de Centro América*, July 29, 1933. For examples of military assistance in the effort to stamp out clandestinismo, see *Diario de Centro América*, December 8 and 13, 1932, and February 24, March 27, and August 18, 1933.

35. Reeves also points to the collusion between local authorities and clandestinistas, so common in the mid-nineteenth century, in *Ladinos with Ladinos*, 106.

36. In a noteworthy comparison from Mexico, the early twentieth-century leader in the Yucatán Bartolomé García Correa enriched himself by using his congressional and even gubernatorial positions to hide his illegal alcohol business. See Fallaw, "Bartolomé García Correa," 561, 562, 564.

37. AGCA, Indice 116, Chimaltenango 1902, Leg. 3F, Exp. 20; AGCA, Indice 116, Chimaltenango 1902, Leg. 3, Exp. 37. See also AGCA, Indice 116, Chimaltenango 1902, Leg. 3F, Exp. 35; and Oxlajuj Ajpu,' 1/19/98, Panabajal, Comalapa, for examples of *comandantes de resguardo* coming from afar and locals serving as their *orejas* (informants, literally ears).

38. *Diario de Centro América*, March 15, 1933. See also *Diario de Centro América*, December 21, 1932.

39. AGCA, Indice 116, Chimaltenango 1903, Leg. 4D, Exp. 47; *Diario de Centro América*, July 22, 1933.

40. AGCA, Indice 116, Chimaltenango 1907, Leg. 8C, Exp. 10.

41. AGCA, Indice 116, Chimaltenango 1900, Leg. 1G, Exp. 41.

42. AGCA, Indice 116, Chimaltenango 1902, Leg. 3F, Exp. 35. See also AGCA, Indice 116, Chimaltenango 1900, Leg. G, Exp. 41.

43. Ix'ey, 6/25/03, Comalapa. As Taylor demonstrates for colonial Mexico, the social meaning of alcohol was intimately connected to the place where it was produced. See Taylor, *Drinking, Homicide, and Rebellion*, 156–57.

44. *Diario de Centro América*, July 29, 1933.

45. *La Gaceta*, June 21, 1931. See also *La Gaceta*, June 30, 1931.

46. *La Gaceta*, February 5, 1933.

47. Wilkinson, *Silence on the Mountain*, 234.

48. To cite one example, whereas Eduarda Colaz was arrested for having a still in her home, Juan Álvarez escaped the police's grasp when agents discovered his still in a canyon. See *La Gaceta*, February 5, 1933. In their study of clandestinistas in Quezaltenango at the turn of the century, Ana Carla Ericastilla and Liseth Jiménez also found that most women operated out of their homes. See Ericastilla and Jiménez, "Las clandestinistas de aguardiente," 16.

49. McCreery, *Rural Guatemala*, 167.

50. *Diario de Centro América*, January 26, 1933.

51. AGCA, Indice 116, Chimaltenango 1900, Leg. 1A, Exp. 36; AGCA, Indice 116, Chimaltenango 1900, Leg. 1D, Exp. 3; AGCA, Indice 116, Chimaltenango 1901, Leg. 2, Exp. 9.

52. AGCA, Indice 116, Chimaltenango 1901, Leg. 2F, Exp. 40.

53. *La Gaceta*, February 5 and 19, 1933.

54. *La Gaceta*, January 1, 1933; Ericastilla and Jiménez, "Las clandestinistas de aguardiente," 16.

55. AGCA, Indice 116, Chimaltenango 1900, Leg. 1A, Exp. 36; AGCA, Indice 116, Chimaltenango 1900, Leg. 1D, Exp. 3; AGCA, Indice 116, Chimaltenango 1901, Leg. 2, Exp. 9; AGCA, Indice 116, Chimaltenango 1916, Leg. 17A, Exp. 3.

56. *La Gaceta*, January 1, 1933.

57. Ibid.; *La Gaceta*, March 26, 1933; Ericastilla and Jiménez, "Las clandestinistas de aguardiente," 16.

58. Ixte,' 8/5/05, Comalapa.

59. *La Gaceta*, June 1, 1941.

60. Huxley, *Beyond the Mexique Bay*, 160–61. For further evidence of this strategy, see Reiche, "Estudio sobre el patrón," 110–11.

61. Ixsimïl, 2/9/05, Comalapa (Ix'ey).

62. Carey, *Our Elders Teach Us,* 206–11.

63. *La Gaceta*, February 19, 1933.

64. See, for example, Vidal Porras's recurrent offenses, documented in AGCA, Indice 116, Chimaltenango 1920–23, Leg. 21, Exp. 20 and Exp. 21.

65. B'eleje' Imox, 6/5/03, Comalapa.

66. *La Gaceta*, February 5, 1933.

67. AGCA, Indice 116, Chimaltenango 1907, Leg. 8b, Exp. 12.

68. Carey, *Our Elders Teach Us*, 210.

69. AGCA, JPC, 1927, Leg. 70A, Escritos presentados por la personas a la Municipalidad de San Martín Jilotepeque, 1927.

70. Archivo Municipal de San Juan Comalapa, "Municipalidad de San Juan Comalapa Libro para actas de sesiones ordinaries y extraordinarias comenzado el 23 de julio de 1928 terminado 1 de enero de 1930," April 19, 1929.

71. Ix'eya,' 8/10/05, Comalapa (Ix'ey).

72. Bunzel, "Role of Alcoholism," 386.

73. AGCA, JPC, 1930, Leg. 73, Indígena Francisca Popol, San Martín Jilotepeque, September 10, 1930. For evidence of such strategies in Quezaltenango, see Ericastilla and Jiménez, "Las clandestinistas de aguardiente," 16.

74. Ixsub'äl, 8/23/05, Comalapa (Ix'ey). Kaqchikel use the term *señora* to denote ladinas.

75. AGCA, Indice 116; *Memoria de los trabajos realizados por la dirección general de la Policía Nacional* (Guatemala: Tipografía Nacional), 1940–44.

76. Bunzel, "Role of Alcoholism," 362; Lincoln, "Ethnographic Study."

77. Sontag, *On Photography*, 156; Tagg, "Evidence, Truth and Order"; Griffiths, *Wondrous Difference*, esp. chap. 3.

78. *La Gaceta*, January 15, 1933.

79. Carey, "'Hard Working, Orderly Little Women.'"

80. Archivo Municipal de Patzicía (hereafter AMP), paquete (hereafter Paq.) 27, Juzgado de Paz Patzicía, 1935, May 14, 1937. See also *La Gaceta,* January 1, 1933, for Adrián Alesio's "grave threats against the police" when his still was confiscated.

81. Lewis, "La guerra del posh," 119, 121.

82. *La Gaceta*, June 1, 1931.

83. AGCA, Indice 116, Chimaltenango 1918, Leg. 19, Exp. 34.

84. AGCA, Indice 116, Chimaltenango 1900, Leg. G, Exp. 75.

85. *La Gaceta*, January 15, 1933.

86. AGCA, Indice 116, Chimaltenango 1902, Leg. 3F, Exp. 20.

87. AGCA, Indice 116, Chimaltenango 1907, Leg. 8B, Exp. 22. For similar arguments about poverty and inexperience from Quezaltecas, see Ericastilla and Jiménez, "Las clandestinistas de aguardiente," 20.

88. AGCA, Indice 116, Chimaltenango 1916, Leg. 17, Exp. 18. Even given the inexpensive nature of such accoutrements as *ollas* (pots), the costs of the materials and equipment meant that clandestine homebrew production often did little more than help families purchase some of their basic necessities. See Reiche, "Estudio sobre el patrón," 121.

89. Ericastilla and Jiménez, "Las clandestinistas de aguardiente," 21; Chambers, "Private Crimes, Public Order," 35.

90. Ixkotz'i'j, 8/6/05, Pamamus, Comalapa.

91. Guillén, "Prólogo, o casi, casi . . . ," 22.

92. Ixsub'äl, 8/23/05, Comalapa (Ix'ey). For their part, clandestinistas from Quezaltenango argued that producing alcohol did not hurt anyone. Some even went so far as to associate it with familial reproduction. See Ericastilla and Jiménez, "Las clandestinistas de aguardiente," 21. Interestingly, becoming intoxicated itself was not considered a transgression among many Mayas. Only when one became violent or failed to provide for their family was intoxication considered a problem. See, for example, Reina, *Law of the Saints*, 298.

93. AGCA, Indice 116, Chimaltenango 1901, Leg. 2F, Exp. 39.

94. AGCA, Indice 116, Chimaltenango 1900, Leg. 1A, Exp. 32.

95. AGCA, Indice 116, Chimaltenango 1918, Leg. 19, Exp. 34. During the Estrada Cabrera regime, the typical punishment for making and selling aguardiente in Chimaltenango was three months in prison, commutable by a fine.

96. AGCA, Indice 116, Chimaltenango 1907, Leg. 8B, Exp. 22. Commutable sentences for moonshiners were not uncommon in early twentieth-century Guatemala. See Gudmundson, "Firewater, Desire," 262.

97. AGCA, Indice 116, Chimaltenango 1907, Leg. 8B, Exp. 22.

98. Ibid.

99. AGCA, Indice 116, Chimaltenango 1918, Leg. 19, Exp. 34.

100. AGCA, Indice 116, Chimaltenango 1901, Leg. 2F, Exp. 40.

101. Ibid.

102. AGCA, Indice 116, Chimaltenango 1909, Leg. 10D, Exp. 5.

103. AGCA, Indice 116, Chimaltenango 1900, Leg. G, Exp. 75.

104. AGCA, Indice 116, Chimaltenango 1902, Leg. 3, Exp. 37.

105. AGCA, Indice 116, Chimaltenango 1900, Leg. G, Exp. 75.

106. AGCA, Indice 116, Chimaltenango 1902, Leg. 3, Exp. 37.

107. Ibid.

108. AGCA, JPC, 1927, Leg. 70A, Marcela viuda de Rodriguez, licencia para tocar

marimba en su establecimiento de licores, January 9. In the same packet, see also licencias to José Angel Gálvez, February 26, 1927; Soledad Morales, March 12 and April 9, 1927; and José Angel Galores, April 10, 1927.

109. *La Gaceta*, January 22, 1933. In truth, the police may have targeted Rubio because the injured drunk was the son of one of Chimaltenango's most influential men, Antonio Solares.

110. *La Gaceta*, February 13, 1931. Women in Costa Rica also routinely owned and ran bars. See Putnam, "Work, Sex, and Power," 144.

111. *La Gaceta*, March 26, 1933.

112. AMP, Paq. 107, Juzgado de Paz de Patzicía, August 10, 1945.

113. *La Gaceta*, January 1, 1933; AGCA, Indice 116, Chimaltenango 1914, Leg. 15D, Exp. 53.

114. AGCA, Indice 116, Chimaltenango 1900, Leg. 1F, Exp. 47. While this incident occurred shortly after the beginning of Estrada Cabrera's dictatorship, a sense of continuity emerges in drunken bouts in light of other incidents such as the one at the beginning of Ubico's dictatorship when Brigida Castellanos watched her nephew get hurt during a fight that broke out in the cantina in her home. See *La Gaceta*, February 13, 1931. See also *La Gaceta*, January 1, 1933 (30), for an example of a *cantinera* whose reaction to a customer who threatened to kill her on various occasions intimated that she had become accustomed to violence.

115. AGCA, Indice 116, Chimaltenango 1907, Leg. 8E, Exp. 17.

116. Ibid.

117. Interestingly, historian Sarah Chambers argues that in early Republican Peru, women felt safe in *chicharías* because they enjoyed the protection of the *chichera* and other women there. See Chambers, "Private Crimes, Public Order," 40.

118. AMP, Paq. 107, Libro de Sentencias Economicas (hereafter LSE) 1943, September 6, 1943.

119. AMP, Paq. 24, Manuel Meses contra Nicolasa Corona, February 24, 1923.

120. Ibid.

121. AMP, Paq. 24, LSE 1929, January 3, 1929.

122. Juárez Muñoz, *El indio Guatemalteco*, 166.

123. Gudmundson, "Firewater, Desire," 276.

124. Reeves, *Ladinos with Ladinos*.

125. Scott, *Domination*.

Conclusion

Community Drunkenness and Control in Guatemala

VIRGINIA GARRARD-BURNETT

Alcohol runs in a steady stream through the literature on Guatemala. We find references to its use and abuse from observers as diverse as early Spanish clergy, colonial authorities, Victorian travelers and missionaries, nineteenth-century statesmen, anthropologists, and twentieth-century revolutionaries. Given its ubiquity, alcohol should appear more often as a serious category of analysis in the scholarly literature on Guatemala, or even on Latin America in general. Like other key social matrixes that twentieth-century scholars often mistook, at best, for markers of other phenomenon—such as religion, for example, or dress—alcohol has mainly appeared as a signifier of contemporary social or political tropes: backwardness, degeneration, ignorance, poverty, antimodernness, or even just folkloric (and therefore dismissible) quaintness. There is, to be sure, a significant body of scholarly literature within sociology and anthropology that addresses alcohol phenomenologically, that is to say, as a pathology or a meme within a given culture. Nevertheless, there are very few studies that speak directly to the role that alcohol has historically played in framing cultural interactions between people and institutions. It is this gap that this book has sought to fill.

That said, our study is not without important precedent. We take our lead from the work of historian William Taylor, who, as he notes in the foreword to this volume, realized through his reading of some ethnographies from Chiapas published in the early 1960s that alcohol played a major role in the framing of indigenous responses to conquest and in social behavior in colonial Mexico. The first to evaluate alcohol use and misuse on its own terms, Taylor's 1979 publication *Drinking, Homicide, and Rebellion in Colonial Mexico Villages* demonstrated how the colonial experience radically transformed alcohol use from a sacred to a social behavior.[1] Taylor also was among the first to track the dual and contradictory function of alcohol in a colonial milieu. The Crown tried to control subaltern drunkenness but benefited from the licensing of *pulquerías*. At the same time that indigenous drinkers used alcohol to try to wash away the pains of conquest and domination, they also exploited social expectations having to do with drinking and drunkenness to engage in violence and subvert Spanish institutions. Taylor's work was enormously influential, especially in its groundbreaking examination of indigenous resistance and agency, but the "drinking" portion of the study failed to attract historians' attention.

During the last decades of the twentieth century, the discipline of history shifted, adapting a postmodern theoretical turn developed somewhat earlier in related fields such as literary criticism, philosophy, cultural studies, and some social sciences to examine much more closely the kinds of local, subaltern themes that Taylor's work had already challenged us to address. Breaking away from an outdated top-down narrative approach, historians began, increasingly, to use new lenses such as (in particular) gender, race, and ethnicity to view history from the bottom up. Yet even when utilizing these new optics, alcohol remained largely outside the historian's gaze. My own 2000 article "Indians Are Drunks and Drunks Are Indians: Alcohol and Indigenismo in Guatemala, 1890–1940," written twenty years after but nonetheless directly inspired by Taylor's book, was among the first historical works to explore the topic per se for Guatemala.[2] The article was a limited attempt to expand upon Taylor's arguments of how alcohol interacts at the nexus of race, class, and power. It described how pro-*indigenista* discourse (*indigenismo* is a movement that concurrently celebrated a prehispanic indigenous past and sought to assimilate contemporary indigenous people) conflated with tropes of indigenous drunkenness in Guatemala at the turn of the previous century. This volume expands upon this and other related themes much more substantially.

Because of their more integral concerns with culture, anthropologists have tended to do better than historians on the topic of alcohol, although they have also frequently made the historian's mistake of confusing the signified with the signifier.[3] Many of the studies were connected with the Harvard Chiapas project, an ethnographic field school that the university operated for many years in midcentury highland Chiapas.[4] In particular, the work of anthropologists Evon Z. Vogt and Frank Cancian typify the theoretical approach of that era by examining alcohol from a functionalist perspective; thus, these studies were more concerned about the ritual and economic functions of drinking than with alcohol per se.[5] A relatively recent and significant exception to this is Barbara Butler's work on Ecuador, *Holy Intoxication to Drunken Dissipation*, which investigates the way that alcohol has shifted its symbolic meaning in recent decades among the Quichua speakers, from a medium of spiritual attainment to one of plain old secular drunkenness, which nonetheless creates a sense of agency and satisfaction during a (contemporary) period of serious economic and structural challenges.[6] Less current but highly germane to our own thinking is Christine Eber's important work, *Women and Alcohol in a Highland Maya Town*.[7] Eber followed a long tradition of anthropological observation of alcohol in a cultural context, but she was groundbreaking in her effort to position alcohol within the context of forming and codifying social interactions. Eber's specific interests in the gendered effects of alcohol and the dynamics of its consumption in Maya communities (in Mexico rather than Guatemala) bear a special salience to the themes that appear in our present work.

This brings us to this particular volume. Here, we have proposed that alcohol in Guatemala, as the preceding chapters clearly show us, is redolent with meaning and implicit contradictions that bring to bear directly upon Guatemalan history. Much more than merely an intoxicant or a source of income, alcohol serves as a lens though which we can observe a variety of negotiated power, moral judgments, economic relations, and turned tables. If alcohol appears in these pages as a pervasive substance of desire, it also functions as a powerful mechanism of control: over state revenue; over community; over labor; over the body. As the chapters of this book demonstrate, alcohol serves as a metaphor and code for divergent and sometimes overlapping issues of race, gender, class, and culture. As such, we position this volume within an emerging historiography of work that explores how a single commodity or idea—such as that of sugar, salt, or coffee, for example[8]—both transverses and elucidates each of these more traditional categories. At the same time, we also hope to engage the ongoing historiographical conversations that test and probe the contest of power and wills that took place between subaltern people and the state. We do not make universal claims for our findings, but we do argue that in Guatemala, at least, alcohol has played a critical role in the nation's history, both as a commodity of exchange and as a marker of status and identity and an important lubricant of social interaction.

Alcohol and the State

The overall thrust of this study indicates that despite a variety of efforts to tame alcohol—that is, not only to manage its consumption and use but also to actually harness its alluring and addictive qualities both to raise revenues for the state and to inure Mayas and poor ladinos into an obedient and compliant labor force—it proved to be as elusive as quicksilver. (Here, we refer not merely to the colonial government or the nation-state but also to local authorities, such as the *cofradías*, described below, and, above all, illegal vendors.) René Reeves's and David Carey Jr.'s chapters illustrate clearly the Guatemalan state's multiple efforts to shut down illegal distilleries; we see, too, in Alvis Dunn's contribution, the importance and chimerical efforts in the late eighteenth century and then the early republic to control and monitor taverns, *estancos*, and any public houses where legal, taxable spirits were sold.

These efforts, generally speaking, did not stem from the state's desire to control alcohol consumption out of concerns for morality or public health. Rather, they came into play so that the state could benefit from the lucrative sale of aguardiente in place of the slightly less potent but locally produced and untaxed corn-based home brew. We can see from the preceding chapters that commodity chains mattered deeply to the Liberal nation, especially by the early twentieth century, when the state apparatus had gained sufficient power to insert itself into regional affairs and the daily life of the Maya. (One of the ironies of this period, as Carey notes, is that modernist dictator Manuel Estrada Cabrera used revenues from alcohol to develop the police state, which he utilized, in turn, to prosecute clandestinistas, whom he viewed as stealing state funds by evading the liquor tax.)

Drunkenness and Ethnic Tropes

But perversely, as nearly all of the contributors to this volume demonstrate, the state also had a direct interest in maintaining high levels of alcohol consumption, including drunkenness. Especially as the nineteenth century transitioned into the twentieth, alcohol had become not only an important source of revenue but also a key conduit for transitioning (usually indigenous) laborers from the subsistence economy into the wage labor force needed for the commercial *fincas*. In this context, it mattered less that people drank taxed liquor than that they drank a lot of it. Against this matrix, racial and ethnic essentializations abounded; by the early twentieth century, the conflation of Indianness and drunkenness was so complete that the two words became virtually synonymous with one another in official discourse and in the public (urban) imagination.[9]

It is important to note that these racialisms were not limited to the Maya population; to some extent, collapsed notions about alcohol and drunkenness also extended to poor ladinos and also to Afro-Guatemalans living on the Atlantic coast. As Frederick Douglass Opie elegantly shows us, social expectations for blacks, heavily influenced by U.S. Jim Crow–era racial stereotypes imported in part by the United Fruit Company, were such that "lowdown culture"—that is, hard drinking, gambling, and general carrying-on—also allowed U.S.-born African American immigrants in Guatemala to easily circumvent national liquor laws with minimal recrimination. Here, alcohol served both as an index of racial stereotyping and as a way of keeping labor content and subservient.

Despite the racial connotations associated with drunkenness, it bears mentioning that in part because Guatemala is historically a Catholic nation, alcohol in and of itself did not carry the kind of moral freight that it did in many Protestant societies. Gestures toward serious reform of its consumption or temperance, therefore, never gained much enthusiasm or traction. Despite hand-wringing on the part of some indigenista, modern-minded reformers in the early twentieth century, in fact, it seems relatively clear that the benefits of alcohol even to the state far outweighed the deficits, even when the state lost revenues because of contraband.

Household Economies of Alcohol

That these benefits came at virtually no cost to the state did not escape the notice of modernist state planners. For example, beyond the significant matter of helping advance the labor draft, the case studies that Carey and Reeves offer of female clandestinistas—a profession that women seemed to have practiced quite freely—show us that the illegal production and sale of home brew had a positive effect on household economies.

Clandestine brewing afforded a woman a culturally appropriate means of augmenting family income, while also allowing her to remain solidly in the sanctioned domestic sphere. Despite their illegality, clandestinistas were crucial to the functioning of many domestic and rural economies. As Reeves points out, distilling alcohol at home, using common materials that were easy to obtain, made sense for women. Like weaving, it was a way to provide supplemental income for the family without intruding into the male social spaces of the field and town. (The fact that many of these women may have been pushed into the enterprise in the first place because their husbands were alcoholics or had contracted while drunk to go work on a distant plantation is yet another contradiction that alcohol brings to the fore.)

Beyond that, the palliative aspect of alcohol in keeping a subservient population docile—recall the tankards of "Victory Gin" that Big Brother provided to the proletarians in George Orwell's *1984*—must surely also have been a factor. Yet this was hardly a case of state conspiracy. On the contrary, the role that local vendors and community leaders played, even to the point of opposing state actors such as the police or the *jefes políticos*, in making sure that alcohol was readily available demands a closer examination of agency. In particular, in rural Maya areas, it was often the local religious brotherhoods—the central arbiters of local custom and authority—that meted out and dictated the consumption of drink in the name of the rituals that helped to define community identity and coherence.

In his chapter on the Q'anjob'al, Stacey Schwartzkopf speaks theoretically to this paradox by suggesting that we look beyond the effects of alcohol to consider its larger meaning within the context of indigenous culture. Here, he draws upon an extensive anthropological literature that focuses on contextualizing alcohol consumption within its distinct cultural and, by extension, political and economic contexts. The strength of this approach, as Schwartzkopf underscores, is that it permits social scientists to examine alcohol use without its often-Puritanical moral baggage and without the stigma of disease pathology that characterizes approaches based in Western, first-world psychology.[10]

Alcohol and Economies of Meaning

While this intriguing conceptual framework lies largely outside the scope of this essay, it directly challenges us to look more closely at the social meaning that alcohol had within the actual communities themselves. As the chapters in this book indicate, because the use of alcohol in rural communities was both ubiquitous and substantial even in the face of a variety of prohibitions and sanctions, its social function must have been quite significant. We can clearly see alcohol's key role in the performative aspects of community, most notably in religious and community rituals and celebrations commemorating a locality's patron saint's day. Alcohol literally helped to distill place and identity into one.

Despite this positive function, there is no question that, over time, for people outside of Maya communities, alcohol and drunkenness were rich signifiers of indigenous degradation and backwardness. For early anthropologists in Guatemala, alcohol and drunkenness provided various metaphors of meaning through which to interpret and judge contemporary Maya culture. North American and European observers, many of them both influenced by and refugees from late Victorian ideas about temperance and liquor, could not fail to notice the widespread use of alcohol in Maya public life. One of the first such notices appears in the work of Alfred Percival Maudslay, the British archaeologist who was one of the first to introduce classic Maya culture to the public. He and his wife, Anne, published a book about their 1885 visit to Guatemala in which they described treating an old man in Copan (more likely, Cobán) for a hangover, which was "too serious for 'the Worcestershire Sauce cure' but which responded to a small solution of opium and beef jelly."[11] After administering this alarming remedy, Maudslay jovially concluded, "Ignorant, lazy, dirty and drunken as these people undoubtedly are, I found them to be cheerful, kindly and honest."[12]

Dismissive and paternalistic, Maudslay's observations nonetheless ran afoul of Guatemalan elites' rising concern with tropes of indigenous alcohol use at the turn of the previous century as they came to define addiction to strong drink as a metaphor for their nation's backwardness and debasement. By the late 1880s, Guatemala's modernist leaders and intellectuals had started to become preoccupied with alcohol as both substance and symbol. In the first decades of the twentieth century, the discourse of alcoholism merged with that of indigenismo. By the early 1930s, during the presidency of Ubico, the theoretical conflation of alcoholism and indigenismo was fully evolved, providing a seamless paradigm for those who credited Guatemala's "drunken" and "racially degenerate" indigenous majority with the nation's underdevelopment. In this respect,

Guatemala rode the cutting edge of the popular eugenic theories of the day wherein, as Nancy Stepan has pointed out, throughout Latin America it seemed necessary to modernity-minded nation builders to identify the "racial poisons" that contaminated the "lesser" populations.[13] As in Bolivia, where anthropologist Rudi Colloredo-Mansfeld has suggested that alcohol was among the many traits that elites used to cleave the population into a popular binary of "dirty Indians" and "clean mestizos," in Guatemala, too, alcohol became a key signifier of indigenous inferiority during the first decades of the twentieth century.[14]

Marking Indigenous and Community Identity

But just how integral, indeed how essential, to indigenous life was alcohol in indigenous life in Guatemala? Certainly, its social role in certain areas of Maya culture, particularly in religion, is well chronicled. There is a well-established body of literature, all written by outsiders, that describes the role alcohol historically played in Mesoamerican religion. In traditional Mesoamerican religions the consumption of alcohol had long been an important component of religious practice, where inebriation (or hallucination) was considered to be an essential part of attaining the proper religious spirit.[15] No less a sympathetic observer than Bartolomé de las Casas described ritual drinking at prehispanic fiestas:

> [The royal lords] danced and leapt before their idols and gave them drink of the best wine that they had, drenching their lips and face with it. And those who held themselves most devout brought vessels and bladders of wine and drank copiously of it, and this they did for no other reason than religious zeal, believing this kind of sacrifice was more pleasing to their gods than any other common acts of devotion, and for this reason the chief one who became intoxicated was the lord or reigning king, and other important lords, among them were some who did not drink enough to become intoxicated, so that they might rule the town and country while the monarch was drunk in his devotions.[16]

As this passage indicates, in prehispanic times, the use of alcohol and hallucinogens was an elite privilege and obligation. But with the arrival of the Spaniards, alcohol's use spread rapidly through the general populace, producing many of the consequences we have seen described in the preceding chapters of this volume.[17]

Although there is a tendency to draw a line between the ancient prehispanic provenance of ceremonial drinking and later community drunkenness, the linkages may not have been quite so direct. The suppression of the institutional Catholic Church in the latter half of the nineteenth and early twentieth century allowed for the dramatic expansion of popular religiosity under the guidance of local cofradías in rural Guatemala, and much of the performance of community-based religion took place around the ritual consumption of alcohol. Although more research is needed on this question, I speculate that the practices of ritual drinking and community drunkenness may have escalated dramatically during the last decades of the nineteenth century. This is not to underestimate the importance of these practices in midcentury; as Schwartzkopf illustrates for Huehuetenango, alcohol was clearly integral to ritual and *compadrazgo* at least as early as 1861, a good decade before the Liberal period initiated by Justo Rufino Barrios in 1871. Nevertheless, it was during this later period when two Liberal reforms—the reduction of the presence of the institutional Catholic Church, thus pushing local religious practice into the hands of cofradías, and the expansion of the wage labor system, which brought cash into some indigenous communities for the first time—made the purchase of aguardiente both possible and, in a manner of speaking, essential.

Central to this was the revival of the cofradía, a colonial institution that had languished badly in the mid-nineteenth century. As historian Douglass Sullivan-Gonzales records, "Scattered reports around the country in the 1860s indicated that cofradías were struggling to survive or even closing due to insufficient funds and lack of popular support."[18] But by the end of the nineteenth century, cofradías were enjoying a hearty revival, flush from cash generated by the new wage-based finca economy and nourished by anticlerical policies that virtually removed the institutional Catholic Church from the daily lived religion of the Maya. The greatly diminished presence of the institutional Church allowed for the cofradías to assert themselves as the central locus of community power and unchallenged authority. Within this revival, alcohol and drunkenness played a central role.

It is important to distinguish between ordinary drinking by individuals (where drinkers were most likely to seek out and purchase illegal home brew produced by the very clandestinistas described in the preceding chapters) and the large-scale, community-based drunkenness that took place during fiestas, much of which centered on the consumption both of homemade contraband liquor *and* commercially produced aguardiente purchased with cash. In the latter case, public drunkenness was not simply a side effect of ritual but an objective of it—an integral part of the performance of community belonging. As one observer described it, "[A]mong the Quichés as among many Central American peoples drunkenness is institutionalized, and runs like a purple thread through all the patterns of ritual."[19]

It was in the context of ritual and fiestas that alcohol seems to have served its most public and social function in the early twentieth century. Certainly, its most basic purpose was and still is to lubricate social interactions—the loosening of inhibitions and loss of care that strong drink brings in any setting. Beyond this, however, drunkenness provided a safety valve for social deviance in small, isolated communities, by providing a context where fighting, adultery, and general fuse-blowing were permitted and even, to some extent, sanctioned. This step outside of ordinary life—what Eber has called a "'time-out' attitude about drinking"—allowed, within reason, maneuvering room for forgivable transgressions.[20] The rare opportunity to vent in small, self-contained communities—where bad behavior, grudges, slights, and missteps committed in a sober light might be remembered for generations—must surely have been significant and, indeed, welcome. In addition, by the last quarter of the nineteenth century, the purchase of liquor (by far, the largest single expenditure for a cofradía member, according to any number of studies), made possible by the introduction of cash into rural communities through indigenous labor on coffee fincas, provided an income-leveling function in villages where envy and greed might otherwise tear at the fabric of community unity.

Consumption in a Liberal World

Alcohol was the *produit moteur* of economic transition in highland communities at the start of the previous century, in its own way perhaps to even a greater extent than was coffee. As anthropologist Ruth Bunzel noted in her work on Chichicastenango in the early 1930s, "[I]n many places alcohol is the chief expense which cannot be met from local industry and trade, and for which outside sources of income are necessary. . . . [I]t is the desire for drink, more than any other need, that drives men to seek outside work."[21] In unpacking this comment, we encounter several themes that appear earlier in this volume. Among other things, it indicates that the expansion of wage versus subsistence labor goes hand in hand with the increased ritual use of alcohol. Does this suggest that the exit of men from their villages to work on the fincas produced an increased need to affirm community identity and cohesion through an expanded fiesta system? In other words, did cash make alcohol more necessary? Or did increased demand for alcohol make cash more necessary?

At the very least, the increase in the purchase of legal alcohol in place of locally produced contraband liquor for ritual purposes in the early twentieth century is a useful measure of the extent to which, in anthropologist Oliver La Farge's words, "[t]he *finca* system [had] upset the native economy and reduced the number and variety of local products."[22] (Clearly, the state was finally winning its long-standing struggle to convert consumption from untaxed, contraband chicha to the licensed, taxed aguardiente that helped fill the national coffers.) In addition, the increased sale and use of alcohol for ritual purposes also suggest something else: that community elders and cofradía leaders may have felt a need to use increased ritual (including community drunkenness) to help assert and reaffirm community values and their own authority at a time when new, modern economic and political forces threatened those communities' autonomy and communitarian identities.

The extremely high financial costs that alcohol incurred at fiestas strongly suggest that there was much more at stake here than simply a "good time." In his early study of economic change in Santiago Chimaltenango, for example, anthropologist Charles Wagley charted the annual household expenditures for a "typical" Mam family in the community. In a reasonably well-off family of six with an annual (cash) income of approximately sixty quetzales,[23] Wagley found that the father, José, spent five to six quetzales for a three-day-long drinking binge during the annual patronal festival of Santiago in 1937; that is, he spent 10 percent of the family's entire annual income on three days' worth of aguardiente. In addition, José also borrowed money from a labor recruiter whom he promised to pay off in return for several months' labor at a finca on the Pacific coast, an effort that would reward him, if the previous year's wage was an indicator, with about fifteen quetzales—all in all, an extraordinary outlay of cash and opportunity to support the fleeting liquid pleasures of the fiesta. Because José did not appear to have a drinking problem overall (the only money that Wagley found that the family spent on alcohol during the entire year was during this single fiesta), José's heavy drinking at the fiesta must have been vested with some larger social value and meaning beyond the simple pleasure of getting drunk.[24]

In a similar vein, anthropologist Sol Tax found during his fieldwork in the late 1930s in Panajachel that liquor accounted for a whopping 40 percent of the town's typical commodity expenditures. That is to say, the people in Panajachel spent on average 60 percent of their cash on household expenses like housing, food, clothing, tools, utensils, and supplies and the remaining 40 percent on alcohol, most of it for ceremonial purposes. "The social cost is much greater," Tax noted, "if one takes into account that Indians frequently continued to drink, to cure hangovers, and the loss of time and money can be very large." Nevertheless, Tax took a sanguine view: by and large, he opined, "[p]eople drink because they should, and it is a symbol of a good, rather than a bad adjustment to society. Liquor is sacred and is used on every occasion of social or religious importance."[25]

This is in no way to overlook the evils that alcohol consumption brought to many individuals and communities but rather to underscore the point that community leaders, particularly cofradía members in the late nineteenth and early twentieth century, largely understood alcohol to be a medium of community cohesion, not dissolution. As late as the mid-twentieth century, anthropologist June Nash observed how this process worked in the selection of a new *alférez* (similar to a mayor): "In order to gain acceptance they got the nominee drunk in a drinking session at the town hall. Liquor was measured out, and all the officials drank only half a cup at each round, but the new alférez was required to drink a full cup. The rounds continued until the new alférez was drunk. If he did not accept at this session, he was put in jail to think it over. Another drinking session took place the next day."[26] She also describes how at the initiation of new civil officers, the regidores were required to purchase two liters of contraband liquor, known as the "gift of the ancestors." Nash continues, "Meeting in the parish church, the new officials ask permission of God to 'receive the gift,' saying, 'give pardon . . . let a little enter and warm your body.'"[27]

Indeed, the ritual drinking of alcohol in cofradía ceremonies to symbolize community cohesion was so central to the cofradía's performance of its moral authority that those who did not drink, for whatever reason, could not participate as cofrades (brothers) and community elders. (The example of pantomime that one finds in Chiapas, where a nondrinker could ritually "drink" by pouring his alcohol through a funnel into a flask hidden in his shirt, is rare in Guatemala, although anthropologist Robert Hinshaw records such a practice by a cofrade in San José Chacayá, Sololá, in the late 1950s.)[28] According to Nash, communal drunkenness was only part of the equation; the material substance of the alcohol itself (as opposed to the drunkenness it produced) was most salient: "[F]lowing blood [in the slaughter of a sheep], water, and liquor are spirit media symbolically linked in ritual behavior."[29]

Community Drunkenness and Social Cohesion

Nevertheless, it was not so much alcohol per se as its effects—drunkenness, and specifically community drunkenness—that caught the eye of many observers in the early twentieth century. Certainly, the spectacle of community-wide drunkenness at Maya fiestas made a deep impression on the early U.S.-trained anthropologists who were among the first to do fieldwork in the Guatemalan highlands in the early 1930s, both immediately before and during the Ubico regime, which inserted the presence of the state much more forcefully into the fabric of daily life in remote rural villages.

There are four U.S. scholars whose work was particularly foundational: Ruth Bunzel, who challenged both convention and gender barriers with her fieldwork in Chichicastenango from 1930 to 1932; Oliver La Farge, who lived in and sensitively observed life in Santa Eulalia in 1932; Sol Tax, who did his foundational fieldwork in Panajachel between 1938 and 1939; and Charles Wagley, who did pioneering research in remote Santiago Chimaltenango in 1936–37. They all recorded and made some attempt to explain the function that alcohol and drunkenness played in Maya society. Although their interpretations reflect the authors' era and their own subjectivities, they also offer if not a window, at least a mirror on the function that community drunkenness may have played. Understanding the limitations of these sources, the anthropologists' observations may still offer us some simulacrum of what community drunkenness actually meant to the drinkers themselves.

All four ethnographers describe in detail fiestas built around ritual dancing and drinking, where, in the words of Bunzel, "[t]he drinking is much more important than dancing, often no one dances at all, but every-one drinks."[30] For La Farge, community drunkenness was the by-product of a traumatic colonial history. "The tragic sight of men and women, the latter sometimes with babies on their backs, so drunk that they could barely walk was all too common," he wrote. "Many sat or lay semicon-scious beside the roads, otherwise were led home by friends slightly more sober. When drunk, these Indians are gay at first, but become gloomy."[31] Criticizing the efforts of Protestant missionaries to stamp out drinking, La Farge poignantly observed, "While these people undoubtedly suffer from drunkenness, one would hesitate to remove the bottle from them until the entire pattern of their lives is changed. They are an introverted peo-ple, consumed by fires which they cannot or dare not express, eternally chafing under the yoke of conquest, and never for a moment forgetting that they are a conquered people. In occasional drunkenness, in dancing, and in the more elaborate ceremonies with their pageantry they find a much-needed release."[32] Bunzel read an even more deeply symbolic, if perhaps over-romanticized meaning, into community drunkenness. She noted how it formed a central part of family celebrations such as wed-dings, served a key role in agricultural rituals, and concluded every fiesta, including the patronal feast of Santo Tomás, where "everyone in town gets drunk and stays drunk for nearly a week."[33] Yet Bunzel also underscored the reverential aspect embodied in festival drinking: "For the drinking in the *cofradías* is an act of worship . . . like dancing or singing in other places. The gods want to see people happy, the joy of drink is, therefore, pleasing to them."[34]

Individual drunkenness for these social scientists was another matter entirely. Bunzel noted that "for drunkenness itself the Indians have no feelings of censure or disgust."[35] By the same token, drinking for drink-ing's sake, outside of the confines of the fiesta, was, in Bunzel's observa-tion, frowned upon: "It is not customary to drink in the *cantones* or in private homes. . . . All the drinking is in the town, on market days, in public places."[36] In this way, community drunkenness seemed somehow to mitigate, even erase in an alcohol fog, the problems that individual drunkenness might otherwise churn up: personal arguments, quarrels, adultery, violence.

The one exception to this was the matter of indebtedness, a problem mentioned in nearly every chapter of this book. Although the Ubico administration in 1934 officially outlawed the *enganche* (that is, labor recruiters loaning money for liquor at a fiesta in return for a drunkard's pledge to work for weeks or months on distant fincas) as well as the sale of liquor on the fincas themselves, both practices remained quite common at least until the mid-twentieth century and probably even longer.[37] La Farge stated in 1932 that "when partway drunk, an Indian will sell his soul for more liquor; upon this the finca system is based."[38] Bunzel seconded this observation: "In this state it is easy to see what easy game they are for the plantation slave-catchers."[39] As late as 1947, during and despite the many reforms of the "Ten Years of Spring," Guatemala's ten-year experiment with democratic government between 1944 and 1954, the gifted amateur anthropologist Maude Oakes took note of the deleterious convergence of drunkenness and debt during the three-day-long November All Saints fiesta in Todos Santos Cuchumatán in Huehuetenango. "When they are drunk the Indians vacillate between joviality and melancholy," she wrote. "They all get drunk especially during fiesta time, and then they are willing to sign contracts to work on the coffee *fincas* or plantations, to will away their possessions, to do anything to buy just one more *trago*, one more drink. And while in this state they are preyed upon by the agents of the *fincas* and their touts, the *caporales*."[40]

The Devil's Brew: Alcoholism and Missionaries

Despite the pervasiveness and perhaps even the social necessity of community drunkenness, alcohol abuse and alcoholism became a serious problem for some individuals, and this in a society in which there seemed to be no other recourse than to drink on required occasions. For example, Oakes noted that early in 1947, the Huehuetenango authorities "removed the Indian who was *Alcalde Municipal* [of Todos Santos] because of his drinking and inefficiency."[41] These culturalist arguments in favor of drunkenness notwithstanding, alcoholism demonstrably *was* a problem in Maya communities in Guatemala in the first half of the twentieth century, although perhaps not a pervasive one. That recorded household expenditures on liquor tended to be clustered around festivals and saints' days rather than throughout the year suggests that alcoholism (that is, problematic drinking on a day-to-day basis) must not have been terribly widespread. Despite the fact that Maya traditions, Catholic culture, and Guatemalan society in general did not encourage the kind of "cultural negativity toward alcohol" that anthropologist Dwight B. Heath describes for rural Mexico, alcohol abuse per se nonetheless proved problematic for certain individuals and their families.[42] It is clear that on an individual basis, people did succumb to the temptations of drink; if alcoholism was indeed a social construction, some certainly learned these tropes by heart. In the words of Eber, indigenous people "learned new drunken comportment from colonists and internalized at least some of these outsiders' views of them when they became drunk."[43]

Evidence of pathological alcoholism shows up most clearly in the records of Protestant missionaries in Guatemala—teetotalers all—who preached a message of absolute temperance and also offered assistance to problem drinkers as part of their larger message. (An important caveat to this is that generally speaking, Protestant missionaries would not have seen a distinction between community drinking and alcoholism; they viewed any consumption of alcohol as universally sinful.)

Although the number of missionaries in the country was not large in the 1930s and 1940s and the number of Protestant converts was smaller still, *evangélicos* (the Spanish term for all non-Catholic Christians) were among the first in the country to offer any kind of alcohol remediation programs. Among their few converts, this appears to have been their most compelling attraction.

From the earliest presence of missionaries in the country, abstemiousness from drink was a central marker and a motivation for conversion to Protestantism. As Hinshaw noted in his early-1970s reevaluation of Tax's work from the 1930s in Panajachel, "The Catholic ceremonial contexts in which drinking is virtually obligatory have precluded until recent years the possibility of Catholics' abstaining completely from alcohol."[44] By contrast, from the earliest days, converts to evangelical churches not only relinquished their membership in Catholic cofradías, but their new identities also required that they eschew alcohol in all its forms and turn their backs completely on any sort of individual or community drunkenness. New converts, particularly men, had oftentimes been heavy drinkers, having drifted into the churches (which lay well outside the bounds of custom and traditional propriety) as a last resort to help with their alcoholism. The missionary records are replete with testimonies of backsliders and alcoholic relapses by members of the flock, whom the congregations variously disciplined and chastised but also offered support and a second chance.[45] The process of working with members' personal and individual shortcomings, *above all* having to do with alcohol, was so commonplace that historian Thomas Bogenschield has written, "The impression is left that the [early missionaries'] primary function was one of social control on a local level."[46]

As early as 1917 or 1918, Presbyterian missionaries established Guatemala's first Sociedad Anti-Alcohólica in Quezaltenango and ten years later founded small branches of the Women's Christian Temperance Union in Quezaltenango and the capital.[47] More tellingly, missionary church membership rolls of virtually every Protestant denomination strongly suggest that many—perhaps even the majority of—converts to the many small evangelical churches that began to dot the landscape of the Maya highlands by the 1930s had joined the churches because of problems with alcohol. In an era just before the dawn of twelve-step programs and clinical diagnoses, Protestant churches offered one of the few avenues of escape from what missionaries called "the slavery of alcohol."[48] Yet this path to sobriety was one chosen by only a very few. As La Farge recalled, "The hatred of most of the Indians for the missionaries and their converts is unbelievably intense."[49] The price for relief from alcohol abuse—exclusion from the elaborate interconnected web of kin, community, religion, identity, and drunkenness that defined community life—was far higher than most, even those with serious drinking problems, were willing to pay.

Social Constructions of Drunkenness: The Wet Debates

Notwithstanding missionary interventions or perhaps even because of them, American anthropologists were largely phlegmatic as to the effects of community drinking—as opposed to "problem drinking" on the part of individuals—even going so far as to suggest that alcoholism, as a problem or a disease, was a culturally constructed phenomenon and that the "problem" of drinking was in the eye of the beholder. (Their work was in conversation with the dramatic expansion of Alcoholics Anonymous in the United States during the late 1930s and early 1940s. Alcoholics Anonymous did not originate but did much to popularize the disease theory of alcoholism.)[50]

One of the first to employ this cultural approach was Ruth Bunzel, whose influential comparative study of Chichicastenango and San Juan Chamula (in highland Chiapas), published in 1940, helped to frame the study of alcohol use within the discipline of anthropology.[51] In this study, written more than ten years after her initial fieldwork in Chichicastenango,

Bunzel attempted to decouple community drunkenness from alcoholism, suggesting that the former is part of a functional social system, while the latter—more common to the highly individualist West—is an illness and a pathology.[52] This engendered a current of ethnographic theory that took the point of view that alcohol abuse is culturally bounded; that is, many cultures (traditional Maya included) do not view drunkenness as a problem, and inebriation serves a specific purpose in discrete environments and contexts, just as we find in the cases described above of community drunkenness on saints' days.[53] As Schwartzkopf, along with others such as Eber, indicates, this theory, first devised to describe Maya community drinking, still largely informs the field.

The intersection of missionaries, alcohol, and culture provides a matrix upon which we can position some larger themes that fix Guatemala within the larger field of alcohol studies. As we have seen, there has been a lively debate within the field of anthropology since Bunzel's early work in the 1940s over the cultural embeddedness of alcohol and its uses and consumption. By the early 1960s, the culturally bounded explanations of alcohol use defined the field. As David Mandelbaum, an anthropologist who worked primarily among the Plains Indians of North America, elucidated in an influential article on alcohol and culture, "Alcohol is a cultural artifact; the form and meaning of drinking alcoholic beverages are culturally defined, as are the uses of any other major artifact."[54]

During the 1960s and later, in an effort to step away from ethnocentric, Protestant-Victorian judgments that informed the "firewater myth" that American Indians were inordinately prone to crave liquor and drunkenness and easily done in by these vices, many scholars, perhaps the most prominent being Brown University anthropologist Dwight B. Heath, firmly advanced this obverse approach. Calling themselves "the wet generation,"[55] these researchers suggested that by looking across cultures and through variations in behavior within a given society, it was possible to observe that there were virtually "no conflicts and problems involved in drinking."[56] Furthermore, as Heath argued in 1975 in a broad theoretical study based in part on his extensive research among the indigenous Camba of Bolivia, "there are very few primitive or other non-Western societies in which habitual drinking in indigenous communities was a major cause of family problems." Rather, he concluded, "'problem drinking' is very rare."[57] In a study done a decade earlier, Heath had suggested that drunkenness was so culturally organic to Camba society that the pathological, even physiological effects of alcoholism were virtually un-known. "Among most peoples whose men are expected to drink heavily and frequently, a man does not do any solitary drinking," he wrote, "nor does he have withdrawal symptoms if he cannot get alcohol. He may not like to do without it, but he does not feel gripped by an iron compulsion to get a drink."[58]

This view, widely held by social scientists well into the mid-1970s (an era not unfriendly to mind-altering substances), was dubbed by one so-ciologist the "reverse firewater myth."[59] As what had been a reduction-ist, almost "noble savage" paradigm became more nuanced in addressing problems of misuse and addiction, one anthropologist later noted, "As abstinence was a self-conscious distinguishing mark of missionaries, it must have been tempting for ethnographers, in their turn, to distinguish themselves from missionaries on the alcohol question."[60] Yet as recently as a generation ago, in the 1980s, social scientists working in the emerg-ing field of alcohol studies (which includes research across anthropology, sociology, public health, policy, and to a lesser extent, psychology and history) argued emphatically that although alcohol could obviously be problematic in specific cases, more often "drinking fits in well with other aspects of local culture and reinforces solidarity," a position that the Gua-temalan case as presented here helps to underscore.[61]

Alcohol and Colonialism

Even within this compensatory theorizing, however, there is room for nuance, which over time has come to replace subjective moralizing with considerations of power, agency, and resistance, as scholars in more re-cent years have begun to use alcohol as a category of analysis with which to view these interrelationships. For a sense of how this works, we may use alcohol to examine postcolonialism. Europeans first introduced al-cohol in many parts of the world (such as Oceania and parts of North America). In places like Guatemala, Mexico, sub-Saharan Africa, and elsewhere, alcohol had a long tradition of proscribed use, but its every-day use expanded dramatically after (and in part as a result of) conquest and colonization. In this sense, alcohol use and/or abuse has undeniably powerful colonial associations. Jeremy Beckett's 1965 work on Australia argues that "Aboriginals had adopted the hard drinking of the frontier to reconstitute their shattered society and . . . in defying official prohibition they were conducting a pre-political resistance."[62] (Beckett later revised his work to take problem drinking into account, offering this mea culpa for his earlier cavalier attitude toward problem drinking: "The people did not take these matters seriously, so neither did I.")[63]

Yet within this framework, it is also easy to fall into what Sally Casswell, writing about the South Pacific, calls the functionalists' "neat equation in which behavior that is seen as produced from within the society is 'good,' while behavior derived from outside is 'bad.'"[64] Although such normative assessments fall hard on postmodern ears, Casswell underscores the point that in the South Pacific (as well as in Guatemala and in many other parts of Latin America and elsewhere in the world), missionaries' efforts to push for abstinence from alcohol have "been described as an effort to alter 'the very fabric' of [indigenous societies] in order to bring it into accord with the values of Protestantism."[65] Yet Casswell pushes further to argue that missionary efforts to eliminate alcohol might also, at least in some situations, be seen as "an attempt to preserve or slow down *others'* efforts to alter the fabric of those societies."[66]

More important, these new ways of thinking about alcohol and drunkenness, Casswell argues, though introduced by missionaries, can nonetheless serve as tools that indigenous people themselves can utilize to "protect their societies from the effect of alcohol," when they see it as "an important facilitator of social and cultural disruption."[67] Casswell concludes, "It seems possible that [changes in attitudes about alcohol] may, at least in part, reflect an actual change in experience relative to the nineteenth and early twentieth century; if so, such a change may have been related to the people's earlier experiences with alcohol and their consequent collective–decision making to reduce . . . alcohol-related problems."[68]

In light of these broader controversies and considerations, then, how should we view the historic role that alcohol has played in Guatemala, especially in rural areas? Should we see the widespread consumption of alcohol in Maya communities as through the lens used by missionaries and indigenistas, as a marker of Maya degradation and backwardness? Or, through the eyes of the state and *finqueros*, as a source of revenue and a means of guaranteeing an inexhaustible supply of cheap labor? Or should we see alcohol instead as a form of resistance and, perhaps, even of cultural vitality—community drunkenness as both a weapon of the weak and a key component in the performance of community cohesion? The inherent contradictions of alcohol use offer us no easy answers to these questions. Alcohol is an elixir that both clouds and illuminates our understanding, a commodity that inspires both desire and revulsion, as contradictory as an object of study as it is of consumption.

Notes

1. Taylor, *Drinking, Homicide, and Rebellion.*

2. Garrard-Burnett, "Indians Are Drunks."

3. I am using these terms in their semiotic sense, as they are defined by Ferdinand de Saussure, to mean real-world object (signifier) and the sign or symbol that stands for it (signified). For example, a tree is a *signifier,* while the mental image of a tree is *signified.*

4. Evon Z. Vogt established the Harvard Chiapas Project in 1957. It ran until 1992 and thus served as a training ground for a generation of Mesoamerican anthropologists. The purpose of the project was to systematically describe and analyze the culture of the Tzotzil Mayas in highland Chiapas, operating under the premise that rich "deep description" and a nearly comprehensive catalog of modern Tzotzil culture might shed light on how contemporary Maya life negotiated the "modern" world and also to investigate ways in which modern Mayas are related to the Classic Maya. For a more complete account of the project, see Vogt, *Fieldwork among the Maya.*

5. See, for example, Vogt, *Tortillas for the Gods.* The literature on alcohol in the Andes is (uncharacteristically) more abundant than that for Mesoamerica, but much of it still maintains a functionalist perspective. See, for example, Valdez, "Maize Beer Production"; Tom Brass, "Beer Drinking Groups"; and Harvey, "Drunken Speech."

6. Butler, *Holy Intoxication to Drunken Dissipation.*

7. Eber, *Women and Alcohol.*

8. See, for example, Mintz, *Sweetness and Power*; Kurlansky, *Salt.*

9. Garrard-Burnett, "Indians Are Drunks."

10. Eber, *Women and Alcohol,* 7; see also, for example, Heath, "Determining the Sociocultural Context."

11. Maudslay and Maudslay, *Glimpse of Guatemala,* 138–39.

12. Ibid.

13. Stepan, *Hour of Eugenics,* 85.

14. Colloredo-Mansfeld, "'Dirty Indians,' Radical Indígenas."

15. The sixteenth century Franciscan friar Bernardino de Sahagún commented on the religious nature of prehispanic ritual drinking; see Gonçalves de Lima, *Alimentos e bebidas.* For another contemporary account, see Chimalpahin Quauhtlehuanitzin, *Codex Chimalpahin.* See also Bruman, *Alcohol in Ancient Mexico.*

16. De las Casas, *Apologética historica de las Indias,* 1:259.

17. See also Taylor, *Drinking, Homicide, and Rebellion,* chapter 2.

18. Sullivan-Gonzales, *Piety, Power and Politics,* 49.

19. Bunzel, *Chichicastenango,* 254–55.

20. Eber, *Women and Alcohol,* 6.

21. Bunzel, *Chichicastenango,* 259.

22. La Farge, *Santa Eulalia*, 28.

23. The value of the quetzal was at that time equal to the dollar.

24. Wagley, *Economics of a Guatemalan Village*, 51–52. Like nearly all the early anthropological works used in this essay, Wagley's fieldwork took place more than a decade before his work came out, since nonessential academic publications were put on hold during World War II.

25. Tax, "Changing Consumption in Indian Guatemala." See also Tax, *Penny Capitalism*.

26. Nash, *In the Eyes*, 173.

27. Ibid., 186.

28. Hinshaw, *Panajachel*, 55.

29. Nash, *In the Eyes*, 17.

30. Bunzel, *Chichicastenango*, 255.

31. La Farge, *Santa Eulalia*, 91.

32. Ibid.

33. Bunzel, *Chichicastenango*, 256.

34. Ibid.

35. Ibid., 257.

36. Ibid., 257–58.

37. "Decreto #1602, Ley de Alcoholes y bebidas alcohólicas y fermentadas," *Diario Oficial*, December 7–8, 1934. See also "Prohibiese el expendido de aguardiente en las fincas," *Liberal Progresista*, October 15, 1940, p. 3. A variation of this practice continued into the mid-1980s, when young men who had already served in the military crafted belt buckles made of fused bullet casings, as a signal that they should not be impressed again when the army did early-morning sweeps after fiestas to recruit drunks who were passed out in the street for military service.

38. La Farge, *Santa Eulalia*, 7.

39. Bunzel, *Chichicastenango*, 259.

40. Oakes, *Two Crosses of Todos Santos*, 32–33.

41. Ibid., 36.

42. Heath, "Historical and Cultural Factors," 155, 175–76.

43. Eber, *Women and Alcohol*, 6.

44. Hinshaw, *Panajachel*, 55.

45. Garrard-Burnett, *Protestantism in Guatemala*, 64.

46. Bogenschield, "Roots of Fundamentalism," 205.

47. Garrard-Burnett, *Protestantism in Guatemala*, 61–65; Bogenschield, "Roots of Fundamentalism," 174–79.

48. Alcoholics Anonymous was founded in 1935 in Akron, Ohio.

49. La Farge, *Santa Eulalia*, 100.

50. Cheever, *My Name Is Bill*.

51. Bunzel, "Role of Alcoholism."

52. See Heath, *Alcohol Use in Latin America*.

53. Eber, *Women and Alcohol*, 6 and 7.

54. Mandelbaum, "Alcohol and Culture," 281.

55. See Room, "Alcohol and Ethnography."

56. Heath, "Reply to Robin Room, 'Alcohol and Ethnography,'" 181. Heath is quoting here, but in this piece he is actually making the opposite argument, that it would be "foolish to ignore a variety of social, psychological, physiological and other deficits that appear to be of significance *even if they are ignored or denied by the people immediately affected*" (italics added). This is a revision and nuancing of some of his earlier work; see Heath, "Alcohol Use among North American Indians," 364.

57. Heath, "Critical Review of Ethnographic Studies," 40–41, 57; Heath, "Peasants, Revolution, and Drinking."

58. Heath, "Drinking Patterns," 31, cited in David Mandelbaum, "Alcohol and Culture," 282.

59. Leland, *Firewater Myths,* quoted in Room, "Alcohol and Ethnography," 170.

60. Casswell, "Reply to Robin Room, 'Alcohol and Ethnography,'" 180.

61. Heath, "Reply to Robin Room, 'Alcohol and Ethnography,'" 181.

62. Beckett, "Aborigines, Alcohol, and Assimilation," cited in Beckett, "Reply to Robin Room, 'Alcohol and Ethnography,'" 179.

63. Beckett, "Reply to Robin Room, 'Alcohol and Ethnography,'" 178.

64. Casswell, "Reply to Robin Room, 'Alcohol and Ethnography,'" 180.

65. Ibid.

66. Ibid. (emphasis in the original).

67. Ibid.

68. Ibid.

Glossary

aguardiente: Distilled sugarcane liquor, or rum
aguardiente clandestino: Moonshine
alcalde: Mayor
audiencia: Colonial court of appeals that also had administrative duties
cabildo: Town council
chicha: Fermented beverage made from some combination of corn, sugarcane, and fruit
chichería: Corn beer establishment
clandestinismo: Bootlegging
clandestinista: Moonshiner
cofrade: Member of a *cofradía,* or religious confraternity
cofradía: Religious confraternity
comisario del real estanco: Commissioner of the royal alcohol monopoly
comiteco: Type of aguardiente made with agave sap manufactured in the Mexican town of Comitán
contrabandista: Smuggler
contratistas: Labor brokers
corregidor: Governor
costumbre: Custom or tradition
creole: Hispanic elite
enganchadores: Labor brokers
estanco: Government-sanctioned alcohol monopoly store
finca: Large landed estate
finquero: Owner of a large landed estate
frasco: Flask; in colonial Guatemala these were ceramic and held approximately 2,250 milliliters
indígena: Indigene or indigenous person
indigenismo: A movement that concurrently celebrated prehispanic

indigenous pasts and sought to assimilate contemporary indigenous people

indio/a: Indian, a term generally used by nonindigenous people to pejoratively characterize Mayas as dirty, drunk, lazy, and retrograde, though at times indigenous people complicated these meanings by self-identifying as indio

intendente: Intendant

Jefatura Política: Governor's Office

jefe político: Governor

juez preventivo: District judge-commissioner

k'uxa: Moonshine

ladino/a: Nonindigenous Guatemalan

mandamientos: Forced labor drafts

mestizo/a: Person of mixed European and indigenous ancestry

milpas: Corn fields/peasant cultivations

mistela: A grape-based and aromatic alcoholic beverage with a slightly higher potency than wine

molendera: Corn miller/grinder

mulatto/a: Person of mixed European and African ancestry

pulpería: Store-tavern

quetzal: Guatemalan currency

regidor: Town councilor or alderman

síndico: Town agent

texel: Member of a religious sisterhood

trapiche: Mill

vinatería: Wine and liquor shop

visitador: Colonial inspector appointed by the Crown

Works Cited

ORAL HISTORY INFORMANTS

Due to the continued political volatility of Guatemala and recurrent human rights abuses, we have preserved the anonymity of oral history sources for their safety. We have used pseudonyms that derive from the Maya calendar. Female informants can be recognized by the "Ix" prefix to their one-word names. In contrast, male names have two words. When research assistants performed the interview, they are listed by their Maya names here and in parentheses in the notes. David Carey Jr. performed all other interviews. Unless otherwise noted, all interviews were conducted in Kaqchikel.

Name	Date	Town/Aldea (Village)	Interviewer
B'eleje' Imox	6/5/03	Comalapa	David Carey Jr.
Ix'ey	6/25/03	Comalapa	David Carey Jr.
Ix'eya'	8/10/05	Comalapa	Ix'ey
Ixkotz'i'j	8/6/05	Comalapa, *Pamamus*	David Carey Jr.
Ixsimïl	2/9/05	Comalapa	Ix'ey
Ixsub'äl	8/23/05	Comalapa	Ix'ey
Ixte'	8/5/05	Comalapa	David Carey Jr.
Oxlajuj Ajpu'	1/19/98	Comalapa, *Panabajal*	David Carey Jr.

ARCHIVAL SOURCES

ARCHIVO GENERAL DE CENTRO AMÉRICA (AGCA), GUATEMALA CITY, GUATEMALA

Indice 116, Criminal Chimaltenango, 1900–1925. This index corresponds to the criminal records generated by the Juzgado de Primera Instancia de Chimaltenango. Citations refer to *legajos* (Leg.) and *expedientes* (Exp.).

Jefatura Política de Chimaltenango (JPC). Department governor's records for Chimaltenango. Citations refer to *legajos* (Leg.) and *expedientes* (Exp.).

Jefatura Política de Huehuetenango (JPH). Department governor's records for Huehuetenango. Citations refer to *registros* (Regs.).

Jefatura Política de Izabal (JPI). Department governor's records for Izabal.

Juzgado de Primera Instancia de Huehuetenango (JPIH). Citations refer to *legajos* (Leg.) and *expedientes* (Exp.).

Ministerio de Fomento (MF), Correspondencia de Los Contratistas del Ferrocarriles.
Ministerio de Fomento (MF), International Railroad of Central America (IRCA). Citations refer to *legajos* (Leg.).
Ministerio de Fomento (MF), Signatura B, 1884–1928. Citations refer to *legajos* (Leg.).
Ministro de Gobernación y Justicia (MGJ), Signatura B, Legajos 1884–1928. Citations refer to *legajos* (Leg.) and *expedientes* (Exp.).
Sección A (colonial section). Citations refer to provenance (for example, A.1 indicates Gobierno Superior, A.2 the Capitanía General, and A.3 the Real Hacienda), *legajos* (Leg.), and *expedientes* (Exp.).
Sección B (republican section). Citations refer to *legajos* (Leg.) and *expedientes* (Exp.).
Sección de Tierras. Citations refer to *legajos* (Leg.) and *expedientes* (Exp.).
Archivo de Gobernación de Quezaltenango (AGQ). Citations refer to *hojas sueltas* unless otherwise indicated.
Archivo Municipal de Patzicía (AMP). Thanks to the work of Edgar Esquit and others, these archives are organized by *paquetes* (abbreviated as "Paq.") and indexed.
Archivo Municipal de San Juan Comalapa (AMC). Because the majority of records were destroyed in the civil war and 1976 earthquake, the extant archives are mainly records from municipal meetings.
Archivo Municipal de San Juan Ostuncalco (AMSJO). Citations indicate the archive section, either "Correspondencia" or "Procesos Judiciales (Criminales)," and the *bulto* (packet) in which the document is located.
Archivo Municipal de Sololá. Because the majority of records were destroyed in earthquakes, fires, and other disasters, only a few books documenting municipal meetings from the 1930s to 1950s survive.

TULANE UNIVERSITY LATIN AMERICAN LIBRARY, RARE BOOK AND MANUSCRIPT DEPARTMENT, NEW ORLEANS

U.S. NATIONAL ARCHIVES (USNA)

Diplomatic Branch. Record Group 84, 1897–1923 Foreign Service Post Records, Washington, D.C.
Executive Documents, vol. 2368, Foreign Relations of the United States, Washington, D.C.
Records Group 59, Records of the Department of State Relating to the Internal Affairs of Guatemala, 1824–1929.

GUATEMALAN GOVERNMENT DOCUMENTS

Memoria de la Secretaría de Gobernación y Justicia 1940, presentada 1941. Guatemala City: Tipografía Nacional, 1941.
Memoria de los trabajos realizados por la dirección general de la Policia Nacional. Guatemala City: Tipografía Nacional, 1940–44.

NEWSPAPERS

Diario de Centro América
Diario Oficial
La Gaceta: Revista de Policía y Variedades
Liberal Progresista
El Norte

SECONDARY SOURCES

Adams, Walter Randolph. "Guatemala." In *International Handbook on Alcohol and Culture,* edited by Dwight B. Heath, 99–109. Westport, Conn.: Greenwood Publishing Group, 1995.

Aguilar, Ernesto Chinchilla. "Antecedentes de la independencia en el partido de Quetzaltenango: Curiosos incidentes y presagios de sublevación en la segunda mitad del siglo XVIII." *Cuadernos de Antropología* 5 (1965): 49–128.

Aguirre, Cesar. *País de alcohol: El problema del alcoholismo en Colombia.* Bogota: Castillo Editorial, 1996.

Akyeampong, Emmanuel. *Drink, Power, and Cultural Change: A Social History of Alcohol in Ghana, c. 1800 to Recent Times.* Oxford, U.K.: James Currey, 1996.

Allen, Catherine J. "'Let's Drink Together, My Dear!': Persistent Ceremonies in a Changing Community." In *Drink, Power, and Society in the Andes,* edited by Justin Jennings and Brenda J. Bowser, 28–48. Gainesville: University Press of Florida, 2009.

Annis, Sheldon. *God and Production in a Guatemalan Town.* Austin: University of Texas Press, 1987.

Appadurai, Arjun, ed. *The Social Life of Things: Commodities in Cultural Perspective.* New York: Cambridge University Press, 1986.

Arnold, Matthew, "'Which way to the honky-tonk?': An Analysis of the Bakersfield and Nashville Sounds." Master's thesis, Department of Humanities and Cultural Studies, University of South Florida, 2009.

Asturias, Miguel Angel. *Strong Wind.* Translated by Gregory Rabassa. New York: Delacorte Press, 1968.

Balderrama, Francisco E., and Raymond Rodríguez. *Decade of Betrayal: Mexican Repatriation in the 1930s.* Albuquerque: University of New Mexico Press, 1995.

Barrows, Susanna, and Robin Room, eds. *Drinking Behavior and Belief in Modern History.* Berkeley: University of California Press, 1990.

Becker, Carl L. "The History of the Political Parties in the Province of New York, 1760–1776." Ph.D. dissertation, University of Wisconsin, Madison, 1907.

Beckett, Jeremy. "Aborigines, Alcohol, and Assimilation." In *Aborigines Now: New Perspectives in the Study of Aboriginal Communities,* edited by Marie Reay, 32–47. Sydney: Angus and Robertson, 1965.

———. "Reply to Robin Room, 'Alcohol and Ethnography: A Case of Problem Deflation?'" *Current Anthropology* 5, no. 2 (April 1984): 178–79.

Belaubre, Christophe, and Jordana Dym. "Introduction." In *Politics, Economy, and Society in Bourbon Central America, 1759–1821,* edited by Jordana Dym and Christophe Belaubre, 1–15. Boulder: University Press of Colorado, 2007.

Bogenschield, Thomas E. "The Roots of Fundamentalism in Western Guatemala: Missionary Ideologies and Local Responses, 1882–1944." Ph.D. dissertation, University of California, 1992.

Brandes, Stanley. "Drink, Abstinence, and Male Identity in Mexico City." In *Changing Men and Masculinities in Latin America,* edited by Matthew C. Gutmann, 153–76. Durham, N.C.: Duke University Press, 2003.

Brass, Tom. "Beer Drinking Groups in a Peruvian Agrarian Cooperative." *Bulletin of Latin American Research* 8, no. 2 (1989): 235–56.

Brennan, Thomas. *Public Drinking and Popular Culture in Eighteenth-Century Paris.* Princeton: Princeton University Press, 1988.

Brintnall, Douglas E. *Revolt against the Dead: The Modernization of a Mayan Community in the Highlands of Guatemala.* New York: Gordon and Breach, 1979.

Brown, Kendall W. *Bourbons and Brandy: Imperial Reform in Eighteenth-Century Arequipa.* Albuquerque: University of New Mexico Press, 1986.

Bruman, Henry J. *Alcohol in Ancient Mexico.* Salt Lake City: University of Utah Press, 2000.

Buffington, Robert. "Prohibition in the Borderlands: National Government-Border Community Relations." *Pacific Historical Review* 19, no. 1 (1993): 19–38.

Bumgartner, Louis E. *José del Valle of Central America.* Durham, N.C.: Duke University Press, 1963.

———. "José del Valle's Unfinished 'Diario de mi viaje de Guatemala a Mexico en 1822.'" *Americas* 18, no. 2 (October 1961): 187–90.

Bunzel, Ruth. "Central and South America: Chichicastenango and Chamula." In *Drinking and Intoxication: Selected Readings in Social Attitudes and Controls,* edited by Raymond G. McCarthy, 73–86. Glencoe, Ill.: Free Press, 1959.

———. *Chichicastenango: A Guatemalan Village.* Seattle: University of Washington Press, 1952.

———. "The Role of Alcoholism in Two Central American Cultures." *Psychiatry* 3 (1940): 361–87.

Burgess, Paul. *Justo Rufino Barrios: A Biography.* Philadelphia: Dorrance, 1926.

Burkitt, Robert. "Explorations in the Highlands of Western Guatemala." *Museum Journal* 21, no. 1 (1930): 41–72.

Burns, Eric. *The Spirits of America: A Social History of Alcohol.* Philadelphia: Temple University Press, 2004.

Butler, Barbara. *Holy Intoxication to Drunken Dissipation: Alcohol among Quichua Speakers in Otavolo, Ecuador.* Albuquerque: University of New Mexico Press, 2006.

Cambranes, Julio C. *Coffee and Peasants: The Origins of the Modern Plantation Economy in Guatemala, 1853–1897.* Stockholm, Sweden: Institute of Latin American Studies, 1985.

Cancian, Frank. *Economics and Prestige in a Maya Community: The Religious Cargo System in Zinacantán.* Stanford: Stanford University Press, 1971.

Carey, David, Jr. "Drunks and Dictators: Inebriation's Gendered, Ethnic, and Class Components in Guatemala, 1898–1944." Unpublished manuscript, n.d.

———. *Engendering Mayan History: Kaqchikel Women as Agents and Conduits of the Past, 1875–1970*. New York: Routledge, 2006.

———. "'Hard Working, Orderly Little Women': Mayan Vendors and Marketplace Struggles in Early Twentieth-Century Guatemala." *Ethnohistory* 55, no. 4 (2008): 579–607.

———. *Our Elders Teach Us: Maya-Kaqchikel Historical Perspectives. Xkib'ij kan qate' qatata'.* Tuscaloosa: University of Alabama Press, 2001.

Casswell, Sally. "Reply to Robin Room, 'Alcohol and Ethnography: A Case of Problem Deflation?'" *Current Anthropology* 5, no. 2 (April 1984): 180.

Chambers, Sarah. "Private Crimes, Public Order: Honor, Gender, and the Law in Early Republican Peru." In *Honor, Status and Law in Modern Latin America*, edited by Sueann Caulfield, Sarah C. Chambers, and Lara Putnam, 27–49. Durham, N.C.: Duke University Press, 2005.

Cheever, Susan. *My Name Is Bill: Bill Wilson; His Life and the Creation of Alcoholics Anonymous*. New York: Simon and Schuster, 2004.

Chomsky, Aviva. *West Indian Workers and the United Fruit Company in Costa Rica, 1870–1940*. Baton Rouge: Louisiana State University Press, 1996.

Christian, David. "Alcohol and Primitive Accumulation in Tsarist Russia." In *Production, Marketing and Consumption of Alcoholic Beverages since the Late Middle* Ages, edited by Erik Aerts, Louis M. Cullen, and Richard G. Wilson, 31–42. Leuven: Leuven University Press, 1990.

Clegern, Wayne M. *Origins of Liberal Dictatorship in Central America: Guatemala, 1865–1873*. Niwot: University Press of Colorado, 1994.

Coe, Sophie D., and Michael D. Coe. *The True History of Chocolate*. New York: Thames and Hudson, 1996.

Colby, Benjamin, and Pierre L. van de Berghe. *Ixil Country: A Plural Society in Highland Guatemala*. Berkeley: University of California Press, 1969.

Colloredo-Mansfeld, Rudi. "'Dirty Indians,' Radical Indígenas, and the Political Economy of Social Difference in Modern Ecuador." *Bulletin of Latin American Research* 17, no. 2(May 1998): 185–205.

Colson, Elizabeth, and Thayer Scudder. *For Prayer and Profit: The Ritual, Economic and Social Importance of Beer in Gwembe District, Zambia, 1950–1982*. Stanford: Stanford University Press, 1988.

Connell, William F. "'Because I Was Drunk and the Devil Had Tricked Me': Pulque, *Pulquerías*, and Violence in the Mexico City Uprising of 1692." *Colonial Latin American Historical Review* 14, no. 4 (2005): 369–401.

Conroy, David W. *In Public Houses: Drink and the Revolution of Authority in Colonial Massachusetts*. Chapel Hill: University of North Carolina Press, 1995.

Cortés y Larraz, Pedro. *Descripción geográfico-moral de la diócesis de Goathelama*, vol. 2, 111–45. Guatemala City: Sociedad de Geografía y Historia de Guatemala, 1958.

Courtwright, David T. *Forces of Habit: Drugs and the Making of the Modern World*. Cambridge, Mass.: Harvard University Press, 2001.

Crump, Thomas. "The Alternative Economy of Alcohol in Highland Chiapas." In *Constructive Drinking: Perspectives on Drink from Anthropology*, edited by Mary Douglas, 239–49. Cambridge: Cambridge University Press, 1987.

Cunningham, Eugene. *Gypsying through Central America*. New York: E. P. Dutton and Company, 1922.

Daniel, Pete. *Lost Revolutions: The South in the 1950s*. Chapel Hill: University of North Carolina Press, 2000.

Daniels, Bruce C. *Puritans and Play: Leisure and Recreation in Colonial New England*. New York: St. Martin's Press, 1996.

De las Casas, Bartolomé. *Apologética historica de las Indias*, vol. 1. Madrid: Serrano y Sanz, 1909 (1552).

Dennis, Philip A. "The Role of the Drunk in a Oaxacan Village." *American Anthropologist* 77 (1975): 856–63.

Dietler, Michael. "Alcohol: Anthropological/Archaeological Perspectives." *Annual Review of Anthropology* 35 (2006): 229–49.

Domine, Andre. *The Ultimate Guide to Spirits and Cocktails*. Bonn: H. F. Ullman, 2008.

Doughty, Paul L. "The Social Uses of Alcohol in a Peruvian Community." In *Beliefs, Behaviors, and Alcoholic Beverages: A Cross-Cultural Survey*, edited by Mac Marshall, 64–81. Ann Arbor: University of Michigan Press, 1979.

Douglas, Mary, and Baron Isherwood. *The World of Goods: Towards an Anthropology of Consumption*. New York: Routledge, 1996.

Dunn, Alvis. "Aguardiente and Identity: The Holy Week Riot of 1786 in Quezaltenango, Guatemala." Ph.D. dissertation, University of North Carolina at Chapel Hill, 1999.

Dunn, Henry O. *Guatimala, or the United Provinces of Central America in 1827–8, Being Sketches and Memorandum Made during a Twelve Months' Residence in that Republic*. New York: G. and C. Carvill, 1828.

Dym, Jordana. "Bourbon Reforms and City Government in Central America, 1759–1808." In *Politics, Economy, and Society in Bourbon Central America, 1759–1821*, edited by Jordana Dym and Christophe Belaubre, 75–100. Boulder: University of Colorado Press, 2007.

Dym, Jordana, and Christopher Belaubre, eds. *Politics, Economy, and Society in Bourbon Central America, 1759–1821*. Boulder: University Press of Colorado, 2007.

Eber, Christine. *Women and Alcohol in a Highland Maya Town: Water of Hope, Water of Sorrow*. Austin: University of Texas Press, 2000.

Ericastilla, Ana Carla, and Liseth Jiménez. "Las clandestinistas de aguardiente en Guatemala a fines del siglo XIX." In *Mujeres, género e historia en América Central durante los siglos XVIII, XIX, XX*, edited by Eugenia Rodríguez Sáenz, 13–24. San José, Costa Rica: UNIFEM; Burlington, Vt.: Plumsock Mesoamerican Studies, 2002.

Fallaw, Ben. "Bartolomé García Correa and the Politics of Maya Identity in Postrevolutionary Yucatán, 1911–1933." *Ethnohistory* 55, no. 4 (2008): 553–78.

———. "Dry Law, Wet Politics: Drinking and Prohibition in Post-Revolutionary Yucatán, 1915–1935." *Latin American Research Review* 37, no. 2 (2001): 37–64.

Foster, Harry L. *A Gringo in Mañana-Land*. New York: Dodd, Mead and Company, 1924.

Fuentes y Guzmán, Francisco Antonio. *Obras históricas de Francisco Antonio Fuentes y Guzmán*, vol. 3. Madrid: Ediciones Atlas, 1972.

Gage, Thomas. *A New Survey of the West Indies*. 3rd ed. London, 1677.

Gall, Francis, ed. *Diccionario geográfico de Guatemala,* vol. 3. Guatemala: Instituto Geografico Nacional, 1980.

García Peláez, Francisco de Paula. *Memorias del antiguo reino de Guatemala.* 3 vols. 2nd ed. Guatemala: Tipografía Nacional, 1943–44.

Garrard-Burnett, Virginia. "Indians Are Drunks and Drunks Are Indians: Alcohol and Indigenismo in Guatemala, 1890–1940." *Bulletin of Latin American Research* 19, no. 3 (July 2000): 341–56.

———. *Protestantism in Guatemala: Living in the New Jerusalem.* Austin: University of Texas Press, 1998.

Garza, James Alex. *The Imagined Underworld: Sex, Crime, and Vice in Porfirian Mexico City.* Lincoln: University of Nebraska Press, 2007.

Gibbons, Robert, Yedy Israel, Harold Kalant, Robert E. Popham, Wolfgang Schmidt, and Reginald G. Smart, eds. *Research Advances in Alcohol and Drug Problems,* vol. 2. New York: Plenum Press, 1975.

Gjelten, Tom. *Bacardi and the Long Fight for Cuba: The Biography of a Cause.* New York: Viking, 2008.

Gonçalves de Lima, Oswaldo. *Alimentos e bebidas no México prehispânico, segundo os manuscritos de Sahagún.* Recife: Ministério da Educação e Cultura, Instituto Joaquim Nabuco de Pesquisas Sociais, 1955.

González Alzate, Jorge H. "History of Los Altos, Guatemala: A Study of Regional Conflict and National Integration, 1750–1885." Ph.D. dissertation. Tulane University, 1994.

———. "State Reform, Popular Resistance, and Negotiation of Rule in Late Bourbon Guatemala: The Quetzaltenango Aguardiente Monopoly, 1785–1807." In *Politics, Economy, and Society in Bourbon Central America, 1759–1821,* edited by Jordana Dym and Christophe Belaubre, 129–55. Boulder: University Press of Colorado, 2007.

González Sandoval, Magda Leticia. "El estanco de bebidas embriagantes en Guatemala, 1753–1860." Master's thesis, Universidad del Valle, Guatemala City, 1990.

Goodman-Elgar, Melissa. "Places to Partake: *Chicha* in the Andean Landscape." In *Drink, Power, and Society in the Andes,* edited by Justin Jennings and Brenda J. Bowser, 75–107. Gainesville: University Press of Florida, 2009.

Gramsci, Antonio. *Selections from the Prison Notebooks of Antonio Gramsci.* Edited and translated by Quintin Hoare and Geoffrey Nowell-Smith. New York: International Publishers, 1971.

Griffiths, Alison. *Wondrous Difference: Cinema, Anthropology and Turn-of-the-Century Visual Culture.* New York: Columbia University Press, 2002.

Griffiths, John. *Tea: The Drink That Changed the World.* London: Andre Deutsch, 2007.

Gudmundson, Lowell. "Firewater, Desire, and the Militiamen's Christmas Eve in San Gerónimo, Baja Verapaz, 1892." *Hispanic American Historical Review* 84, no. 2 (2004): 239–76.

Gudmundson, Lowell, and Héctor Lindo-Fuentes. *Central America, 1821–1871: Liberalism before Liberal Reform.* Tuscaloosa: University of Alabama Press, 1995.

Guillén, Flavio. "Prólogo, o casi, casi. . . ." In *El indio Guatemalteco: Ensayo de sociología nacionalista,* by J. Fernando Juárez Muñoz, 5–27. Guatemala City: Tipografía Latina, 1931.

Haefkens, Jacobo. *Viaje a Guatemala y Centroamérica*. Translated by Theodora J. M. van Lottum. Edited by Francis Gall. Guatemala: Editorial Universitaria, 1969.

Hames, Gina. "Maize-Beer, Gossip, and Slander: Female Tavern Proprietors and Urban, Ethnic Cultural Elaboration in Bolivia, 1870–1930." *Journal of Social History* 37, no. 2 (2003): 351–64.

Hamilton, Dr. Alexander. *Gentleman's Progress: The Itinerarium of Dr. Alexander Hamilton*. Edited by Carl Bridenbaugh. Chapel Hill: University of North Carolina Press, 1948.

Harpelle, Ronald. "White Zones: American Enclave Communities of Central America." In *Black and Blackness in Central America: Between Race and Place,* edited by Lowell Gudmundson and Justin Wolfe, 307–33. Durham, N.C.: Duke University Press, 2010.

Harvey, Penelope M. "Drunken Speech and the Construction of Meaning: Bilingual Competence in the Southern Peruvian Andes." *Language in Society* 20, no. 1 (March 1991): 1–36.

Hayashida, Frances. "*Chicha* Histories: Pre-Hispanic Brewing in the Andes and the Use of Ethnographic and Historical Analogues." In *Drink, Power, and Society in the Andes,* edited by Justin Jennings and Brenda J. Bowser, 232–56. Gainesville: University Press of Florida, 2009.

Heath, Dwight B. "Alcohol Use among North American Indians: A Cross-Cultural Survey of Patterns and Problems." In *Research Advances in Alcohol and Drug Problems,* vol. 7, edited by Reginald G. Smart, Frederick B. Glaser, Yedy Israel, Harold Kalant, Robert E. Popham, and Wolfgang Schmidt, 343–92. New York: Plenum Press, 1983.

———. *Alcohol Use in Latin America: Cultural Realities and Policy Implications.* Providence, R.I.: Center for Latin American Studies, Brown University, 1987.

———. "Anthropology and Alcohol Studies: Current Issues." *Annual Review of Anthropology* 16 (1987): 99–120.

———. "A Critical Review of Ethnographic Studies of Alcohol Use." In *Research Advances in Alcohol and Drug Problems,* vol. 2, edited by Robert Gibbons, Yedy Israel, Harold Kalant, Robert E. Popham, Wolfgang Schmidt, and Reginald G. Smart, 1–92. New York: Plenum Press, 1975.

———. "Determining the Sociocultural Context of Alcohol Use." *Journal of Studies on Alcohol,* supplement 9 (1981): 9–17.

———. "Drinking Patterns of the Bolivian Camba." In *Society, Culture, and Drinking Patterns,* edited by David Joshua Pittman and Charles R. Snyder, 22–36. New York: John Wiley and Sons, 1962.

———. "Historical and Cultural Factors Affecting Alcohol Availability (and Consumption) in Latin America." In *Legislative Approaches to Prevention of Alcohol-Related Problems: An Inter-American Workshop,* edited by Alan K. Kaplan, 127–88. Washington, D.C.: Institute of Medicine, National Academy Press, 1982.

———. "Peasants, Revolution, and Drinking: Interethnic Drinking Patterns in Two Bolivian Communities." *Human Organizations* 30 (1971): 179–86.

———. "Reply to Robin Room, 'Alcohol and Ethnography: A Case of Problem Deflation?'" *Current Anthropology* 5, no. 2 (April 1984): 180–81.

Hernández Palomo, José Jesús. *El aguardiente de caña en México, 1724–1810*. Seville: Escuela de Estudios Hispano-Americanos, 1974.

Hinshaw, Robert E. *Panajachel: A Guatemalan Town in Thirty-Year Perspective*. Pittsburgh: University of Pittsburgh Press, 1975.

Huarcaya, Sergio Miguel. *No os embriaguéis . . . borracheras, identidad y conversión evangélica en Cacha, Ecuador*. Quito: Universidad Andina Simon Bolivar, 2003.

Huertos Vallejos, Lorenzo. "Historia de la producción de vinos y piscos en el Perú." *Revista Universum* 19, no. 2 (2004): 44–61. http://www.scielo.cl/scielo.php?pid=S0718-23762004000200004&script=sci_arttext. Accessed July 19, 2010.

Hughes, Langston. *Not Without Laughter*. New York: Scribner Paperback Fiction, 1995 (1969).

Hurston, Zora Neale. *Their Eyes Were Watching God*. New York: Harper Perennial Modern Classics, 2006 (1937).

Hurt, Douglas, ed. *African American Life in the Rural South, 1900–1950*. Columbia: University of Missouri Press, 2003.

Huxley, Aldous. *Beyond the Mexique Bay*. New York: Harper and Brothers, 1934.

Ingersoll, Hazel. "The War of the Mountain: A Study of Reactionary Peasant Insurgency in Guatemala, 1837–1873." Ph.D. dissertation, George Washington University, 1972.

Ishii, Izumi. *Bad Fruits of the Civilized Tree: Alcohol and the Sovereignty of the Cherokee Nation*. Lincoln: University of Nebraska Press, 2008.

Jennings, Justin, and Brenda J. Bowser, eds. *Drink, Power, and Society in the Andes*. Gainesville: University Press of Florida, 2009.

Jennings, Justin, and Melissa Chatfield. "Pots, Brewers, and Hosts: Women's Power and the Limits of Central Andean Feasting." In *Drink, Power, and Society in the Andes*, edited by Justin Jennings and Brenda J. Bowser, 200–231. Gainesville: University Press of Florida, 2009.

Juárez Muñoz, J. Fernando. *El indio Guatemalteco: Ensayo de sociología nacionalista*. Guatemala City: Tipografía Latina, 1931.

Kaplan, Alan K. "Legislative Approaches to Prevention of Alcohol-Related Problems: An Inter-American Workshop." Washington, D.C.: Institute of Medicine, National Academy Press, 1982.

Kennedy, John. "The Role of Beer in Tarahumara Culture." *American Anthropologist* 60 (1978): 620–40.

Kicza, John. *Colonial Entrepreneurs: Families and Business in Bourbon Mexico City*. Albuquerque: University of New Mexico Press, 1983.

Kramer, Wendy, W. George Lovell, and Christopher H. Lutz. "Fire in the Mountains: Juan de Espinar and the Indians of Huehuetenango, 1525–1560." In *Columbian Consequences*, vol. 3, edited by David Hurst Thomas, 263–82. Washington, D.C.: Smithsonian Institution, 1991.

Kurlansky, Mark. *Salt: A World History*. New York: Walker Press, 2002.

Lacoste, Pablo. "Wine and Women: Grape Growers and *Pulperas* in Mendoza, 1561–1852." *Hispanic American Historical Review* 88, no. 3 (August 2008): 361–91.

La Farge II, Oliver. *Santa Eulalia: The Religion of a Cuchumatán Indian Town*. Chicago: University of Chicago Press, 1947.

La Farge II, Oliver, and Douglas S. Byers. *The Year-Bearer's People*. New Orleans: Tulane University, 1931.

Leland, Joy. *Firewater Myths: North American Indians Drinking and Alcohol Addictions*. Monograph 11. Rutgers, N.J.: Rutgers Center of Alcohol Studies, 1976.

Leonard, Irving Albert. *Don Carlos de Sigüenza y Góngora, a Mexican Savant of the Seventeenth Century*. Berkeley: University of California Press, 1929.

Lewis, Stephen E. "La guerra del posh, 1951–1954: Un conflicto decisivo entre el Instituto Nacional Indigenista, el monopolio del alcohol y el gobierno del estado de Chiapas." *Mesoamérica* 46 (2004): 111–34.

Licht, Walter. *Working for the Railroad: The Organization of Work in the Nineteenth Century*. Princeton: Princeton University Press, 1983.

Lincoln, Jackson Steward. "An Ethnographic Study of the Ixil Indians of the Guatemalan Highlands." Microfilm Collection of Manuscripts on Middle American Cultural Anthropology, University of Chicago, no. 1, 1945.

Little-Siebold, Todd. "Decaffeinating Guatemalan History: Perspectives from the Periphery, 1850–1950." Paper presented at the American Historical Association Annual Meeting, Chicago, Illinois, January 1995.

———. "Guatemala and the Dream of a Nation: National Policy and Regional Practice in the Liberal Era, 1871–1945 (Chiquimula, San Marcos)." Ph.D. dissertation, Tulane University, 1995.

Lomnitz, Larissa. "Alcohol and Culture: The Historical Evolution of Drinking Patterns among the Mapuche." In *Cross-Cultural Approaches to the Study of Alcohol: An Interdisciplinary Perspective*, edited by Michael E. Everett, Jack O. Waddell, and Dwight B. Heath, 177–98. The Hague: Mouton, 1976.

Lutz, Christopher H. *Santiago de Guatemala, 1541–1773: City, Caste, and the Colonial Experience*. Norman: University of Oklahoma Press, 1994.

MacLeod, Murdo J. *Spanish Central America: A Socioeconomic History, 1520–1720*. Berkeley: University of California Press, 1973.

Mallon, Florencia. *Peasant and Nation: The Making of Postcolonial Mexico and Peru*. Berkeley: University of California Press, 1995.

Mancall, Peter C. *Deadly Medicine: Indians and Alcohol in Early America*. Ithaca, N.Y.: Cornell University Press, 1995.

Mandelbaum, David G. "Alcohol and Culture." *Current Anthropology* 6, no. 3 (1965): 281–93.

Mangan, Jane E. *Trading Roles: Gender, Ethnicity, and the Urban Economy in Colonial Potosí*. Durham, N.C.: Duke University Press, 2005.

Markman, Sidney David. *Colonial Architecture of Antigua Guatemala*. Philadelphia, Penn.: American Philosophical Society, 1966.

Márquez, Graciela. "The Stamp Tax on Alcoholic Beverages: Continuities and Discontinuities of Indirect Taxation in Mexico, 1875–1930." Paper prepared for the Latin American History Workshop, DRCLAS, Harvard University, November 2005.

Maudslay, Anne Cary, and Alfred Percival Maudslay. *A Glimpse of Guatemala, and Some Notes on the Ancient Monuments of Central America*. London: John Murray, 1899.

McCreery, David. *Rural Guatemala, 1760–1940*. Stanford: Stanford University Press, 1994.

Menéndez, Eduardo, ed. *Antropología del alcoholismo en México*. Mexico City: Centro de Investigaciones y Estudios Superiores en Antropología Social, 1991.

Meneray, Wilbur E. "The Kingdom of Guatemala during the Reign of Charles III, 1759–1788." Ph.D. dissertation, University of North Carolina, 1975.

Metz, Brent E. *Ch'orti'-Maya Survival in Eastern Guatemala: Indigeneity in Transition*. Albuquerque: University of New Mexico Press, 2006.

Miller, Daniel. "Consumption and Commodities." *Annual Review of Anthropology* 24 (1995): 141–61.

"Ministerio general del Supremo Gobierno del Estado de Guatemala. Departamento de Gobernación. El Jefe Supremo del Estado de Guatemala." *Boletín de noticias de la colera morbo*. April 21, 1837. Guatemala: Imprenta de la Nueva Academia de Ciencias, 1837.

Mintz, Sidney W. *Sweetness and Power: The Place of Sugar in Modern History*. New York: Penguin Books, 1986.

Mitchell, Timothy. *Intoxicated Identities: Alcohol's Power in Mexican History and Culture*. New York: Routledge, 2004.

Mora de Tovar, Gilma Lucía. *El aguardiente y conflictos sociales en la Nueva Granada durante el siglo XVIII*. Bogotá: Universidad Nacional de Colombia, Centro Editorial, 1988.

Nardone, Jennifer. "Roomful of Blues: Jukejoints and the Cultural Landscape of the Mississippi Delta." In *Perspectives in Vernacular Architecture*, vol. 9, *Constructing Image, Identity, and Place*, edited by Alison K. Hoagland and Kenneth A. Breisch, 166–75. Knoxville: University of Tennessee Press, 2003.

Nash, June. *In the Eyes of the Ancestors: Belief and Behavior in a Mayan Community*. Prospect Heights, Ill.: Waveland Press, 1970.

Navarrete Pellicer, Sergio. *El aguardiente en una comunidad maya de los altos de Chiapas*. Mexico City: Instituto Nacional de Antropología e Historia, 1988.

Oakes, Maud. *The Two Crosses of Todos Santos*. New York: Bollingen Foundation, 1951.

Okrent, Daniel. *Last Call: The Rise and Fall of Prohibition*. New York: Scribner, 2010.

Opie, Frederick Douglass. "Adios Jim Crow: Afro–North American Workers and the Guatemalan Railroad Workers' League, 1884–1921." Ph.D. dissertation, Syracuse University, 1999.

———. "Afro North American Migration to Latin America, 1880–1932." Unpublished paper presented to the Latin American Studies Association Conference, Guadalajara, Mexico, April 1997.

———. "Black Americans and the State in Turn-of-the-Century Guatemala." *Americas* 64, no. 4 (April 2008): 583–609.

———. *Black Labor Migration in Caribbean Guatemala, 1882–1923*. Gainesville: University Press of Florida, 2009.

———. "Foreign Workers, Debt Peonage and Frontier Culture in Lowland Guatemala, 1884 to 1900." *Transforming Anthropology* 12, nos. 1–2 (2004): 40–49.

Pardo, J. Joaquín. *Efemérides para escribir la historia de la muy noble y muy leal Ciudad de*

Santiago de Los Caballeros del Reino de Guatemala. Guatemala: Tipografía Nacional, 1943.

Peiss, Kathy. *Cheap Amusements: Working Women and Leisure in Turn-of-the-Century New York*. Philadelphia: Temple University Press, 1986.

Perlov, Diane C. "Working through Daughters: Strategies for Gaining and Maintaining Social Power among the *Chicheras* of Highland Bolivia." In *Drink, Power, and Society in the Andes,* edited by Justin Jennings and Brenda J. Bowser, 49–74. Gainesville: University Press of Florida, 2009.

Piccato, Pablo. *City of Suspects: Crime in Mexico City, 1900–1931*. Durham, N.C.: Duke University Press, 2001.

———. "'El paso de Venus por el disco del sol': Criminality and Alcoholism in the Late Porfiriato." *Mexican Studies/Estudios Mexicanos* 11, no. 2 (Summer 1995): 203–41.

Pilcher, Jeffrey M. *¡Que vivan los tamales! Food and the Making of Mexican Identity*. Albuquerque: University of New Mexico Press, 1998.

Pine, Adrienne. *Working Hard, Drinking Hard: On Violence and Survival in Honduras*. Berkeley: University of California Press, 2008.

Pineda de Mont, Manuel, ed. *Recopilación de las leyes de Guatemala*. 3 vols. Guatemala: Imprenta de la Paz, 1869–72.

———. *Recopilación de las leyes emitidas por el gobierno democrático de la República de Guatemala*, vols. 1 and 2. Guatemala: Imprenta de la Paz, 1874.

Pittman, D. J., and C. R. Snyder, eds. *Society, Culture, and Drinking Patterns*. New York: John Wiley and Sons, 1962.

Pompejano, Daniele. *La crisis de antiguo régimen en Guatemala (1839–1871)*. Guatemala City: Editorial Universitaria, Universidad de San Carlos de Guatemala, 1997.

Pozas, Ricardo. *Juan the Chamula: An Ethnological Recreation of the Life of a Mexican Indian*. Translated by Lysander Kemp. Berkeley: University of California Press, 1962.

Putnam, Lara E. "Eventually Alien: The Multigenerational Saga of West Indians in Central America, 1870–1940." In *Black and Blackness in Central America: Between Race and Place,* edited by Lowell Gudmundson and Justin Wolfe, 278–306. Durham, N.C.: Duke University Press, 2010.

———. "Work, Sex, and Power in a Central American Export Economy at the Turn of the Twentieth Century." In *Gender, Sexuality and Power in Latin America since Independence,* edited by William E. French and Katherine Elaine Bliss, 133–62. Lanham, Md.: Rowman and Littlefield, 2007.

Quauhtlehuanitzin, Chimalpahin. *Codex Chimalpahin: Society and Politics in Mexico: Tenochtitlan, Tlatelolco, Texcoco, Culhuacan, and Other Nahua Altepetl in Central Mexico: The Nahuatl and Spanish Annals and Accounts Collected and Recorded by Don Domingo de San Antón Muñón Chimalpahin Quauhtlehuanitzin*. Translated and edited by Arthur J. O. Anderson, Susan Schroeder, and Wayne Ruwet. Norman: University of Oklahoma Press, 1997.

Reay, Marie. *Aborigines Now*. Sydney: Angus and Robertson, 1965.

Rebolledo, Raquel. "Pícaras y pulperas: Las otras mujeres de la colonia." *Cyber Humanitatis* 19 (Winter 2001).

Reeves, René. *Ladinos with Ladinos, Indians with Indians: Land, Labor, and Regional Ethnic Conflict in the Making of Guatemala.* Stanford: Stanford University Press, 2006.

Reiche, Carlos Enrique. "Estudio sobre el patrón de embriaguez en la región rural altaverapacense." *Guatemala Indígena* 5 (1970): 103–27.

Reina, Ruben E. *The Law of the Saints: A Pokomam Pueblo and Its Community Culture.* New York: Bobbs-Merrill, 1966.

"Relaciones Geográficas—1740." *Boletín del Archivo General del Gobierno* 1 (1935): 9–28.

Roberts, Morley. *On the Earthquake Line: Minor Adventures in Central America.* London: J. W. Arrowsmith, 1924.

Rodríguez Sáenz, Eugenia, ed. *Entre silencios y voces: Género e historia en América Central (1750–1990).* San José, Costa Rica: Centro Nacional Para el Desarrollo de la Mujer y la Familia, 1998.

Room, Robin. "Alcohol and Ethnography: A Case of Problem Deflation?" *Current Anthropology* 25, no. 2 (April 1984): 169–78.

Rosaldo, Michelle Zimbalist. "Woman, Culture, and Society: A Theoretical Overview." In *Woman, Culture, and Society,* edited by Michelle Zimbalist Rosaldo and Louise Lamphere, 17–42. Stanford: Stanford University Press, 1974.

Rosenbaum, Brenda. *With Our Heads Bowed: The Dynamics of Gender in a Maya Community.* Austin: University of Texas Press, 1993.

Ruhl, Arthur Brown. *The Central Americans: Adventures and Impressions between Mexico and Panama.* New York: Charles Scribner's Sons, 1928.

Salinger, Sharon V. *Taverns and Drinking in Early America.* Baltimore, Md.: Johns Hopkins University Press, 2002.

Sanders, James E. *Contentious Republicans: Popular Politics, Race, and Class in Nineteenth-Century Colombia.* Durham, N.C.: Duke University Press, 2004.

Scardaville, Michael C. "Alcohol Abuse and Tavern Reform in Late Colonial Mexico City." *Hispanic American Historical Review* 60 (1980): 643–71.

Schivelbusch, Wolfgang. *Tastes of Paradise: A Social History of Spices, Stimulants, and Intoxicants.* New York: Pantheon Books, 1992.

Schwartzkopf, Stacey. "Maya Power and State Culture: Community, Indigenous Politics, and State Formation in Northern Huehuetenango, Guatemala, 1800–1871." Ph.D. dissertation, Tulane University, 2008.

Scott, James C. *Domination and the Arts of Resistance: Hidden Transcripts.* New Haven, Conn.: Yale University Press, 1990.

Sharer, Robert, with Loa P. Traxler. *The Ancient Maya.* 6th ed. Stanford: Stanford University Press, 2006.

Singer, Merrill. "Toward a Political-Economy of Alcoholism: The Missing Link in the Anthropology of Drinking." *Social Science and Medicine* 23, no. 2 (1986): 113–30.

Siverts, Henning. *Drinking Patterns in Highland Chiapas: A Teamwork Approach to the Study of Semantics through Ethnography.* Bergen: Univeritetsforlaget, 1973.

Skinner-Klee, Jorge, ed. *Legislación indigenista de Guatemala.* Mexico City: Instituto Indigenista Interamericano, 1954.

Smart, Reginald G., Frederick B. Glaser, Yedy Israel, Harold Kalant, Robert E. Popham, and Wolfgang Schmidt, eds. *Research Advances in Alcohol and Drug Problems*, vol. 7. New York: Plenum Press, 1983.

Smith, Frederick H. *Caribbean Rum: A Social and Economic History*. Gainesville: University Press of Florida, 2005.

Smith, Waldemar R. *The Fiesta System and Economic Change*. New York: Columbia University Press, 1977.

Sontag, Susan. *On Photography*. New York: Farrar, Straus, and Giroux, 1973.

Soustelle, Jacques. *Daily Lives of the Aztecs on the Eve of the Spanish Conquest*. Stanford: Stanford University Press, 1961.

Stepan, Nancy. *The Hour of Eugenics: Race, Nation, and Gender in Latin America*. Ithaca, N.Y.: Cornell University Press, 1991.

Stephens, John Lloyd. *Incidents of Travel in Central America, Chiapas and Yucatan*, vols. 1–2. New York: Dover Publications, 1969.

Stoll, David. *Between Two Armies: In the Ixil Towns of Guatemala*. New York: Columbia University Press, 1993.

Sullivan-Gonzales, Douglass. *Piety, Power and Politics: Religion and State Formation in Guatemala, 1821–1871*. Pittsburgh: University of Pittsburgh Press, 1998.

Tagg, John. "Evidence, Truth and Order: A Means of Surveillance." In *Visual Culture: The Reader*, edited by Jessica Evans and Stuart Hall, 244–73. Thousand Oaks, Calif.: Sage, 1999.

Takaki, Ronald. *Strangers from a Different Shore: A History of Asian Americans*. Boston: Little, Brown and Company, 1989.

Taracena Arriola, Arturo. *Invención criolla, sueño ladino, pesadilla indígena: Los altos de Guatemala; De región a Estado*. Costa Rica: Editorial Porvenir y CIRMA, 1997.

Tax, Sol. "Changing Consumption in Indian Guatemala." *Economic Development and Cultural Change* 5, no. 2 (January 1957): 147–58.

———. *Penny Capitalism: A Guatemalan Indian Economy*. Washington, D.C.: Smithsonian Institution, 1953.

Taylor, William B. *Drinking, Homicide, and Rebellion in Colonial Mexican Villages*. Stanford: Stanford University Press, 1979.

Thatcher, Richard W. *Fighting Firewater Fictions: Moving Beyond the Disease Model of Alcoholism in First Nations*. Toronto: University of Toronto Press, 2004.

Thompson, Edward P. "The Peculiarities of the English." In *The Poverty of Theory and Other Essays*. New York: Monthly Review Press, 1978.

Thompson, J. Eric. *Maya History and Religion*. Norman: University of Oklahoma Press, 1990.

Thompson, Peter. *Rum Punch and Revolution: Taverngoing and Public Life in Eighteenth Century Philadelphia*. Philadelphia: University of Pennsylvania Press, 1999.

Thorpe, Daniel B. "Taverns and Tavern Culture in the Southern Frontier: Rowan County N.C., 1753—1776." *Journal of Southern History* 61, no. 1 (November 1996): 661–88.

Tozzer, Alfred M. *Landa's Relación de las cosas de Yucatán*. Cambridge, Mass.: Peabody Museum of Archaeology and Ethnology, 1936.

Valdez, Lidio M. "Maize Beer Production in Middle Horizon Peru." *Journal of Anthropological Research* 62, no. 1 (Spring 2006): 53–80.

Van Binsbergen, Wim M. J., and Peter L. Geschiere, eds. *Commodification: Things, Agency, and Identity (The Social Life of Things Revisited)*. Münster: Lit Verlag, 2005.

Van Oss, Adriaan C. *Catholic Colonialism: A Parish History of Guatemala, 1524–1821*. New York: Cambridge University Press, 1986.

Viqueira Albán, Juan Pedro. *Propriety and Permissiveness in Bourbon Mexico*. Translated by Sonya Lipsett-Rivera and Sergio Rivera Ayala. Wilmington, Del.: Scholarly Resources Imprint, 1999.

Vogt, Evon Z. *Fieldwork among the Maya: Reflections on the Harvard Chiapas Project*. London: Routledge, 1994.

———. *Tortillas for the Gods: A Symbolic Analysis of Zinacanteco Rituals*. Cambridge, Mass.: Harvard University Press, 1976.

Wagley, Charles. *Economics of a Guatemalan Village*. Menasha, Wis.: American Anthropological Association, 1941.

Warren, Kay B. *The Symbolism of Subordination: Indian Identity in a Guatemalan Town*. Austin: University of Texas Press, 1978.

Webre, Stephen. "Conclusion: Change and Continuity in Bourbon Central America." In *Politics, Economy, and Society in Bourbon Central America, 1759–1821*, edited by Jordana Dym and Christophe Belaubre, 265–73. Boulder: University of Colorado Press, 2007.

———. "Water and Society in a Spanish American City: Santiago de Guatemala, 1555–1773." *Hispanic American Historical Review* 70, no. 1 (February 1990): 57–84.

Weismantel, Mary. "Have a Drink: *Chicha*, Performance, and Politics." In *Drink, Power, and Society in the Andes*, edited by Justin Jennings and Brenda J. Bowser, 257–77. Gainesville: University Press of Florida, 2009.

Wilkinson, Daniel. *Silence on the Mountain: Stories of Terror, Betrayal, and Forgetting in Guatemala*. New York: Houghton Mifflin Company, 2002.

Williams, Ian. *Rum: A Social and Sociable History of the Real Spirit of 1776*. New York: Nation Books, 2005.

Williams, John L. "The Rise of the Banana Industry and Its Influence on Caribbean Countries." M.A. thesis, Clark University, 1925.

Willis, Justin. *Potent Brews: A Social History of Alcohol in East Africa, 1850–1999*. Nairobi: British Institute in East Africa, 2002.

Wilson, Iris H. "Pineda's Report on the Beverages of New Spain." *Journal of the Southwest* 5, no. 1 (Spring 1963): 79–90.

Wilson, Peter J. *Crab Antics: The Social Anthropology of English-Speaking Negro Societies of the Caribbean*. New Haven, Conn.: Yale University Press, 1973.

Winter, Nevin O. *Guatemala and Her People of Today*. Boston: L. C. Page and Company, 1909.

Wolfe, Justin. *The Everyday Nation State: Community and Ethnicity in Nineteenth-Century Nicaragua*. Lincoln: University of Nebraska Press, 2007.

Woodward, Ralph Lee, Jr. *Central America: A Nation Divided*. 3rd ed. New York: Oxford University Press, 1999.

———. *Rafael Carrera and the Emergence of the Republic of Guatemala, 1821–1871*. Athens: University of Georgia Press, 1993.

Wortman, Miles. *Government and Society in Central America, 1680–1840.* New York: Columbia University Press, 1982.

Yarrington, Doug. "Román Cárdenas, the Liquor Tax, and Fiscal Modernity, 1913–1935." Paper presented at the Rocky Mountain Conference on Latin American Studies, Flagstaff, Arizona, 2008.

Yentsch, Anne. "Excavating the South's African American Food History." In *African American Foodways: Explorations of History and Culture,* edited by Anne L. Bower, 59–100. Urbana: University of Illinois Press, 2007.

Contributors

David Carey Jr. is professor of history and women and gender studies at the University of Southern Maine. His publications include *Our Elders Teach Us: Maya-Kaqchikel Historical Perspectives, Xkib'ij kan qate' qatata'*; *Ojer taq tzijobäl kichin ri Kaqchikela' Winaqi'* (A History of the Kaqchikel People); and *Engendering Mayan History: Mayan Women as Agents and Conduits of the Past, 1875–1970*. He is also the author of over a dozen peer-reviewed articles and essays and the coeditor of *Latino Voices in New England*. He is currently working on a manuscript about gender, ethnicity, crime, and state power in Guatemala, 1898–1944.

Alvis E. Dunn has taught at the University of North Carolina, Duke University, East Carolina University, and North Carolina A&T University, and he currently chairs the Department of History at Guilford College in Greensboro, North Carolina. Dunn has also worked on more modern topics regarding Guatemalan history and immigration to the United States, contributing to the research that resulted in the publication of *The Maya of Morganton: Work and Community in the Nuevo New South*, by Leon Fink.

Virginia Garrard-Burnett is professor of history and religious studies at the University of Texas. Her books include *Terror in the Land of the Holy Spirit: Guatemala under General Efraín Ríos Montt, 1982–83*; *Viviendo en la Nueva Jerusalém*; *On Earth as It Is in Heaven: Religion and Society in Latin America*; *Protestantism in Guatemala: Living in the New Jerusalem*. She was also coeditor of *Rethinking Protestantism in Latin America*. She has more than two dozen peer-reviewed articles and chapters in edited volumes and is currently coediting the *Cambridge History of Religion in Latin America* with Paul Freston.

Frederick Douglass Opie is professor of history and foodways at Babson College. He is the author of *Hog and Hominy: Soul Food from Africa to America* and *Black Labor Migration in Caribbean Guatemala, 1882–1923.* He is also a blogger at http://www.foodasalens.com/, where he does daily musings on the history of traditions, culture, and systems and the history of campaigns and movements for, about, and involving food. His forthcoming book is titled *Black and Latino Relations in New York, 1959–1989.*

René Reeves is professor of history at Fitchburg State College in Fitchburg, Massachusetts. His research focus is nineteenth-century Guatemala, in particular how ethnic conflict, regional identity, and gender affected national politics. He is the author of *Ladinos with Ladinos, Indians with Indians: Land, Labor, and Regional Ethnic Conflict in the Making of Guatemala.*

Stacey Schwartzkopf is visiting assistant professor at Hendrix College. His research examines the anthropology and history of Maya peoples, with a particular focus on community, indigenous political activity, and the relationship between culture and political economy in nineteenth-century Guatemala.

Index

Page numbers in *italics* refer to illustrations